The Missing Pieces of Mum

The Missing Pieces of Mum

SALLY HERBERT

MARDLE

First published in hardback in 2021 by Mardle Books
This edition published in 2022
15 Church Road
London, SW13 9HE

www.mardlebooks.com

Paperback 9781914451010
eBook 9781914451102

A CIP catalogue record for this book is available from the British Library.

Every reasonable effort has been made to trace copyright-holders of material
reproduced in this book, but if any have been inadvertently overlooked the
publishers would be glad to hear from them.

Printed in the UK

10 9 8 7 6 5 4 3 2 1

Cover image: Sally with her Mum, Phyllis

For my darling Mother
~ until we meet again

This book is dedicated to all those
who have been brought up in institutions
and long to know who their families are.

CONTENTS

This is a true story but some of the names,
dates and places have been changed to protect
the identity and privacy of some individuals

PART ONE

Phyllis Little – Orphan

Chapter 1

Where Do I Begin?

Catching sight of her winding her way down the hill from the station to meet me, as she often did, you could have easily mistaken my mother for one of life's misplaced people. The moment I caught her eye, I felt a sense of elation that she was here again, and yet a pang of sadness, too. I laughed when my partner Philip joked that she could be Mr Bean's mother; I knew exactly what he meant. Other boyfriends in the past had been less kind. I remembered her showing off at a Christmas party once and I must admit it was entertaining, as her dancing was more tribal than disco. At least I understood her little eccentricities, but to some people she may have appeared odd; she certainly wasn't your average mother, that's for sure. How she managed to get stranded in a lift in the Savacentre at 10 o'clock at night, when the store had already closed, or ended up being dropped off by a taxi driver in the middle of nowhere in London when she only wanted to go a few miles down the road, I will never know. Things seemed to just happen to her.

Dressed in a teenager's graffitied parker coat, her ebony hair cut in a boyish style, and weighed down by a ton of carrier bags, she drifted along aimlessly in a world of her own. I couldn't help but wonder what had changed her. When I was growing up she cared about her appearance, even when she had very little money, but now it was as though she had let everything go. That's not to say she was an unhappy person, on the contrary, full of the Irish banter and a cheery smile, nothing ever got her down. Even the checkout girls in Tesco would ask after her, as did the man in the dry cleaners whom she used to buy charity pin badges from.

"How's your mother? Haven't seen her lately," he said, checking the number on my ticket. "She's a real character you know. Cracks me up with the things she comes out with."

That didn't surprise me, since she tended to say exactly what she thought, which, to my relief, most people found amusing. Nothing she said was ever meant to offend, it was just her being her.

As she plodded nearer, I scuffed my feet on the pavement and buried my head in my scarf, trying to shake off the biting wind. I checked my watch and breathed a sigh. As usual, I had been waiting for quite a while, but at least now, with her in sight, I could stop fretting about whether something had happened to her. My eyes followed her movements as she stopped at the lights to cross the road and negotiate the fast-moving traffic. She was puffing heavily on her cigarette and dragged her feet as she ambled along, painful arthritis having caused her left foot to splay out to one side, making her walking slow and laboured. But as soon as she saw me she forgot about her ailments and her face lit up. I couldn't help but smile as I watched her wave her hand in the air like an excited child.

"Sal! Sal!" she called out, trying to be heard above the din of buses and heavy lorries thundering past.

Coming down to see me was the highlight of her week, when she knew that she would be looked after and could completely switch off for a couple of days; it was our little routine. Even though I was now in my mid-40s, I still needed her as much as she needed me, and throughout my adult life she had been my pillar of support when things had gone wrong.

"It's not about you," my ex-husband announced, as he stormed out of the door. "It's about me, and whether I still want to remain married to you!"

She was there that day he left, cradling me in her arms like a broken doll as I sat cross-legged on the floor in a shower of glass and debris. And it was her who gave me the strength to move on when, eventually, I decided to relocate to Sussex and start over.

"Don't worry, darling," she said. "No matter what happens in life, you've always got your Mammy. You don't need a man to make you feel happy. I'm telling you, they're not worth a light – the lot of them. Just believe in yerself and be strong. You know I'll always be by your side."

My marriage break-up, when I least expected it, had been earth shattering, leaving me feeling like a discarded toy; all my hopes and dreams crushed beyond recognition and making me look at my life in a different way. Now I was on my own and it felt very lonely. I had no children and no family, apart from my brother who I didn't see very often, and that was it.

There were some relatives on my dad's side, but he had become estranged from them many years before, so we grew up never knowing them. It was only now, after all this time, that I had begun to rekindle a tentative relationship with them because of my genealogy research.

I thought of Mum. We were both in a similar situation. Her own marriage had ended after a long spell of unhappiness and misery but, unlike me, she had no one to turn to. It was then I began to really understand her suffering; what it felt like to be rejected and to feel unloved.

Abandoned as a baby by her mother, Mum was raised in an orphanage in Ireland. The not knowing who she was or where she came from had a devastating effect on her, leaving her distrustful of the world. But for that, her life could have been so different. Now I began to wonder about the family she never knew and why she'd been given up. Just who was her mother and could she still be alive?

So much had happened to us through the years that our lives were intertwined. My childhood was dysfunctional and insecure. I craved normality and a sense of belonging, but they were absent. Perhaps that's why I used to attach myself to other families as a teenager. When I was married I became part of my husband's family. While it lasted, it was great, the feeling of being accepted and knowing that people cared. But now I felt abandoned, just like she had felt as a child. There was no one to relate to. I had friends, but it's not the same as having family who cares. But why? How were we both born into worlds where we did not know our own families, I wondered. Who were they and what had happened? These questions had always been there, but now in middle age they seemed more important than ever, which made me realise that for my own peace of mind, as well as hers, I needed to find answers, before it was too late.

Mum's health was a nagging issue, giving me many a sleepless night and often sending my mind into overdrive. The thought of losing her terrified me. I loved her so much, I thought I would never cope if anything happened to her.

Walking over to the car, she stubbed her cigarette out on the pavement before opening the passenger door.

"Hello, Petsey," she said, manoeuvring herself and several bulging carrier bags.

"Are you alright, Mum?"

"Yes, I'm fine, Sal – just not as fast as you, Pet. I'll be there in a minute. Mammy's cold. Can't you put the heater on?"

"Yes, alright. It'll be warm soon. Have you been buying again?"

"Buying what?"

"The bags. What's in all the bags?"

"Oh, Petsey, I just popped into the second-hand shop on the way down. They had some crocheted blankets and I thought they'd do your cats for the winter, to wrap them up and keep them warm."

"Oh, that's kind—"

"And then I popped into the Savacentre before I got the train, and would you believe it naw, they had boil-in-the-bag cod in seafood sauce on special offer in the frozen aisle, so I couldn't resist."

"Boil-in-the-bag *what*? You don't mean... not for the cats, surely?"

"And Sal, hey, wait till I tell you this. Here listen, you'll never guess what?"

"What?"

"They've selected me for a Sunny Award, for carer of the year. Well, would you believe that?"

"A what? You mean the care home where you work?"

"Yeah, that's great, don't you think? There's going to be a big award ceremony in a hotel in Gatwick... and I've been invited along to collect it."

"Wow, that's great Mum. I'm so proud of you. Well done! It's about time, I'd say, after all the hard work you put into that place."

Although supposedly retired, she was working all the hours God sent in a care home for elderly people. Work, it seemed, was the one thing that kept her going and which she seemed to thrive on. It also meant she didn't have to think about the past.

My father had died 20 years previously. At the time, they had been separated, but remained on good terms while still living apart. No matter how badly he treated her over the years she never held a grudge, even lying beside him holding his hand during his final hours when he was fearful of death. Her capacity to forgive never ceased to amaze me. If only I could have felt that way about him when he was alive. But I couldn't. I could not forget the past. My own relationship with him was strained, and to be in his presence for more than five minutes was intolerable. Just hearing him talk irritated me. I never went to visit him and we rarely spoke. Even on the odd occasion when he called at my flat there was an evident distance between us. I simply felt numbness, indifference, nothing. The only thing I cared about was the unbearable strain his illness put on my mother. I wish I could have felt differently, but I just wanted it to end.

When his death finally came, I thought it would bring her some relief. Instead, all it did was create a vacuum. Mum became like a lost soul drifting in and out of second-hand shops along the high street and visiting cafés, with nothing to do except people-watch, smoke and drink tea.

"How was work, Mum?" I asked.

"Oh, alright, although they asked me to do some extra shifts this week because some of the others went sick. There's a lot of them that's lazy, you know."

"Not again?"

"But I got invited to four funerals – four funerals, Sal! Would you believe it naw?" she said, sounding ecstatic, as if she had won the top prize in a competition.

"Several of the residents' relatives requested me. But, of course, I couldn't go to all of them."

"Oh Mum, I wish you'd slow down; you know you're not in the best of health. You shouldn't be doing so much at your age. Let the others go to the funerals. I don't want you standing around getting cold."

As if on cue, she started to cough; a really wheezy cough that seemed to go on and on. I could hear the catarrh rattling around on her chest as she choked copious amounts of mucus into a tissue and then examined the contents. *Lovely*, I thought.

"Have you got another chest infection?" I asked.

"Ah no, don't worry about me now. I'm grand. There are plenty worse off people than me. I love my job and I'm very lucky still to be employed at my age. Did I tell you about Mary?"

"No."

"Poor Mary – ah, now, she's gorgeous…"

"But Mum —"

"God bless her, I love her. She's just so sweet, but the poor thing has dementia and has no family. Makes me realise how lucky I am to have you and Will. You know, I felt so sorry for her I bought her a little teddy the other day, out of my own money, and she was delighted – oh, delighted she was!"

"That was really kind of you, Mum, but you shouldn't be forking out your own money. Let the home do that."

"Ah, Petsey, I know what it feels like to have no one in the world, just like Mary. No one to even come and see you. Sure, it's nothing; only a few pounds – so what? You know money doesn't mean anything to me."

"Oh, Mum, what am I going to do with you?" I really wish you'd pack up work and come and live down here with me."

It was no use. She had already switched off and was deep in thought as usual, not listening but looking out of the window at people we passed in the high street as we headed for the winding country road to take us home.

*

"Sal, darling, tell me how you're getting on with your father's family tree. Have you found out any more yet?"

I knew she wasn't really interested and only mentioned it for something to say but, having recently caught the genealogy bug, I had been keeping her updated about my progress.

"Yes, I've found out quite a lot and managed to go way back. But what I'd really like to do is find your family."

"You mean my mother?"

"Well – yes! And who knows what else?"

"Oh, Sal, that would mean the world to me, if I could just find out what happened to her. But I doubt I ever will. You know, I believe that the orphanage changed the date of my birth deliberately so she'd never be found."

"But that doesn't make sense, Mum. Why would they do that?"

"Oh, darling, everything was well hidden in those days. No one ever talked about anything. It's not like it is today. They didn't care about you as a person. I was a nobody – the lowest of the low – that was how it was in life back then."

"Mum, that's so sad. But surely there must've been a good reason? I can't believe they'd hide the truth from you like that."

"I don't know. Perhaps it was something to do with my aunt's family. They never liked me – certainly Edna Carter never approved, and Bunty could never look me in the face. But my aunt always said there was money put aside for me. In fact once, she actually said that a mother 'would never leave her daughter out of her will'."

"But she wasn't your real aunt, was she? She was only your guardian. Do you think you might be related then?"

She stared out of the window.

Mum had been such a loving mother to me and my brother. Selfless and giving, she poured affection into our lives. The thought of no one offering her the love that she had so unconditionally shown us greatly saddened my heart. Being so close allowed me to still see that lost child in her. I often noticed how she needed to clutch objects like a lighter or pen tightly in her hand, as though for comfort, and how her facial expressions would give away her struggle to work out something being said, as if it was a difficult puzzle.

Her life was a whirlwind of mayhem: bills unpaid, never being on time for anything, spending every spare minute on the go without allowing proper time to eat or rest. Unfailingly, she would pretend everything was alright because she never wanted me to worry, which of course I did, often wondering *Why is she like this? Why can't she slow down and be like normal mothers of her age?*

But it would take several more years and experiences in my own life before I realised that the reason she was like this was the legacy of her childhood, one that would never go away or be forgotten. She had learnt at an early age to supress her pain but I knew that, underneath, the absence of any nurturing in her childhood meant she still suffered inside.

Those thoughts were pressing heavily on my mind as I pulled into the drive. I took a deep breath and examined my face in the rear-view mirror, quickly wiping the corner of one eye with my finger so Mum wouldn't notice. She smiled and waved through the window at my two silver tabbies who pattered out to greet us with their tails high.

The cats purred and rubbed their furry bodies against the side of the car as Mum opened the car door to greet them.

"Look, Sal, the cats. Hello, my darlings. Yer Mammy is home. Oh, I'm so cold and dying for a cup of tea. Petsey, will you put the kettle on when we get in?"

"Of course, just give me a minute."

She started to cough again. It never seemed to go away and was getting worse, if anything. Even the antibiotics didn't always work. It became of great concern to me. Somewhere in the back of my mind, although I tried to dismiss it, I felt a clock ticking away the time we had left. I knew I needed to ask her for as much information as she could recall, but it wouldn't be easy as she was always reluctant to talk about the past.

After several refills of tea and a bite to eat, we sat down on the sofa together.

"Right, Mum, I want you to tell me as much as you can remember about your time as a child."

"Oh, Sal, quite honestly I'd rather not think about that. It was a long time ago… my memory isn't what it used to be, you know."

"Look, I know it's difficult for you, but it's our only hope of piecing any information together. There must be a way of finding out about your mother… why you were brought up in an orphanage. You want to know the truth, don't you?"

"The truth?" she asked incredulously. "Darling, I've thought of nothing else for the last 60 years. Do you not know what it feels like to think your mother never wanted you? Never loved you. Never cared. You were lucky – you had me to love and protect you – but I had no one." And then, as an afterthought, "Perhaps she wanted a boy."

"Oh, don't be ridiculous. Now you're being irrational. You may have been a mistake, but for all you know your mother was forced to give you up. Times weren't like today. You know that, don't you?"

"Yes of course, Pet. Life was hard then. That I *do* know."

She blinked as she cupped the hot tea tightly in her hand as though to gain warmth. I realised how difficult it was for her to recollect a past she would rather forget. I understood that feeling of abandonment and how raw the pain still felt, years later, after having left its scars, but still I needed to press her.

"Things don't just happen without a reason. Look, neither of us is getting younger. If we keep putting off talking about it, one day it may be too late. You're always telling me, we never know what's around the next corner. And, for all we know, your mother might be still out there somewhere. Can you try and think back... for me? How old were you when she left you at the orphanage? Try Mum, please."

Chapter 2

The Orphanage

Phyllis

It was the loneliness and fear I felt at night that I remember the most. I was about six or seven at the time. Staring up at a lofty ceiling and listening to an angry wind howling a gale outside and fighting to get in, I slid down under the refuge of the covers trying to make myself seem small. The room was dark and there was no light, except moonlight filtering through the high-up windows and casting eerie shadows on the wall. All I could hear was my own heart thudding. Although I was in a dormitory with 12 other girls, I might as well have been on my own as talking was forbidden when the lights went out. God help you if you were caught by the staff. I only had to hear their footsteps on the creaking floorboards outside and I felt fearful. Laying there with my eyes tightly shut and holding my breath, I hoped and prayed I would drift off soon so as I wouldn't get into trouble.

At times like this I often used to wonder about my mother and why she had given me up. I couldn't understand why she'd leave me in a place like this and I prayed that, whatever had happened in her life, she would come back for me one day and take me home with her. I wanted her so much, my heart physically ached for her love. I imagined her tucking me in, stroking my hair and saying, "Go to sleep, Phyllis." But it was just a dream. Instead, I'd bury my head in the pillow and rock myself backwards and forwards for comfort until eventually I'd fall asleep.

It was the early 1940s, and this was the place I called home, The North Dublin Female Orphan House. It was the place I had grown up in since I was nearly three years old when I was transferred from the Bethany, a mother and baby home for unmarried mothers. The orphanage was not a place of love. There was no talk of love. There was never any talk of mothers or fathers either. It was just accepted that you had been conceived out of wedlock and so this was your lot in life. Several other girls who had never known their parents came from the same place, and they were all like me. It was a Protestant orphanage, run by a Reverend Parsons who ruled us with an iron rod – quite literally – and he was responsible for the religious indoctrination of our souls.

Church was three times on a Sunday. In between church, dinner and tea, we were marched in all weathers on long arduous walks up to Phoenix Park and back. By the end of the day we were fit for nothing. Our life in the orphanage was structured so that little time was left for ourselves.

"Will you all stand for hymn number 93, *What a Friend We Have in Jesus*," the reverend ordered, and I watched him narrowing his eyes to observe the two of us like a hawk.

Patsy, my best friend, was huddled close to me. I could smell the musty dampness of her coat from the rain, and her stale breath. She had the giggles that morning.

"Ah no, Patsy – don't naw!" I mouthed, trying to control the smirk on my face.

I only ever had to note that twinkle of devilment in those eyes of hers to know there'd be trouble. I'm sure it was that unruly mane of red hair that made her so bold. It certainly wasn't me as

I was mostly a quiet child, although I did have my moments. The place made you that way; always being told you mustn't do this, you mustn't do that. Every task was done in complete silence and obeying all the rules, or there were severe consequences.

For a moment my mind wandered, as it often did, and I watched the sun's rays illuminating the stained-glass window. The bright colours were beautiful and had me transfixed until my thoughts drifted away wondering what the outside world was really like. I thought about when I'd be old enough to leave and be free. Free as a bird, I was thinking – how wonderful that would be. The reverend, noticing I was distracted, gazed down and shot me a glare of disapproval. *Oh, God, why was it me? Why always me?* Quickly, I buried my face in the hymn book.

His sermons were always fervent: he lectured us from the pulpit, working up a sweat and dabbing his brow with a handkerchief. *When is it ever going to end?* I thought. It was a relief when we could file out of the church.

"Phyllis Little, come back here," he summoned.

"Yes, reverend," I replied.

"Was it you, I saw fooling about during my sermon?"

"No, reverend."

"Well, I hope not. God's house is not a place to be mocked and if I ever catch you behaving disgracefully, there will be all hell to pay. Am I clear?"

"Yes, reverend. Of course, reverend."

I turned to go, but he hadn't finished.

"Little, your hair is like a haystack! Show some respect in the house of our Lord. Remember, cleanliness is next to godliness. I know all about you. I'll be watching you – just remember that."

My aunt (who wasn't my real aunt, but acted as my guardian) never cared for him. She always sensed something untrustworthy about his character, especially when he complained to her about me. Perhaps she was right. He was full of airs and graces to people who came to visit, offering a warm handshake and an earnest smile, but behind closed doors we knew what he was really like.

His office was a place you dreaded being sent. Usually it was matron who dished out the corporal punishment, with a big stick kept in a tall cupboard. She used it to make an example of you, but if you were deemed to have committed a more serious offence you were sent to the reverend.

There was talk of something we called the 'inkwell'. It was a sort of pot he kept, which had a flame burning from within. He used the flame to heat up the pointy end of his stick and then, when he considered it hot enough, he lashed you on the palms of your hands. I never saw it – he never used it on me – but its existence was legend.

There were plenty of unsavoury rumours about him too. I remember how Patsy once told me how she had witnessed him coming into her dormitory one night in an awful rage. He had it in for a girl in the next bed to her. He whipped back the bedclothes and beat her with violent sweeps across her backside. There was no stopping him as his force rained down on her again and again. The more she cried, the harder he struck his blows.

While she was wriggling about trying to avoid being beaten, his stick caught her sanitary towel, but he didn't care. You would have thought he could have seen it was her time of the month and left her alone, but still he carried on. Bits of bloodied cotton wool were strewn all about the room in a million pieces as he lost control. Patsy, who witnessed it all, lay there like a corpse, pretending to be asleep and too scared to move. It wasn't until he had exhausted himself that he finally stopped. His limp, lacklustre hair stuck to his brow and he wiped spit from his mouth with the back of his hand. Patsy's friend was left distraught and uncontrollably sobbing, surrounded by a mass of bloodied white sheets. Listening to her friend's pain was torturous. Patsy told me later she was never going to tell anyone when her periods started; she didn't want the same thing to happen to her.

However, we got our own back one day. It was a Saturday afternoon and we had been hard at work cleaning rooms on the first floor. The reverend, who thankfully we didn't see that often, was walking about the building looking for Mrs Pritchard. She was in charge of housekeeping and liked to keep us all in our place. Patsy and I peered over the bannisters to see what was going on.

"Have you seen herself, Mrs Pritchard?" we heard him enquiring, his voice echoing upwards.

"Sorry, no, reverend," came the reply. "Maybe she's upstairs."

"Will you tell her I'm looking for her if you see her? I've some urgent business to talk about," he said.

He strode towards the front door as if he was going back to his clergy house, but then changed his mind.

"I'll just dash upstairs and check to see if she's there for myself," he said and bounded upstairs, two steps at a time.

"Quick, Patsy, quick! He's coming – hide!" I said.

Oh, sure, we both had the devil in us that day.

"Let's get him!" urged Patsy. "Right, I'll get this big stick and lay it on the floor. You get in that doorway opposite and I'll get in this one. We'll hide behind the doors and when he's close I'll shove it over to you, so as when he runs along the corridor he'll trip up. And then we'll run for it. What do you say?"

"Aww, that's absolutely brilliant Patsy!" I said, suppressing my fear with laughter.

His fast-paced walk grew louder and louder the nearer he came. I could hear my heart fiercely pounding and my hand trembled uncontrollably as I held the stick. It was a daring plan, and I'm not sure why we did it. Maybe it was the thrill of being able to get away with something, anything, as our lives were so repressed; or perhaps just the chance to get our own back on him for the way he treated us. Either way, we knew if we were caught we'd receive the beating of our lives.

Dizzy with excitement, my head started to spin as his footsteps drew closer. Patsy winked to me from the doorway opposite. All I could see were a flash of sapphire eyes and a set of pale fingernails cupped around the edge of a large oak door. I winked back. You could hear the metal heel-plates on the soles of his shoes tap-tap-tapping on the wooden floor. I held my breath.

In a moment of unbridled madness, Patsy shoved the stick along the floor at great speed. Quickly, I grabbed it, lifting it slightly and – wham! He tripped and stumbled then fell into a dishevelled heap on the floor, his round-rimmed spectacles flying off at random and his white wispy hair in a state of disarray.

"What the hell...?" he cried, attempting to pull himself up from the floor. "Who in the name of all that's holy...? Wicked children that y'are. When I find out who it is you won't hear the end of this, I can assure you!"

We raced back along the corridor laughing our heads off, not daring for a second to glance behind us, and then ran swiftly down the back stairs, slamming out through a fire escape door and down the iron steps adjacent to the side entrance. We ran like we'd never run before.

Somehow, we managed to avoid being seen by sneaking through a black wrought-iron gate that led to the orchard. Once among the trees we felt safe because it was partially out of sight of the main building. At last we caught our breaths and relaxed. We sat there, cross-legged under the apple trees, still panting like a pair of restless greyhounds. At last, lying flat with my arms outstretched behind me, I felt vindicated. It was a rare satisfaction which I haven't felt since, and a bloomin' miracle that we got away with it.

Everyday life was hard though. It always started with a bell – a very loud bell that rang in the hallway – followed by one of the staff marching around shouting for us to get up. You knew you had to jump out of bed fast or else. Every single activity was signalled by the sound of a bell: breakfast, dinner and tea; time to go to school, time to go to bed, and so on. We knew the routine. Immediately we rose in the morning we had to say our prayers before we did anything else, then make our own bed and keep our clothes and shoes clean. It was a fixed regime that resulted in severe discipline if we didn't stick to it. This was all before breakfast.

When I was younger, bed-wetting inspections took place first thing every morning. If you were found to have wet the bed, you faced being chastised and humiliated. Then you were made to hold the sheets above your head for everyone to see and sent to the laundry room to wash them yourself. Some girls would throw them out of the window onto the fire escape, in anticipation of this, then rush down two flights of stairs to retrieve them and wash them before they were found out. But wetting the bed was common in those days because we lived in constant fear. Fear of everything. The staff barely looked at us before giving out a slap round the face. They'd hit us even for having mud on our shoes when we came in from the garden. They really didn't need an excuse.

One time, I had got into trouble for something – although it wasn't for wetting the bed, as I was a bit older – I can't quite remember the incident now, but my punishment was to clean the back stairs.

The building, built around the end of the 18th century, was on three floors and had six flights of stairs with a shiny wooden bannister from top to bottom, that always smelt of lavender beeswax. It took me all day on my hands and knees, and well into that dark winter evening, to make it from one end to the other.

My back ached and I had pins and needles, and stiffness in my knee caps from kneeling in the same position for so long. The worst of it though was that it was eerie. That is, no doubt, why it was given as a punishment.

We were always telling each other ghost stories at night before the lights went out, and used to imagine the place was haunted. The electric lighting didn't help either because the voltage was very low and only lit the place dimly. The bulbs constantly flickered, which made the whole place creepy. We could hardly see what we were doing and sometimes I imagined they were going out completely and was beside myself with fear. When the wind got up outside and started to whip around the building, every groan and every creak left my mouth dry and I remember my heart almost pumping out of my chest. I was more scared of that than of facing a beating from any of the staff.

Life at the orphanage was like being incarcerated. Sure, there are some who will say we weren't so hard done by because we got sixpence pocket money every week when some orphans didn't get any, but then again you could say that we earnt our keep for being used as skivvies. We had trips to the seaside, to Bray and Greystones in the summer holidays. Oh, they were great! I remember eating sandwiches on the beach and being allowed to the shops on our own to buy sweets with the pocket money we had saved. Father Christmas even came a couple of times, bearing gifts. He'd bring us cast-off toys that nobody in the outside world wanted anymore wrapped as Christmas presents. Mine, one year, was a doll. It didn't matter that she only had one arm and one leg and an eye missing. I was overjoyed! I was grateful for anything.

But I think a lot of those niceties were done for show. The orphanage was run as a charity and well-to-do people were encouraged to donate. They wanted the world to see the orphans being well looked after, but they had no idea what a hard existence we endured. The orphanage's ethos was based on servitude, and much of our time was learning how to be domestic servants for when we left to get a job at 16.

Every moment before school was taken up with cleaning the dishes and scraping out the big industrial-sized pots that the porridge was cooked in. After school we did our homework, and more cleaning or scrubbing on our hands and knees. On top of that we did the laundry and cleaned the communal bathrooms with their 28 porcelain sinks. It never seemed to end.

I hated all the cleaning and, I suppose because of that, I wasn't good at it. Maybe that's why housework was never my thing later in life. My head was often in the clouds, dreaming about the day I'd be free and reunited with my mother. I used to wonder what she looked like and if I took after her in any way. Did I get my raven hair and dimpled cheeks from her? And why did my front teeth slightly protrude? Were they like hers? What made her give me up and let me grow up in a place like this? What had I done that was so bad – that made her abandon me? Or did she simply not love me enough? Oh, I longed for her so much.

During one of my daydreams Mrs Pritchard was patrolling the corridors for signs of idleness and caught me in the act.

"Wake up, Phyllis! Are you daydreaming again?" she exclaimed.

"Call this clean? By my soul, you are the laziest child I think I ever met. Lazy, good for nothing and useless. Don't you know how lucky you are to be here instead of out there on the streets? Well?"

"Sorry, so I am, Mrs Pritchard. I'll do the sinks again, I will so. I promise."

"I think you will, my girl, and I'll be back to inspect them shortly," she warned, rushing off to persecute more victims.

It was no place for a child. We were made to feel grateful for a bed to sleep in and food on our plate. It was continuous work and very little play. Recreation was only allowed on Saturday afternoons once we had finished our chores for the day but, even then, we were encouraged to attend knitting and needlework classes that prepared us for our future domestic life when we left the orphanage. Some Saturdays, a lady known as Auntie Joan, who used to teach these skills, came up to the dormitories and threw sweets on the beds for us all to clamber for. Ah, there were occasionally a few nice ones like her, but no sooner did you get close than they left – and that broke your heart.

We also had to look after the younger children. A special room was designated for learning to change nappies and how to wash and dress them. Aww, I loved the little ones, and looking after them made me want some of my own when I grew up. By the age of 12 I'd already decided I wanted to be a children's nurse.

And then there was never enough food. When it was our turn to scrub the potatoes in the scullery we'd eat them raw if no one was looking, as we were so constantly hungry. Oh sure, they gave us three meals a day, but they were meagre portions, never enough, and the older girls stole mine off my plate whenever they could.

"Give it here!" one would say, snatching it when I wasn't looking. "If you don't wannit, I'll have it."

I was never quick enough to realise what was happening. Being the smallest, I found it difficult to retaliate, especially against older girls who were meant to be looking out for us. Thinking back, I don't blame them now. It was the way it was. You'd chance anything if you thought you could get away with it. Sometimes, we'd sneak down to the orchard and steal apples from the trees and stuff them down our knickers. Thankfully, I never got caught.

Every morning we stood in the refectory hall with its cavernous ceiling and high windows, waiting patiently at the long-benched tables for permission to sit down. It was always a stressful time and quite often I fainted while waiting. That happened to me a lot when I was younger and I never understood why. Once matron had finished saying grace, we could start breakfast. It was always the same; controlled and very disciplined. A bowl of porridge, a slice of bread and marmalade and a cup of tea. Dinner was a small dish of some sort of vegetable stew, with a tiny bit of meat in it if you were lucky. Tea was a piece of cheese and another cup of tea. It was never enough, not with all the energy we used scrubbing the place down all day.

The staff sat on a separate table, watching us continuously, scrutinising us to make sure there was no talking or laughing.

"The girl Betts and the girl Little! You will stop all that chatter now, so you will, and eat your food in silence," was a common command.

God, you couldn't breathe. We all saw that, unlike us, they had pots of honey and jam and whole loaves of bread, so they could help themselves to as much as they liked. They had nice china too, not the chipped mugs we were given.

We were certainly forced to understand our place in life. Even the outside world looked down on us, especially if they knew we were illegitimate. I remember one time when we had a rare outing and were marched up to visit the zoo, paid for by a local Lady Somebody-or-the-other, there'd been a motor accident right outside the main gates. We were instantly recognisable in our dark green gaberdine coats with hats pulled well over our heads, holding hands and marching two by two. People always stopped and stared. A group had crowded round the scene of the accident where an elderly lady was lying in the road. Immediately, we were picked on by a group of boys from a local private school, who jeered at us. It was the first time I became acutely aware of how people from the outside world judged us.

"Orphans, orphans, dirty little orphans!" taunted the boys.

"Aww, look at them now. It's the poor little orphan girls. What's the matter orphans? Didn't yer mammies want yer now?"

They snickered and ridiculed while the adults in the crowd turned their heads and looked away. There was not the merest glint of compassion in their eyes – sure, we were only orphans to them, which meant 'nothing'. Luckily an ambulance arrived swiftly, because all I wanted was to disappear and for the ground to swallow me up. I lowered my head and stared at the paving stones, I felt so sad and ashamed. It felt so unfair to be treated like this, even if they were only silly school boys.

State school was the worst, so it was. The teacher thought nothing of singling us out. She hated anyone who she thought was the offspring of a fallen woman, particularly if she knew you were from a place like the Bethany Home. Thankfully for me, I only had to attend there until I was 12 years old and then, for some lucky reason, my 'aunt' paid for me to go to private school. Out of the whole orphanage only two of us were privileged enough to be sponsored. That in itself caused a problem though, with repercussions I never envisaged.

*

By the time Mum finished telling her story, it was past nine o'clock and she had started to fade. I left the room for five minutes and when I returned she had nodded off, still sitting upright.

When I called her the following morning she was still weary from the day before. The curtains were drawn but a spear of light pierced its way into the darkness, revealing an array of black garments scattered about the room. An opened carton of skimmed milk, some boxes of antibiotic capsules, a half-used tube of cream for athlete's foot and several AA-sized batteries littered the bedside cabinet.

"Mum, Mum, are you getting up? I've made you a cup of tea."

Beneath the duvet she stirred and coughed.

"Are you okay? You don't sound very good today."

She coughed again and pulled back the bedclothes.

"Ah, Petsey, I'm alright. I'm not awake yet. What time is it?"

"It's a quarter past 11."

"Is it now? Where are the cats?"

"The cats are downstairs – they're fine. I've got the day off, so I thought we could maybe go to the garden centre and have a bite to eat when you are up. What do you think?"

"Oh, that would be grand, darling."

Two hours later we were comfortably eating lunch in the garden centre, Mum pushing her fork around a small plate of scrambled egg and me enjoying my cheese sandwich.

"So, Mum… carrying on from last night… How did it all start, your relationship with Auntie Bea?"

She took a gulp of tea and wiped her mouth with a tissue.

"My aunt? Oh, yes, she was so good to me. She used to come over from Ireland and babysit occasionally when you were small. And she helped out when Will was born.

"That's interesting. She obviously still cared for you, even though you were an adult and had a life of your own. Why would she do that? I'm intrigued. Can you remember when you first met her?"

Chapter 3

Auntie Bea

Phyllis

You know, it's so long ago that I don't recollect when I was first introduced to my aunt, but I guess it must have been by the time I started school. The local Protestant churches in Dublin used to encourage the congregations to take an interest in us orphans, by befriending us. The orphanage often used to hold open days when they encouraged visitors and patrons to come and meet the staff and us girls. Sometimes we put on a play and dressed up, or demonstrated some Irish dancing. Then we'd hand round tea and cakes, along with bright cheery smiles, praying for someone kind to take pity on us and want to be our sponsor. It was a wonderful accolade for any girl who received attention, because if someone decided to take an interest in you, then they might pay for you to attend private school instead of the nightmarish state school that we all dreaded. But for those who were ignored it was the ultimate humiliation. Our mothers didn't want us and neither did anyone else. But I was one of the lucky ones.

Miss Beatrice Davidson, or Auntie Bea as I used to call her, was an independent single lady who lived with her mother on the outskirts of North Dublin. She had no interest in marriage and worked as a legal secretary and drove a car, which was unusual for a woman in those days. One of her main interests was photography and she was always taking pictures of me when she got the chance. Her life, though, revolved very much around the Church and she was a devout Christian. If anyone should ask, she told me to say she was my great aunt, and she acted as my guardian for the remainder of my days in the orphanage. Always dressed in black, and never without her kid gloves and clutch bag under her arm, she had an air of refinement about her. She was slim and elegant with compassionate eyes and was the kindest person I ever knew. Yet she had a steely attitude about her and wouldn't tolerate nonsense from anybody. I had nothing but admiration for her. Why she showed such an interest in me and picked me out of all the others, I'll never know.

Then her mother died, when I was 11 or 12 years old, leaving her the house and making her substantially well off. Around this time, I saw more and more of her, and some weekends or holidays she took me out and bought me things. She paid for my private school and even introduced me to members of her family. I believe she also paid the reverend a fee for me to reside at the orphanage. Her warm-heartedness and generosity knew no bounds.

"Phyllis, dear, if there is anything you ever want − it doesn't matter about the cost − don't be afraid to ask," she used to say.

I never did ask for anything, but I used to wonder about this. Auntie Bea was talking as if money had been put aside for me. But why, and who could have done this? Could it be my father showing some responsibility for me being born out of wedlock? I would never know.

Before she decided to sell the house, she even asked if I'd like to go and live with her. However, by then I had become too institutionalised and was afraid of change. Despite the orphanage's shortcomings, it felt safe and it was the only home I'd ever known. I couldn't work out why she'd even want me to live with her. Surely, all she'd done for me was enough. Was there a deeper reason that she was hiding from me? Perhaps she couldn't tell me. I had many unanswered questions in my head, but these were topics of conversation that I wouldn't dream of entering into.

Sometimes, she took me to her sister's house in Monkstown for a visit. Her sister, Edna, never approved of me, a fact she made blatantly obvious. When I entered her house, she'd turn a certain picture around on the wall. It was of a beautiful woman, and I always admired it. It made me wonder if it had some connection to me. Were they trying to keep something from me? I was puzzled.

"Can I talk to you outside – in private?" Edna would say, or "...*not* in front of Phyllis," as she ushered Auntie Bea out of the door. This only made me more suspicious. Why didn't they want me to hear what they were saying?

Edna's daughter, who was called Bunty, never looked me in the face if she visited. In fact, if she saw I was there she made her excuses and left the room.

It was always the same and I grew convinced there was a secret. Easter often fell in March, the time of year that Bunty went to England for a month, and also the school holidays, when I spent more time with Auntie Bea. Was this deliberate avoidance on Bunty's part, I wondered? And if so, why?

I had the clear impression that although my aunt wanted me to know the family, they didn't actually want anything to do with me.

Auntie Bea greatly improved things for me in many ways. Going to private school meant I made different friends outside the orphanage, but I wasn't interested in studying. I was a bit of a dunce when it came to most subjects, especially maths and science where I came bottom of the class. But I did well at religious studies, which I loved.

Geraldine was my best friend at school and used to take me up to her parent's farm in Skerries for the holidays. It was great being freed for a while from the orphanage's strict regime and all its chores. But I didn't realise how much bad feeling it would cause in my fellow orphans. I could only see what was happening in my world and, perhaps, looking back now, I should have seen it through their eyes. After all, I was the lucky one with a guardian aunt. Back then, I didn't think like that; life was just about getting through each day and surviving.

One Saturday afternoon when I returned from a shopping trip with Auntie Bea, Patsy and Joyce, another friend, were on their hands and knees cleaning the hallway floor.

"Been out with your Auntie 'gain Phyllis? Wat did she buy you this time then?" said Joyce, petulantly looking up from her bucket with a floor cloth dripping from her reddened hand.

"Auntie Bea took me to Grafton Street and she bought me a coat and some sweets," I said, as though it was nothing. I tried to get past them, but they blocked my path.

"Grafton Street, was it?" enquired Patsy. "Oooh, she must be well off then?"

She squeezed the floor cloth of every last drop and then slapped it hard on the stone-tiled floor in front of me.

"No, not at all," I said, as I began fiddling with the buttons on my coat.

"You've changed, Phyllis. You're not the same as you used to be," said Joyce.

"No, I haven't."

"Sure, yer have. You're at private school now."

"We're not good enough for the likes of yous anymore," said Patsy, joining in.

"Patsy, don't be like that. You're my best friend, yer know you are. It's not true. Of course, you're good enough for me. Please let me pass, Pats, please."

"Not until you've cleaned yer shoes," said Joyce, spitefully flicking the floor cloth, heavily saturated in dirty grey water, over my feet. My shoes and socks were completely soaked through, and I squelched as I walked.

"What d'you do that for!" I exclaimed. "My feet are soaked now!"

"Oops! How clumsy of me. I'm so sorry now... I didn't mean it," mocked Joyce.

"Can we have some of your sweets, Phyllis?" asked Patsy.

"Well, I don't know why I should after what you've just done, but I don't want you to be angry with me. Sure, I'm sorry if I upset you now. Pats, please let's still be friends... cam on now."

"Ah, Phyllis, yer know we didn't mean it. Sure, we're only having a laugh now." Patsy was trying to sound sincere and I genuinely wanted to believe her.

I bent down, feet standing in a dripping puddle, and offered them both a sweet.

Joyce grabbed a handful, then Patsy. Then Joyce went back for more, before finally snatching the paper bag from me.

"No!" I cried. "Give it back. Auntie bought them for me." I lunged for the bag in a state of panic and upset. "Give it to me! Give it back here."

With that, Joyce grabbed my hair by the roots and pulled my head down as far as she could, while Patsy held the bag in the air so I couldn't reach the sweets.

"Aargh! Stop! Stop! You're hurting me," I screamed.

In all the commotion, the galvanised bucket filled with the dirty disinfected water was knocked over creating a mini pond on the floor. With that, my ankle twisted sideways and I slipped and landed in the puddle, my coat soaking up the wet. The bag of sweets was propelled into the air and its contents scattered far and wide, far-flung into the corners of the room. To make matters worse, with all the screaming and shouting going on, Mrs Pritchard appeared, looking more than a little disgruntled.

"And what is the meaning of this then? I see no work, that's for sure. Fooling around. You're a disgrace, so the lot of you are! What have you got to say for yerselves?"

"Sorry, so we are, Mrs Pritchard," I blurted out. "It won't happen again."

She folded her arms and had a self-assured look on her face. "Right, so, I'm sure it won't happen again. I wonder what himself the reverend will have to say about this."

I was so upset I was unable to answer. The brand-new coat that Auntie had so lovingly bought me was ruined.

"Get up child," commanded Mrs Pritchard. "I want all of you to go and stand outside the reverend's office – now!"

We stood there with nothing to say, looking down at the floor and shuffling our feet. Tears trickled down my face. I felt so hurt that Patsy and Joyce could behave like that when I thought we were friends.

Mrs Pritchard knocked at the door.

"Enter!"

Mrs Pritchard flicked a wave of white coiffured hair back from her forehead and opened the door. She seemed to be gone for ages but eventually reappeared with the reverend, both looking very stern.

"Step inside all of you – now!" he barked.

We traipsed in to await our fate, trying to avert our gaze from his eyes.

"Mrs Pritchard tells me there has been tomfoolery going on in the main hallway instead of work and the place is now flooded. Is this correct?"

We all looked up and nodded slowly. It was no use trying to defend ourselves, not with him. He wouldn't listen anyway.

"Now, I would like you to give me one good reason why you don't deserve to be punished for your actions, please."

There was silence. My whole body was trembling.

"Hmm? I'm waiting and I can't hear anything," he said sarcastically in a sing-song voice, cupping his hand to his ear.

No one dared answer.

"Hmm, right. It's just as I thought. Well, you know how God views unrepentant sinners, don't you?"

He paused for a moment and walked behind his desk, turning his back on us as he reflected at length by gazing out of the window. There was a deafening silence. We looked at each other, unsure what he'd do next, but it wasn't long before he had formulated his grand speech.

"You are only here but for the grace of God. Your aim is to learn how to support yourselves when you leave us and go into the world, to be *some* use to society. At the moment, I would say you are not fit for purpose for any future employer – and may never be!"

We stood there completely still, too scared to speak. I could hear the sleeves of my coat drip, drip, dripping onto his parquet flooring, forming a wet patch where I stood.

"Phyllis Little, take off that coat and leave it on the floor," he barked.

Slowly I peeled the sopping wet sleeves from my arms. My beautiful new coat dropped to the floor in a crumpled soaked heap. I was just heartbroken.

"Stand in line and hold out your right hands, all of you," he ordered.

Out of nowhere he produced the longest wooden stick I had ever seen. He paced briskly up and down a few times, swiping it through the air as though to test its force. My bottom lip trembled and my hand shook as he drew near. My innards tightened and my knees grew weak.

"Remember then, that God is love; merciful and kind," he said, clasping his hands behind his back as though deep in thought. "Repent, then turn to God, so that your sins may be wiped out. The times of refreshing may come from the Lord. If we confess our sins, He is faithful and just and will purify us from all unrighteousness."

We stood shuddering, tolerating the wrath that he was drawing out as long as possible.

"Now, keep very still and do not move, or I will be forced to do it again. This is to teach you a lesson that one day you will, I have no doubt, thank me for."

Whack. Whack! WHACK. He struck each one of us in turn three times with brutal force. I recoiled in pain, with a burning sensation that pierced like a knife right down to the bones in my hand. The pain brought instant hot tears flooding into my eyes and I felt convulsed to the pit of my stomach, as though I was going to be sick. Patsy let out a loud fearful cry, wincing with the pain. Joyce, the most resilient of us three, just stood there biting her lip, refusing to give in, although I could see even her eyelids begin to redden and blink as watery tears blinded her eyes.

"Now, I want you to report to Mrs Pritchard and clear up that mess. When you have finished you will go to your dormitory where you will remain without any form of sustenance until you have learnt how to behave and to appreciate your good fortune to live in a place like this. Remember, you are only here because of the kindness and generosity of this charity and the staff that run it, otherwise you would be on the streets. I hope I have made myself clear."

It was a long couple of weeks before I saw Auntie Bea again. It was bad enough that the beautiful coat she bought me had somehow disappeared, but trying to disguise the truth about how it had happened was much worse.

I tried to hide my hand from her, but it was only a matter of time before she saw it. The physical pain remained unbelievable, and the three red welts where I had been struck so brutally were still swollen and angry-looking. But the ache I felt in my heart was far greater for the loss of my friendship with Patsy, whom I loved like a sister. Now, neither Patsy nor Joyce would speak to me. Somehow, it was made to seem all my fault that the reverend had given us a beating. Even some of the others hardly spoke to me at breakfast. It was as though word had got around that I had a benefactor and was receiving privileges they could only dream about. I felt so alone and longed for things to be back to the way they were.

"Phyllis, dear, what an earth happened to your hand?" Auntie enquired, trying to prise open my clenched fist.

I didn't want to tell her the truth in case it got Joyce and Patsy into trouble and life became even worse, so I said nothing.

"Phyllis, tell me who did this to you?"

"It doesn't matter," I said.

"Oh yes, it does matter. Now who was it? Was it the Reverend Parsons?"

"It's nothin' really," I said, keeping my head bowed.

"Phyllis? Now you know God would want you to tell the truth, don't you? Was it that awful man?"

I nodded reluctantly.

"The reverend? Really? I would have thought better of a man of the cloth, than to do such a cruel thing." Her expression said it all – it was one of complete disgust.

Tenderly, she stroked my head. "Oh, my dear child," she exclaimed. "You must be in such pain. Your hand looks so sore. No child deserves to be punished in this way."

I could tell that Auntie wasn't happy at all about what had happened and that this wasn't going to be the end of the matter. It wasn't even her first time of being displeased with him either. On a previous occasion she had queried how much food I got to eat there as she had noticed how thin my arms were, and she complained to him that I was suffering from malnutrition. He didn't like that in the least, I can tell you. Her needling must have pricked his conscience. But she was a very gifted lady: she could always see through people instantly and there was something about his character that she didn't like.

"Right," she said. "I'm going to get to the bottom of this. Phyllis, I am going to have a word with him."

Before I could stop her, she had marched off to his office. I trailed behind, cautiously, scared of the outcome and how it might affect my daily life.

She gave three firm angry knocks on his door.

"Enter!" He was curt as usual, not realising it might be a visitor.

As the door swung open, I glimpsed him standing up, greeting her warmly and offering her a seat.

"Ah, Miss Davidson! How delightful to see you again. To what do I owe this extraordinary pleasure?"

The door slammed shut. Bang! A few moments later there were raised voices coming from inside. I pressed my ear to the door, eager to hear the conversation. But the only words I could make out were "withdrawing substantial donations...", "...cruelty" and "...will take it further."

I jumped back when the door knob turned unexpectedly, not wanting them to know I had been listening in. Out spilled my ruffled aunt, impatiently fiddling with the hairpin in her hat and pursued by a red-faced reverend. Not so smug and righteous now, I thought.

"I'll see you to the door, Miss Davidson," he said, looking flustered.

Auntie dusted her hands.

"That won't be necessary, thank you, reverend. I want to say goodbye to Phyllis myself. Come, Phyllis, come," she said as she marched back down the hallway, throwing her stole across her shoulder.

"Is everything alright Auntie?" I asked hesitantly.

"Now don't you worry, Phyllis dear. Everything is fine. I have had a nice little chat with the reverend and I imagine he will think twice before he decides to inflict corporal punishment again on defenceless children."

My mouth dropped open. "What did you say?"

"Well, I might have suggested that the parochial committee (of which I am head), should perhaps divert some of their fundraising activities to other needier causes in the future."

Thankfully, it was some while before I saw the reverend again. It was the summer holidays and we all spent six weeks by the sea at Greystones. It was a welcome break from the drudgery, but flew by quickly and soon we were back in the routine of back-breaking hard chores before and after school. When we returned, the reverend was away attending a seminar, so it gave me breathing space.

By now I was coming up to 13. Patsy and I had eventually made it up and were relishing spending our time in the nursery with the little ones. We both loved babies and toddlers and used to fantasise that one day we would become children's nurses, although the mere mention of such a dream to any of the staff was laughed at unmercifully.

"What *you*?" chortled Mrs Dooley. "Ah, go on naw! You're pulling my leg. How in the name of all that's good, would the likes of you become a nurse? You wouldn't know where to begin. You have to have proper training and take exams, and no one is ever going to employ an orphan now. Best stick to what yer know. I'm sure one of the big houses would be more than happy to take you in when the time comes for a domestic job."

This put down from Mrs Dooley was typical. We were conditioned into thinking that we had no right to feel good about ourselves. We were told it so often that I began to believe it was true. Our lives were to be all about suffering, as Christ had suffered on the cross, and being grateful for small mercies. As the years drifted by, all I wanted was escape from this life of drudgery and undermining; to be my own person.

Before I knew it, I had turned 14 and finished my time at private school. My aunt now decided it would help me get a better start in life if I attended a finishing school in Central Dublin. As usual, she paid for everything. Of course, that caused more contention with my fellow orphans, so that I was ignored and shunned by some of them, which was very hard to bear. One, who I thought was my friend, shoved me across a table and pulled my hair, which ended in a nasty tussle on the floor. I quickly learnt the best thing to do was to keep out of their way.

A year trying to learn the French language and improve my cooking skills was a complete disaster. I never had any interest whatsoever in domestic science or cooking. And as for French, the only thing I learnt to say was *du fromage*, and *merci beaucoup*. That was not going to take me far in life. Funnily enough though, I did enjoy the deportment and elocution lessons. But, at the end of the day, all this finesse was only going to catch me a job as a glorified maid.

Life went on as before, but as we got older they had a slightly more relaxed attitude towards us. Everyone knew everyone and, being older, we were allowed out of the door by ourselves.

By the 1950s there were fewer than 20 of us, and eventually it was my time to leave the orphanage for good. I was sweet 16, with not the slightest idea of what lay ahead for me. That Friday morning arrived and we waited apprehensively outside the boardroom not knowing what to expect. There was myself, Patsy, Joyce, Kitty, Winnie and Una; all fidgeting and feeling anxious in our best frocks and white ankle socks. Inside, the reverend headed a long, highly polished table with matron and Mrs Pritchard either side of him. They were preparing our papers for leaving the orphanage and had managed to find us some form of employment as our first job.

First Kitty was called in. About 10 minutes later, she opened the door and returned to us.

"How did it go then?" I asked.

"Sure, they were alright, I suppose. Could have been worse. I got my birth certificate and they've found me a job as a domestic at Dr Steeven's Hospital with live-in accommodation in the nurses' wing. It's something, I guess. At least I'll be free of this place at last."

"Are you going straight away?" asked Joyce.

"Fine, so, there's nothing left for me here naw. I just need to pick up my belongings and find my way there. The job starts tomorrow."

"Ah, Kitty. I'm gonna miss you, Pet," I said, feeling as though an era was over and a new one about to start.

"I'll be missing all of yous too, won't I? But we can all keep in touch," said Kitty with tears in her eyes.

We hugged in turn, sadly, and said goodbye. It felt as if the years of camaraderie and suffering we'd endured together was finally coming to an end. We were like birds being freed from a cage for the first time, and the unknown world felt scary.

The door knob turned with force and matron appeared.

"Next please. Phyllis, that's you," she beckoned.

"Come in Phyllis, and please sit down," greeted the reverend, giving me one of his sanctimonious looks over the top of his glasses. I looked back at him for one last time.

"Now Phyllis, you will be pleased to know – and it's only by the graciousness of God – that we have found you some employment. You will start on Monday at a children's home in Blackrock as a general helper, to include some domestic work as well. You wanted to work with children, didn't you?"

"I did, I did. Thank you so much. That'll be grand. I'd be delighted to take it," I said enthusiastically, not believing my luck. What! Was he actually trying to be considerate?

"It has live-in accommodation but is only for the term of six months. How will that be for you?"

"Oh, that will be grand, reverend. I am sure that will be fine. I'm very grateful. Thank you."

"Well, I'm sure you'll do well since you love little children, and if you put your trust in the Lord, He will guide the way for you."

"That I will. Thank you."

"Here is the address for the children's home, directions to find it, and who to report to, along with a reference from matron and myself. This is your birth certificate with your particulars on. You may need this in later life, so don't lose it."

"Yes, make sure you look after it, Phyllis. We know how scatter-brained and untidy you can be," reminded Mrs Pritchard.

"Don't worry, I will. I'll treasure it always," I said, feeling totally ecstatic and trying to take it all in.

I was overwhelmed. At last I was free from this place and I had a job to go to, working with children. I couldn't have been happier. Not only that, but for the first time in my life I had my birth certificate and could see the name of my mother. I was all grown up at last. I thought how proud Auntie Bea would be of me. I undid the envelope with nervous anticipation and pulled out the birth certificate, which was written in Irish with English underneath. It said:

Sex – girl
Name – Phyllis Maud Little
Mother's name – Margaret Little
Father's name –
Place of residence at time of birth – Bethany Home
Date of birth – 30 March 1937

I read it again. "Date of birth – 30 March 1937!" I couldn't quite take it in. The *thirtieth* of March? My birthday had always been 23 December. Surely, they must have made a mistake. It was wrong. I stared blankly at the stony-walled faces in front of me. I wanted to tell them how I felt, make them understand, but I couldn't get out the words that were lodged in my throat.

"Is something wrong Phyllis?" asked matron, detecting my uncertainty.

I stared at it in disbelief.

"No, matron. Well – I'm not sure. My birth date… it's not… it's always been…"

"Yes, it is correct. Checked and verified." She spoke with clenched authority.

"But…"

"It is all correct now, Phyllis," agreed Mrs Pritchard.

My head was in turmoil. I was in a state of total confusion. Was this some sort of conspiracy? In one single instant my life had been thrown up in the air. What was going on? This was not my date of birth. Even knowing my mother's first name seemed to pale into insignificance compared to this. For 16 years my birthday was in December and now they were telling me it was in March. March, for goodness sake? I couldn't comprehend it. Were they trying to hide something? Was it to do with my mother? They were carrying on as if everything was normal and it had always been that date, but they knew full well that every year near Christmas, my aunt would call and take me out for a special high tea for my birthday on 23 December. The staff knew that. They all knew!

There was a silence before the reverend started tapping his fingers on the desk and glanced pointedly at the wall clock.

"Is there anything else Phyllis? I'm afraid we are going to have to hurry you now, as we have other leavers to get through this morning," he said.

I was stunned, with a burning sensation behind my eyes and a lump in my throat, but I held it all back. I wasn't going to let them see my pain.

"No. Well, yes… No – nothing. Just to say thank you for everything you have done for me all these years. I am very grateful indeed."

My time was up and the five minutes I had been allocated to ask all the questions about my entire life had passed. They wanted me gone.

"Well, you are very welcome. Good luck in life Phyllis and may God be with you," said the reverend as he shook my hand and ushered me to the door.

"Well, goodbye then, reverend, matron, Mrs Pritchard."

*

Another week passed leaving me keen to see Mum and ask more questions about her life. Why I had never asked her before is still a mystery to me. Maybe it was because when I was married, we never had much time alone. I had dedicated myself to being the perfect wife, and my husband came first in everything. I thought it would make him love me more, but in hindsight I realised that was a mistake. Now, I didn't have to worry about anyone else. It was all about Mum and me.

Due to a delay with the trains we arrived home later than usual. Mum was looking pale, cold and shivery. Her hair was damp, sticking to her face from the rain, and she was short of breath.

"I'm exhausted, Sal," she said, taking her coat off and plonking herself down on the sofa. "Oh, it's good to be in the warm. My chest has been playing me up again you know."

"Has it? You're pushing yourself too hard, Mum."

"Ah, Sal, don't keep on. Your Mammy's fine. I'll be all right when I see the doctor."

I heaved a reluctant sigh. "Look, I only say it because I care."

"I know, Pet, but you don't need to be worrying about me naw. I enjoy my work. I've been working all my life since I was 16, and I'm not going to stop now."

"Yes, I know, it's your life. It's just that I'm always thinking about you. That reminds me… you never finished telling me what happened after you left the orphanage and started work.

"Just let me get my breath back for a minute. Ah, the children's home at Blackrock? Yes, that's right. I hadn't thought about that place for a long while. But you got me thinking."

"Oh yes… what about?"

"My first job, when I ventured out into the big wide world. Oh, Sal, I was so green then, you'd never believe it. But I guess we all learn by our mistakes, don't we?"

"Did you regret having to leave the orphanage then?

"Ah no, I didn't have any regrets. Why would I? But I did have mixed feelings. I was glad to be free… but now I wondered who I could trust."

Chapter 4

The Land of Milk and Honey

Phyllis

Monday morning arrived and I felt a strange mixture of excitement and trepidation for my new adventure into the unknown. Yet, at the same time, I felt an overwhelming sadness at leaving the place I called home. It was the only home I'd ever known. I said farewell to a few of the staff – some of them had mellowed over the years and now they didn't seem as bad as they once were.

I eased on my woollen coat, checked my beret in the hall mirror and made my way to the bus stop with my small suitcase carrying just a few items. There was quite a nip in the air, despite the sun smiling down. People were wearing their overcoats and the trees weren't in leaf yet, although the sight of pink blossom promised it wouldn't be long.

At precisely 9:45 am the bus arrived. I climbed aboard and pressed my face against the window, watching men pass by tipping their hats, dogs pulling on their leads and shopkeepers laying out their wares for the day ahead. There was a woman pushing a pram with a little boy running ahead who tripped over and started to cry. She picked him up, hugged him and rubbed his back. I remember thinking how wonderful that must feel, to have a mammy who cared; someone to sooth your woes and make you feel better. I felt my heart sink, and wished that child had been me.

As the bus jollied along, clinging to the coastal road, I couldn't help but think about my birth certificate again. Why had they given me a different date of birth, knowing full well that it was not the birth date I had all my life? No explanation. Nothing! They wanted rid of me now I had turned 16. They didn't care that I had no one; no mother, no father, no family. My feelings meant nothing to them. And here I was, a naive young girl without a clue, being dropped off the edge of a cliff, just like that, and expected to get on with life. I tried not to let it gnaw away at me, but it did – constantly. I was frantic to know who I was and where I came from, but now my whole life felt like a lie. Changing the date on my birth certificate had been done on purpose. It was the cruellest action: to deny me the ability to find a mother who I so longed to know. What chance did I stand now of ever finding her? I bit my lip as I tried to take control, and pushed all my pain and anxiety deep down inside.

As we rounded a bend, I spotted the sea and my spirits began to lift. A row of traditional cottages opposite peeped across at the long sandy stretch of beach. *How nice it must be to live here and run barefoot along that beach*, I thought. Before long I saw a sign for Blackrock, so I knew my journey wouldn't be much longer. Sure enough, after 10 minutes, the bus screeched and ground to a halt, jolting me out of my faraway sadness. I hopped off and followed my paper directions to the address I had been given.

And there it was. I had arrived at the Blackrock Home for Little Children – a large Victorian building with storm porches to the front and the side. I went on through what I thought was the main entrance, under a lych-gate, and dropped my suitcase abruptly on the path. In front of me was an old pulley bell from when the house was first built. I gave it a sharp pull and it released a delightful *ding-ding*, like the sound of cow-bells. After a while of waiting, a plump jolly-looking woman in her early 30s answered the door. She wore a dark green patterned apron and was covered in flour, which she had somehow managed to get on her face as well. Filtering through the half open door was a faint sound of children's laughter.

"Hello," I greeted her. "My name is Phyllis Little and I am here about the job. The orphanage sent me."

"Ah yes, that'll be right, to be sure. Come in, Phyllis, come in. My name is Mary, by the way. Sorry about the flour," she said, as she shook my hand, scattering flour dust everywhere. "Here, give me your case. I'll show yous round. You know the job is only for the six months, don't yous?"

"Oh yes, I know, but that'll be grand. We all have to start somewhere, and I'm sure something will come along afterwards." I remember saying that.

"Well, let's hope for you then. The reason it's only six months is that you are replacing our Mrs Gold, who has to be taking care of her husband. He recently suffered a serious accident at work."

"Oh dear," I said, wondering what sort of accident.

"Yes, well, I think he will be alright eventually, but he has some broken bones and is still suffering from concussion. Anyways, let me show you upstairs to your room."

We climbed a steep wooden staircase to an attic room. Then Mary gave me a tour of the rest of the building and invited me into the staff sitting room for a cup of tea. It seemed a homely place and nothing like the orphanage that I had grown up in.

"So, Phyllis, what would you like to do when you finish here?" asked Mary.

"Well I don't know exactly, but I have a dream."

"Oh yes?"

"I want to go to England and become a children's nurse."

"England? Don't you mean 'the land of milk and honey where the streets are paved with gold'?" Mary said, in a slightly mocking tone.

"Are they really?" I asked, naively.

Mary spluttered her tea halfway through a mouthful. "Nooo!" she said laughing. "Ah sure Phyllis, I'm only pulling your leg naw. But that's what you'd like to do, is it?"

"Yes, it is. I just love children. But the orphanage never encouraged us to take up a profession. They thought we were only suitable for domestic duties."

"Well Phyllis, I'm not gonna lie to yous naw. There'll be some cleaning here too, but we will need you to look after the little ones. I'm sure you'll be grand on both counts."

And I was, although better with the children than the cleaning. My first job and I loved it there. It felt more like a family home than a place of work and the children were gorgeous; my little pets. I had such fun playing and spending time with them that it was totally rewarding. It made me even more sure that I wanted to become a nurse and have my own children one day, but that was just a dream back then.

Mary became like a patient older sister, guiding me and teaching me as we went along. She never scolded, but she found everything I did highly amusing, especially when I struggled with menial tasks.

"Phyllis, would you look at you naw? What are you doing?" laughed Mary. "Do you not know how to boil an egg? You need water in the pan first. Sure, did they teach you nothing at that finishing school for goodness sake?"

"No. How stupid of me," I said, feeling like an idiot. "Well, to tell you the truth, Mary, I never was very interested in cooking."

"No matter. I'll teach you the basics; at least to boil an egg if nothing else. I'm sure you'll be fine."

And she did. She helped me enormously, not just with cooking, but many other things of which I knew nothing, not being worldly-wise. I learnt how to apply make-up and wear the latest fashions. I learnt how to smoke. She'd listen with empathy to my stories of the orphanage and how I was aching to find the truth about my past and who my mother was. It was as if she understood. Like she was my friend.

Those six months passed all too quickly. Mrs Gold was returning to work and soon it was my time to leave. It was a real wrench, but I had no choice as they had no permanent vacancies. Mary told me to keep in touch and said if I didn't find anything else to come back. But I knew it wouldn't be as easy as that, because she wasn't in charge. I thought that was it and I'd never return there. But we can't ever see into the future, can we? 16 years later, I did go back, under a completely different set of circumstances.

People weren't exactly falling over themselves for me, but I managed to find an au pair job, working for a banker and his wife in Killiney. They had four children and it was great while it lasted. Unfortunately, they also had a very aggressive Alsatian dog that used to constantly bark for attention. One day, after having some teeth out at the dentist, I bent to take something out of the oven and the dog bit me on the face. I think it smelt the blood from my extractions. That experience frightened me so much that I retained a fear of big dogs for years. Of course, that was the end of that job.

I tried various things, including shop work, but I was no good with money so went back to more cleaning and au pairing, but they never lasted. The fact that I hated cooking and cleaning, and was sometimes accused of being slovenly, didn't really help matters. No one wanted to take a girl on who was good with children but useless at housework. All I had my heart set on was becoming a nurse. I think Auntie Bea must have sensed my frustration, as one day she picked me up in her car and took me to Phoenix Park for a walk.

"Phyllis dear, I've something to tell you," she said, as we walked along arm in arm towards the tea rooms.

"Oh, yes, Auntie... what's that?"

"Well, I've been thinking about your future and I can clearly see that you've not been happy in the types of employment you've found. Am I right?"

"Well, yes, but..."

"Your heart is purely set on becoming a nurse, is it not?"

"Yes, it is..."

"So, I have paid for you to do a training course in England."

"A what... in England?" I repeated, unable to believe what I had just heard.

"Yes, it has all been arranged, so you needn't worry about the money or anything. My youngest sister, Flory, who lives in Liverpool, will meet you at the station and put you up for a night. Then, on Tuesday morning, you will catch the train to Euston and change for Epsom in Surrey. After a day to acclimatise yourself, you will start your training at the general hospital there, which, by the way, has live-in accommodation."

"Oh Auntie. England!" I exclaimed. "I can't believe it! It's my dream come true. That's truly wonderful and I don't know what to say. But it's all too much... I'll pay you back for all your kindness to me when I start working."

"No, you won't, now," she said, in a very assured tone. "Now remember, Phyllis, I told you a long time ago that money had been put aside for you?"

"Well, yes, I do."

"This is what you really want to do, so now is the time to spend it on something that you want and that will benefit your future life. The only thing that I ask is that you put your trust in God and make sure you attend church whenever you can. If you do, and you put Him first, He will guide and protect you."

"Sure, I will, Auntie. I'll say my prayers every night without fail. And you don't have to worry about me going to church. I would've done anyway."

"And, Phyllis, if you get into any difficulty or are unhappy, you're to telephone me at Edna's and reverse the charges. I will send Bunty to keep an eye on you every so often. She works as a ward sister in another hospital not far from Epsom. Is that all clear now?"

"Yes Auntie, it is very clear and so awfully kind of you that I can't say thank you enough." I gave her the biggest hug ever. My heart was overcome with joy.

"Oh Phyllis, my dear child, you don't have to thank me. I would give you the world if I could," she said, as she gently steered my arms back. "I only wish you hadn't grown up in that bleak place for so long."

We walked towards the tea rooms, where she gave me the documentation for my journey, including the boat ticket from Dún Laoghaire and train tickets for England. I was leaving on Monday, in two days' time, and would start the following Thursday morning. I remember telling myself, *In two days I will be in the land of milk and honey, where the streets are paved with gold!*

Curiosity encroached on my thoughts. Just why was my aunt so caring and generous? Why did she feel an obligation to guide my way even though I was fast approaching adulthood? Although still pressing me, I put these questions on hold while preparations to leave grasped my immediate attention. There wasn't even time for proper goodbyes, although I did manage to get a message to Patsy, who was now working as a hotel maid in Lower Leeson Street.

Departure day arrived quickly and I was all fired up with feverish excitement for my new adventure. Auntie picked me up from my boarding house lodgings; the sky was a buoyant blue and a warm air current whisked us along. I jumped in the car beside her and calmly we drove down to the harbour. There in the distance, waiting at the quayside, I could just make out my dearest Patsy, her flaming-red hair flapping around in the wind like a flag against a sea of sparkling topaz.

Delirious with excitement, I stuck my head out of the window to attract her attention.

"Pats! Pats!" I yelled. "Look Auntie! It's Patsy."

Auntie Bea gave two boisterous beeps on the horn as she parked and I leapt out.

The moment Patsy spotted us, she tore up the quayside path and ran straight into my arms.

"Phyllis!"

"Pats!"

We clung to each other like survivors of a tsunami who were about to be prised apart forever. Auntie watched us with understanding, and I saw her dab the corner of her eye with her white handkerchief.

Patsy had tears streaming down her flushed cheeks.

"Oh Phyllis, yer goin', really goin'! I can't believe it. Just what am I gonna do without yous naw?" she sobbed.

"Ah Pats, you'll be fine. Don't cry, Pet. You can always come over and visit me. You know this is what I've always wanted to do."

"But Phyllis, I work long hours in that shabby hotel, 'n I earn a pittance. I never get time off and I'd never be able to afford the boat trip. As it is, I lied this morning and said I was going to a funeral. I'll have to get back soon or they'll miss me."

Auntie interrupted. "Patsy, my child, pray to God and he will find a way. I know Phyllis is lucky to have me and it is not the same for you but, trust me, miracles do happen."

"Do they?"

"Yes, indeed they do," reassured Auntie.

Just then, a gust of sea air blew up and tried to snatch Auntie's netted pill-box hat off her head. She managed to hold on to it, but only just, as our dresses fluttered around trying to fight the south-westerly breeze.

"Phyllis, stand close to Patsy and I'll take a picture of you both with the ship in the background," requested Auntie.

And right at that moment the ship's funnels thundered a long roar.

"Quick now, move closer, we haven't got long. That's it… right there. Now to the left a bit…" Auntie said, gesticulating. The camera clicked.

The ship's funnels sounded again.

"I think that's telling you it's time to go, Phyllis," said Patsy.

"Oh no!" I blurted out, and burst into tears, overwhelmed by our separation.

Auntie put her arm around me. "Come now, dear, it's time to leave. You know it's for the best."

Together, we hurried towards the ship, with Patsy carrying my case and Auntie guiding me towards the point of entry where a queue was forming and a man in naval uniform was checking everyone's tickets. I stood solemnly in line.

"Bye then, Phyllis," choked Patsy, giving me a final hug.

"Pats…" I started.

"Don't worry about Patsy, dear. I'll be taking her back to her place of work and will also make sure she has your address in England so she can come and see you one day," said Auntie.

"Thanks Auntie. What would I have done without you?"

I put my arms affectionally around her neck and pressed my cheek tightly against hers. But showing outward affection did not come naturally to Auntie Bea. She held me at distance and looked intently into my eyes.

"Phyllis, listen to me. You are a very fine, attractive young woman and I wouldn't want anything to happen to you now. There are men out there who I am sure would take advantage of a naive Irish girl like yourself. I want you to be happy, but please be wary, won't you?"

"Sure, of course I will."

"And if you have any trouble, just give me a call."

"Fine, so I will. I will."

"Right then. Well, goodbye and good luck." And she kissed me on both cheeks.

"Bye, Auntie – bye, Patsy."

"Goodbye dear."

"Bye!"

It was now my turn to have my ticket checked. I picked up my case and walked up the slight incline towards the ramp and onto the ship. Every so often I turned back to see if they were both there. They were; both still waving, with Auntie looking jubilant and Patsy blowing her nose. In a moment or two they were out of sight. My new journey of discovery had begun.

After a whirlwind couple of days with Flory and her family in Liverpool, it was time to make the final part of my journey. I caught the train to London's Euston station. A signal failure delayed me by several hours, but eventually I hopped onto the tube to Waterloo and picked up the over-ground train to Epsom. By the time I reached the hospital accommodation it was getting late. I was let in by the night staff and shown to my bland, but functional single room, and told that if I arrived back after 10:30 pm in future I would be locked out. Everyone was highly respectful of the matron and sisters in charge then. I think they expected nurses to be chaste, and certainly no one was allowed to be married and still keep their job. It was seen as a calling and you had to be totally dedicated to the profession in order to get on.

The next day was a Wednesday, but not just any old Wednesday. It was Derby Day – the famous Epsom Derby, frequented by the Royal Family. After familiarising myself with the hospital layout and the staff quarters, I decided to amble up to the town and take in some of the lively atmosphere. I wasn't starting my induction for another day, so it was a good opportunity to find my way around.

There wasn't a cloud in the sky on that first gladsome day in Epsom. I was bursting with pride and happiness that, at last, I was going to do a job I knew would make me happy and that I'd be good at. The sun's rays were scorching my shoulder blades, so I sought the shelter of shop canopies to escape the rising heat. I flitted from one shop window to another, mesmerised by the array of tempting, expensive-looking fashions and shoes with stiletto heels.

It was June 1957, and everywhere was teeming, cafés and coffee bars were packed out and the smell of greasy food drifted out onto the bustling pavements. I felt such a vibrant atmosphere everywhere: street vendors selling goods, excitable children tearing along with their mothers tottering behind trying to keep up, shady spiv characters doing deals in darkened doorways and gypsies loitering on street corners accosting passers-by with bunches of lucky heather.

"Hello, my lovely," said one who caught my eye. "You're a very pretty gal, aren't you? Would you like a bunch of my heather to bring you some luck? Catch you a rich young man maybe?"

"Oh, I don't know about that," I laughed. "Ah, go on then! Perhaps I need the luck, as it's my first time here," I said, giving her a penny.

"Bless you, my lovely. Be sure, good fortune is about to come your way."

I continued down the High Street looking for a café with space to sit down for a cup of tea. A blast of Bill Haley and the Comets belted out of a passing music shop:

Nine, ten, eleven o'clock, twelve o'clock rock...

We're going to rock around the clock tonight...

A group of teenage boys dressed in drainpipes and long jackets dawdled outside, tapping their feet and preening their slicked-back coifs in the reflection of the glass window. They were angling for a group of giggling girls who mooched along pretending to be unimpressed. I smiled to myself remembering how I was at their age, not at all long ago.

Eventually, I stumbled upon Joe's Café, and went in for a smoke. Everybody smoked in those days and I'd adopted the habit too under Mary's influence at Blackrock.

A large middle-aged man with Brylcreemed hair and sideburns came to take my order, with a pen behind one ear and a cigarette dangling from his mouth. While he was waiting for me to make my mind up, he cleaned down the table-tops in vigorous sweeping movements. I can still smell the sickly body odour wafting from two large wet patches under his arms as he moved closer.

"Wotcha having then, love?" he asked. "Made up yer mind yet?"

"Yes, I'll have a cup of tea and a currant bun," I decided, straining at the blackboard behind the counter for the prices.

"Thruppence ha'penny, love," he replied.

I gave him the right money and he shouted across to a woman who was pouring cups of tea from a metal urn.

"'Ere, Dot! Bun and a cuppa char for this young lady."

"Right you are Joe," she called back.

Somebody put a record on the jukebox. It was *Take Me Home Kathleen*, which I'd heard a lot on the radio back home.

The man brought over my order. "There you go, love."

"Oh, *merci beaucoup*," I joked.

"Mercy-bo-wot?" he echoed back at me, looking puzzled.

"Ha-ha! Oh, I'm sorry. That's French, so it is. What I meant was 'thank you'. Ah, sure naw, I knew that all that money spent on me having French lessons at finishing school was a waste."

The jukebox music took me straight back to Ireland. As I stared out of the window, cupping the milky tea in my hand, I found myself drifting off into another world, thinking about the mother I might never find and why keeping the truth from me could be so important. And as the words tenderly played, the sadness in my heart moved up into my throat and it seemed hard to swallow anything.

A voice behind me brought me back down to earth.

"Was that a Dublin accent I recognised?"

"It is, to be sure," I said, turning around to see who it was.

"Hallo. My name's June, June Byrne, but you can call me Juney, if you like – they all do," she said, offering a handshake. "I'm a trainee nurse at Epsom District, up the road."

"Oh, so am I!" I said smiling, thrilled to have found a fellow Irish person. "The name is Phyllis Little, by the way, and I only arrived late last night."

"Well Phyllis, I think we'll get on just great! Here, listen to this a minute, I'll put on another record. D'you like Peggy Lee? *Mr Wonderful*?"

"I don't know that one. I grew up in an orphanage and we never had music except for hymns – or the traditional, when we did Irish dancing."

"Oh, you don't know what you're missing. This is great, just listen."

Juney put some money in the jukebox.

"Which part of Ireland do you come from, Juney?" I enquired, intrigued as to why she was here.

"Originally Tipperary, but we moved to be near the River Liffey because Daddy was a docker, so we lived along the North Wall until I was about six; but later we settled in Stoneybatter."

"And now you find yourself here in England, like me?"

"Well Ireland hasn't got much to offer these days. I thought I'd give it a go and seek my fortune here."

"What, where the streets are paved with gold?" I quipped, only semi-laughing.

"Oh yes, the streets of gold," she laughed. "Been here nine months now and never looked back. But I do miss my family from time to time."

The record started playing and Juney sang along.

Why this feeling? Why this glow?

Why the thrill when you say hello?

A man's voice behind us, finished off the words.

It's a strange and tender magic that you do...

"Mr Wonderful! Yeah that's me. That's me alright baby."

"Charlie!" Juney exclaimed, jumping up and throwing her arms round him. "What are yous doing here?"

A tall man wearing a checked shirt, with a black T-shirt underneath, stood in the doorway wearing a cheeky smile.

"Hello, Doll. Got let out early for good behaviour – or so the guvnor says. Going up the downs for the Derby this afternoon. Coming?"

"The Derby? Well, for the life of me, how did you manage to wangle that?"

Charlie stood inspecting his reflection in the café window and slicking back his hair with a comb.

"Oh, ya know, work hard, keep ya nose clean," he said, with a wink and a grin. "The boss is closing the garage for the afternoon."

"But I thought you didn't have any money?"

"I haven't."

"So?"

"So, baby girl, I was wondering if you could see yourself to lending me 10 bob until payday?"

"You're joking, aren't you? What happened to the money you were meant to pay me back last week?"

"Well, me mother collared the lot for me keep, didn't she?"

"Did she, I wonder? Hmmm. Are you sure that wasn't the pub now?"

"Ah, go on Juney. You know I love ya, dontcha?"

Charlie sidled up and wrapped his strong arms around Juney from behind. He looked as if he knew exactly how to persuade her.

"Ah, go on with you now, yer useless hunk of mouldy mutton," she chastised, giving him a playful slap. "I haven't got 10 bob. You'll have to make do with three – and that's it! In case you didn't realise, I don't earn that much. This is Phyllis by the way.

Phyllis is starting work at the hospital tomorrow. Phyllis, this is Charlie, my boyfriend. He's a car mechanic."

Charlie stooped, bowed, and very politely kissed my hand.

"*Enchanté*," he said.

I laughed nervously and fiddled with my cigarette packet. "Oh, you speak French, Charlie, do you?"

"Not bleedin' likely. It's all those romantic films she keeps dragging me along to with that French bloke – what's his name?"

"Paul Henreid, 'interrupted Juney. "You know, *Casablanca* and *Now, Voyager*. They're a few years old but I still like them."

"Oh yes," I said, trying to sound convincing though I hadn't a clue what she was talking about.

Charlie sat down and put his arm around Juney.

"Hey, Phyllis, wanna come with us? Have a little bet on the gee-gees? What d'ya say?"

"Well, no, I don't think so. I was brought up to believe that drinking and gambling are sins of the flesh. You go and enjoy yourselves. I'm fine."

"Sins of the what? You're 'aving a laugh, ain't ya?"

"Well, I was brought up very strictly." I took a long drag on my cigarette and looked for the door.

Juney stepped in as she could sense I wasn't used to men like Charlie. "Ah, come on, Phyllis. You don't have to have a bet, you can just soak up all the atmosphere. There's a funfair too. It's a great day out and what else are yer going to do anyway?"

"I don't know."

"Please, Phyllis, please. It'll be a good way to get to know you," she cajoled.

So, with a little more persuasion, I gave in. We jumped in Charlie's old banger and the three up us sped up to the Epsom Derby.

The Derby was like another planet to me. The mingled smell of cut grass, hot dogs and candyfloss was enticing. We worked our way through to the public part of the racecourse where you could get in for nothing. The fair was not far from the finishing post. The whole place was magical; alive, teeming with dazzling colours and exuberance. There were stalls and rides, jugglers and musicians in flamboyant outfits and clowns pretending to trip over themselves. Children ran chasing each other, laughing and screaming, and carousel music played wherever we walked. Tic-tac men in white gloves were signalling the odds to their bookies, while a suspicious-looking character wearing a purple skirt over brightly-coloured trousers, and a feathered turban, was shouting out, "I gotta horse! I gotta horse!" to excite punters into placing a bet.

"Who's that funny-looking fellow? "I asked Juney as he walked past.

"Prince Monolulu. He's a tipster. He tells you the best horse to pick. Charlie's going to put a bet on for Crepello, ridden by Lester Piggott. Would you like him to do one for you Phyllis?" coaxed Juney.

"No, I don't think so. Better not."

"Ah, go on... go on!"

"I shouldn't really – but alright, just a small one... a shilling then," I said relenting. So that was it, my first venture into the world of gambling. Thank goodness my aunt couldn't see me. She would not have approved at all.

Juney dragged me into a tent to have my fortune read by Madame Zanzibar. We were laughing and giggling so much, that although I had been warned to stay away from such places, all I could think about was having a good time. As we headed back to find Charlie, my head was buzzing about her prediction that I would meet an older man who would change my life. A relationship with anyone was the last thing on my mind, but still it was intriguing. Then, with a flutter of anticipation, we all settled on a long wooden bench to watch the horses gallop past and I watched excited beads of sweat trickling down Charlie's face.

"Come on Crepello! Come on boy!" he shouted, jumping to his feet.

Juney and I found ourselves joining in.

"C'mon Crepello. C'mon naw, horsey!" I cried, as I timidly waved a programme.

He was coming up to the final furlong and the air was electric with a nervous expectation. The crowds were on their feet shouting and waving their fists as the horses raced past them and closer to the finishing line.

"Ye-es!" screamed Charlie, on his feet and punching the air. "We've done it! Bleedin' well done it! Whey hey!" With that, he lifted Juney off the ground and spun her round.

I clapped with excitement – I'd never seen anything so thrilling! The three of us hugged each other. It was a triumphant end to a day where the hours had passed so quickly. My first day in England and I had made new friends, was about to start the job of my dreams and had won my first bet on a horse. We celebrated with frothy milkshake and I couldn't have been happier. My life had finally changed for the good.

*

I was still at work when my mobile rang. I missed the call but there was a voicemail.

"Darling, it's Mammy here. I'm helping them out with a few extra hours today, so don't wait for me… I'll be late. I'll get a taxi from the station. Perhaps we could drive to Epsom tomorrow and

I could show you where I used to work. I won't say anything more on the phone. Mammy will see you later... Beep—"

Next day we did as she suggested. I had worked for the Gas Board in Epsom during the 1980s but never thought of visiting Mum's training hospital, the place she lived when she first came to England. As we drove along, she recognised some of the landmarks.

"Look Sal, look! That's the Spread Eagle pub on the corner where Juney, Patsy and I used to go. And there's the clocktower where we arranged to meet sometimes."

She coughed.

"Are you okay? Your chest's not getting any better, is it?" I asked. And what's that plaster on your forehead? You look like the walking wounded."

"My chest will be fine, now I've got different antibiotics. The plaster is just to cover up a little mole that's itchy and bleeds every so often."

I gripped the steering wheel tightly.

"Bleeds? A little mole that's itchy and bleeds? For goodness sake Mum, do you know how serious that could be? You really should get that looked at by a doctor. I'll come with you."

"Ah, no naw, I'm not a guinea pig to be played around with. I'm not having any old doctor tampering with me. Oh, look Sal. We're here!"

"But Mum..."

"Sure, you know this place brings back so many happy memories. It was real hard work and we got paid a pittance, but it wasn't about the money."

Chapter 5

A Dream Come True

Phyllis

After a lengthy morning interview with matron, which seemed to go quite well, I collected my new stiffly starched uniform and tried it on. Standing in front of a long mirror with my hands on my hips, I beamed with pride at the petite reflection staring back at me. I had a nice little figure in those days, never weighing more than seven stone, and had turned into quite an attractive young woman, if I do say so myself. Make-up was frowned upon by the matron, so I kept it to a minimum with a quick dab of face powder and rouge. But I didn't really need much anyway due to my olive skin and large green eyes that made some people think I was more Italian than Irish. I wonder what my mother would have thought? If only she was here with me now, there'd be so many things I'd say to her. Who would have thought a poor orphan girl could make it this far? Now I felt ready for the world. And so, with a smile on my face and new-found confidence, I started my first day's training to be a State Enrolled Nurse.

The next few months were spent in lectures and learning practical skills, including how to deal with a difficult patient and how to bite my tongue when told off by sister. It was all about the bedside manner in the 1950s. Respecting patients as individuals and showing that you cared were the most important requirements.

Once I was working on the wards it reminded me of being back at the orphanage because everything had to be meticulously cleaned down, from bedsteads to sterilising instruments and everything in between. We did every little thing ourselves in those days, from making tea to mopping the floors. The sluice room became my second home and I sometimes felt I spent most of the day emptying bed pans. And lifting patients was back-breaking work. But even saying all that, I loved every minute.

I settled well into life in the nurses' home and began to make friends. Juney and myself often met up with other girls in the High Street coffee bars. When we were a bit short of money to go out we hung around in each other's rooms, smoking and listening to the latest Connie Francis or Johnny Mathis records, on a record player a previous occupant had left behind. My favourites were *Who's Sorry Now?* and *A Certain Smile*, though secretly I preferred the Irish ballads from back home.

Auntie Bea wrote every month to begin with, and often popped in a few pound notes with her letter so I could treat myself.

Get yourself something nice, Phyllis. I know you don't earn a great deal there. Sent with love, Auntie Bea.

She was so kind and thoughtful it made me wonder about her. Could she be hiding a secret? She used to check up if I was attending church regularly by arranging for me to meet with her niece Bunty for a cup of tea, "to see how I was getting on". Although she dutifully obliged, she had nothing to say to me. We sat in stony silence; Bunty tight-lipped and eyes downcast as she stared long and hard into her empty cup, and me, trying to make polite conversation with a brick wall. I don't think either she or her mother approved of orphans, especially illegitimate ones.

Out of the blue one day, I received a phone call. Sister was down on the next floor so Juney picked up the phone, which was just as well as we weren't allowed private calls.

"Phyllis, it's for you!"

"Who is it?"

Juney had a quizzical look on her face.

"Can't tell. Its sounds like a woman… and there's a lot of street-noise in the background. I think she's calling from a phone booth."

"Hallo," I said, as she passed the receiver.

"Is that yerself, Phyllis? It's Patsy! Guess what? I'm in London. I'm in Piccadilly Circus, I think, and I'll be with you soon."

"Wh–at?" My voice was shocked and loud. "Pats… it can't be!" A couple of startled patients sat up, diverted by my conversation.

"Nurse… nurse! I need the bedpan." I might have guessed.

"Alright Mr Taylor, I'm sorry. I'll be with you in a little moment," I replied, putting my hand over the phone.

I tried to speak in a whisper. "Sorry about that Pats. I'm really busy and I shouldn't be talking. But how? How did you get the money?"

"Listen, I'll tell yer when I see yer later. Let's just say that a bit of good luck came my way. I am going to be training in the same place as yous. If all goes well, I should be at the nurses' home this evening."

"Well, would you believe it naw? That's great! It'll be wonderful to see you again. I've missed you so much, you know."

My patient called me for a second time.

"Nurse! Please, nurse!"

"I'm coming now, Mr Taylor. Sorry Pats… going to have to fly. I'll say goodbye and see you tonight. Can't wait!"

"Me neither."

I was dumbfounded. It was 18 months since I'd last heard from Patsy, apart from a sad little note she sent saying how unhappy she was working at the hotel. How on earth had she managed to get on the same training course as me, I wondered?

My shift finally came to an end at eight o'clock, but it was nearer nine by the time I had handed over to the night staff. When at last I was able to go, I hurried back to the nurses' home and eagerly changed out of my uniform.

About 10 to 10, the front door bell rang in the communal lobby. I raced downstairs, jumping the last few, so impatient to see Pats again. The first thing that hit me when the heavy front door swung open was her perfume.

"Phyllis!"

"Pats! Mmmm…You smell gorgeous," I said, throwing my arms around her and getting a mass of red hair caught in my mouth.

"Thanks. *Evening in Paris*."

"I knew – I recognised it."

"I thought I'd treat meself for a change, since I came into a bit of money."

"Money? Did you find yourself a rich sugar daddy or something?"

"Ah no. I wouldn't be doing with the likes of no men naw."

"So how did you manage…"

"Well…" Pats hesitated. "You're not going to believe this, but one day, while I was working at the hotel, a strange package arrived in the reception – for me. I thought, who-in-the-name-of-what, would be sending me a package, naw? I hardly know anyone outside the orphanage. Anyway, I opened it and there inside was a form for me to fill in to apply for nursing training at this hospital – and *several* 10-pound notes. I nearly died!"

"I bet you did. But who sent it?"

"I have no idea. There was no name no note attached – nothing. Perhaps it was a rich hotel guest who felt sorry for me."

"That's very strange."

"It surely is, but I'm not complaining. It meant I could apply to come here, and have enough money to keep me going for a couple of months and I've already applied and got meself a room on the second floor. Obviously, someone had my best interests at heart, but I'm not even going to try and work out who would do that. I am just so happy to be free of the hotel – and I gets to be with you again. It'll be just like old times."

And indeed, it was. Patsy started her training and, although we were now on different courses and working different shifts, we still found time to meet up and chat, even if it was only in the staff canteen. I introduced her to Juney and the three of us would go out window shopping, arm in arm. Parading along in our high heels and petticoat dresses, we were like a trio of naughty schoolgirls, stealing admiring glances and the occasional wolf whistle from the Teddy Boys who hung about outside the pubs. But I wasn't really interested in boys back then. I remembered how my aunt had warned me about men, and I was so in love with my nursing that it didn't even cross my mind what the opposite sex thought of me.

Those two years in England passed very quickly. Although I had intended to become a children's nurse, the sight of seeing seriously sick children suffer was too much to bear and tugged at my heart. I knew from my own experience what it felt like to suffer; to be a child and lie there with no one understanding your fears, your loneliness, and to wonder how to make it through another day. And to watch them slowly die, so young, so innocent, and no chance to live their lives to the full. I wanted to give them hope, I wanted them to have the chance I had. But it was too heart-breaking for words and all it made me do was cry. So, after a lot of deliberation, I decided to specialise in geriatric nursing instead. At least the elderly had already lived a life.

Six months later a post came up at Cuddington Cottage Hospital, a few miles away, which had originally been an isolation hospital for fever and TB patients. It was linked to Epsom District, and in the late 1950s it opened some new geriatric wards.

The original hospital was built in Victorian times on the site of a farm. It had been extended and added to over the years and now consisted of several low-level blocks set in gardens that had seen better days, but despite its grand iron-gated entrance it still had a homely feel. Perhaps that was to do with the staff. There was an easier going, less formal feel than Epsom District. Film shows, talks and plays were put on for the patients, and staff acted more like family than work colleagues. Everyone knew everyone, and even the doctors seemed more approachable than in the hierarchy in Epsom.

As Cuddington was out in the sticks, it made sense to live in the nurses' home again. Money was tight after board, lodging and laundering my uniforms was deducted, and I was left with just a few shillings for cigarettes. And being pretty hopeless with money didn't help either. But I was having such a ball it didn't really matter. It wasn't long before Patsy joined me and then it became a riot!

One night, when the two of us were working a shift together, I got a mad idea to scare her by pretending to be a ghost. You'd never get away with anything like that now – times have changed. The only light visible came from a desk-lamp in the middle of the ward where Patsy was writing up her notes. Seeing her engrossed, I took my opportunity and crept up behind her with a fresh white sheet over my head.

"...whooooOOOoooo..." I moaned in the eeriest voice I could muster, raising my hands inside the sheet.

Patsy nearly jumped 10 feet in the air!

"Argh, For goodness sake! Wat in heaven's name d'yer think yer doing?" she yelled.

Mrs Merrifield woke up with all the shenanigans. "Nurse... nurse!"

But by now I was bent over double, with laughter.

"Nurse... are you there, nurse?" Mrs Merrifield called again. "I think I've just seen my mother."

"Now you've done it, Phyllis! She's confused at the best of times. This is all we need," chided Patsy.

"Ha-ha-ha..." I couldn't stop. The tears were streaming uncontrollably.

"Nurse, I think my mother just came to me in a vision. She was wearing all white."

"It's alright, Mrs Merrifield. No need to get out of bed. It was a dream. Your mother isn't here, there was a bit of a commotion, but nothing to worry about," reassured Patsy, coaxing her back to bed and tucking her in.

"But she was – I saw her!"

"Well done, Phyllis. We'll never hear the end of this, naw," said Patsy.

I felt a sudden pang of guilt.

"There, there, Mrs Merrifield, it's alright," I said. "Here, let me get you a nice cup of cocoa, to help you get back to sleep."

Patsy was not amused at first, but did eventually see the funny side. However, Mrs Merryfield hadn't forgotten the apparition early next morning when the consultant geriatrician and his team made their daily ward round, escorted by matron. I realised how stupid I'd been. What was I thinking? Poor Mrs

Merrifield had been quite agitated because of me and my ridiculous prank and now the doctors would be wondering what was going on with her. Oh hell!

"And how are you this morning, Mrs Merrifield?" boomed Dr Forster.

He examined her notes at the foot of her bed, as a team of pubescent-looking junior doctors crowded around hanging onto his every word and Mrs Merrifield scrabbled for her false teeth in a glass of water on her bedside cabinet.

"Oh, I'm fine, doctor. I saw my mother last night. You know, it's been nearly 45 years since we laid her to rest."

"Did you, indeed?" he replied, looking slightly bemused.

Patsy and I were opposite each other making the next bed along and bit our lips hard listening to the conversation. Even so, we could barely hold it together.

"She was dressed in white, doctor."

"Who was dressed in white?"

"The bride. That's what they wear. Don't you know anything?"

One of the junior doctors let out an uncontrolled snigger, but instantly changed it to a cough when he was struck with an icy glare from Dr Forster, who was not amused.

"Matron, have you tested her urine lately?" he enquired. "It might be as well to test it later on and check her blood levels at the same time; see if anything is going on that we should know about."

"Yes of course, Dr Forster. I'll arrange it today."

Minutes later, before my shift finished, matron asked me to call a porter to take Mrs Merrifield to outpatients for a blood test. By now, I felt full of remorse that she was going through all this unnecessarily, but there was nothing I could do about it.

The porter arrived. It was Eric. I often passed him in the corridor and he always gave me a friendly nod and a wink. He was older than me, in his mid-30s; always full of charm and ready to have a laugh and a joke.

"Hello Phyllis – again," he said, as he wheeled a chair in beside Mrs Merrifield's bed. "We'll have to stop meeting like this. People will talk you know!" We both helped Mrs Merrifield get comfortable in the wheelchair.

"Ah, go on with you naw," I laughed back, brushing off his remark.

Mrs Merrifield remained confused. "Have you come to take me to the wedding?" she asked.

Eric grinned, "What wedding would that be then?"

"My mother's," she replied.

"Your mother's?" Eric looked puzzled.

"Yes, Mrs Merrifield is going to be the bridesmaid. And I'm going to make you look beautiful for the occasion," I assured her, running a comb through the delicate strands of white hair that barely covered her head. "Isn't that right?"

"Yes, that's right," she agreed.

"Well, we better get you to the church on time. Your carriage awaits, milady," added Eric, playing along.

I tucked a crocheted blanket around her legs and gave her a little hug. Ah, she was gorgeous and I loved her.

"See you later then," said Eric as he quick-footed it down the ward, still grinning and turning his head to see if I was looking at him.

"I'd watch that one," warned Patsy following me into the sluice.

"What d'you mean, Pats?"

"Yer know he has an eye for the ladies, don't you?"

"No. I've never paid much attention really. But he is very charming, don't you think?"

"Charming, my foot. Huh! As if butter wouldn't melt… And he's way too old for you anyway, Phyllis. Just be careful, is all I'd tell yer."

A couple of weeks later, I bumped into Eric as I was rushing to go on duty. I was on an early shift and after my alarm went off I'd gone back to sleep. I panicked, threw my uniform on, dragged a brush through my hair, and raced to the ward. As I ran, I managed to drop the entire contents of my handbag in the corridor.

"Oh, dash!" I said, gathering up the spillage in a hurry.

"Would you like a hand with that?" said a voice behind me.

I looked up and it was Eric, who seemed to have appeared from nowhere.

"Ah, yes, that would be grand. Thank you, Eric," I replied, blushing.

He knelt beside me and helped gather my precious remnants that were strewn across the polished floor. I felt the knuckle of his hand brush against mine as we put them back in my handbag. It was an awkward moment because I wasn't sure if it was deliberate or not, but I felt a shock of electricity dart through my skin making the hairs stand on end. I looked up at his face. It was mature and knowing, with a confident smile.

I looked for my escape route. "All done then," I said, feeling flustered. "Thanks again, Eric. Must hurry, I'm late already."

"My pleasure, Phyllis. I'll see you around then."

"Yes, see you. Bye."

We passed him again as Patsy and I were off on our tea break and he was wheeling someone to X-ray. As soon as he spotted me down the corridor he waved and beamed a huge smile.

"Oh, Phyllis, I think you've got an admirer there," teased Patsy.

"Ah, don't be daft. He wouldn't be interested in the likes of me."

"I think he is, naw. Remember to be careful, Phyllis. You don't know anything about him."

She was right of course. But the more I bumped into him, the more my curiosity grew and the more my curiosity grew, the more I longed to bump into him.

It was fast approaching the end of the year. The cold wet winter weather had set in, making it less appealing to catch the bus into Epsom for a night out. It meant evenings were mainly spent chatting and smoking in the staff dining room, with nothing to do but swap stories about our working day. The only chance to go out in comfort was if anyone had a car and could give us a lift. Being stuck out in the middle of nowhere meant we were a bit cut off from civilisation. One particular chilly evening though, a crowd was going up to The Downs pub to celebrate Dr Ackerman's birthday. Thankfully, both he and a couple of others had cars.

He had just turned 30 but was unmarried, which I thought was strange considering his Scandinavian good looks. Although he liked women, they came second place to his fancy cars and obsession with train spotting.

The pub was loud and rowdy, so we were all squeezed together in our damp coats by the bar as Dr Ackerman ordered drinks all round. All I could hear was raucous laughter and the tinkling of glasses – and the place absolutely stank of beer and cigarettes. He grew impatient and clicked his fingers in the air to attract the bartender's attention, and then I cringed to feel him nonchalantly rest his hand on my back.

"Phyllis, has anyone ever told you that you look just like Elizabeth Taylor?" he said turning to study my face. "I think it's something about the eyes. Hmm, yes, the eyes." A dreamy look came over him.

My ears felt as if they were burning, and I needed a cigarette.

"Ah, well, no… I don't think so,' I said, eager to get away.

"What would you like?" he asked, changing the subject.

"I don't drink I'm afraid. Do they do milk?"

"Milk?"

"Yeah, sure. You can always ask for milk when you go to the pubs in Ireland. Not that I ever go in any."

He laughed at me. "Good God, woman – milk? No, I don't think they do that here. It's not the same. How about a Babycham or a miniscule glass of sherry? What do you say?"

"No thanks, doctor. Tap water will be fine."

"Oh, come on, Phyllis! It's my birthday, just a little tipple now. It's not often I get my wallet out, so you should make the most of it. I'll get you a sherry. If you don't like it, you don't have to drink it."

"Alright then. Just a little one," I said, finally giving in.

"Outstanding! Good girl. You grab a seat on that round table with the others and I'll bring the drinks over."

So, we all sat round the table laughing and joking, but I still felt uneasy. The pub was dimly lit and so thick with cigarette smoke that you could've cut the air with a knife.

Dr Ackerman fought his way through the crowd, splattering a wobbly tray of drinks.

"Budge up. Make room for a little one," he ordered, and squeezed into a tiny gap next to me. "Ah, that's better."

"I think he likes yer," Patsy whispered in my ear.

"Och, no. He's just being friendly. He's always full of the old blarney with the girls."

"Yes, and we know why that is, don't we?" said Patsy.

Just then I felt a hand on my knee. I flinched and tried to move closer to Patsy.

"Drink up, Phyllis. See what you think. There's more where that came from, if you like it."

I tried a sip, but was repulsed by the burning sensation in my mouth. "Urgh, no… I don't think this is for me I'm afraid." And I pushed the glass away.

"You haven't given it a proper try. Give it another go. It takes a while if you're not used to it. I'm sure you'll love it if you try a little at a time."

He was talking loudly now and I was aware of everyone watching my reaction as I shrank back in my seat.

"Go on, Phyllis," encouraged Audrey. "There's always a first time."

"Mother of God! You know she doesn't drink," snapped Patsy. "Why don't you just leave her alone?"

"What, are you her mother now?"

Patsy gave Audrey a piercing glare, enough to spear her through the heart. "No, but if she doesn't want to drink, she doesn't have to. Okay?"

All eyes were on me. "Alright, alright, I'll try it once, to keep you all happy."

My hand was trembling but I took a deep breath and knocked it back – in one.

"Urgh!" I said, gulping and catching my breath. It was ghastly. The alcohol felt like lighter fuel searing its way down my gullet and burning a hole in the pit of my stomach.

"Outstanding! There we go. Not so bad after all, is it?" Dr Ackerman chuckled and gave me a pat on the back.

I pretended to laugh and looked away only to spot Eric propping up the bar with Johnny Butters and Nobby Boyle, a couple of hospital maintenance men. They all had pints in their hands and looked as if they were having a good laugh. Oh, how I longed to be in their company and not Dr Ackerman's.

Eric carried on chatting for quite some time before he spotted me through the barricades of people who had nowhere to sit. I made my excuses to use the ladies' room.

"Hurry back," urged Dr Ackerman. You don't want to miss the next round."

Thank God I've managed to escape, I thought, pushing my way through the hordes and heading for the way out. There was no way I was going to sit with a bunch of people getting tipsy all night and put up with Dr Ackerman being frisky with his wandering hands.

At last I was out in the fresh air. It was dark now, and the stars were like tiny jewels twinkling on a cushion of black velvet over the downs. The pub was opposite the grandstand and set back off the road; no street lights, only the dazzling glare of the odd car and tiny dots emanating from distant surrounding towns and villages. It felt cold and the car window screens were beginning to frost over. I shivered and watched my breath form vaporising clouds in the air, until I sensed someone standing by my side and smoking a cigarette.

"Good here, innit?" he said, with a cheeky smile. It was Eric.

I felt a hot flush sweep over me and my heart beating erratically.

"What're you doing here?" I asked.

"I could ask the same of you. Want a fag?"

He handed me a lit cigarette and I told him about the ordeal in the pub. There was something about him being older that appealed to me and we seemed to connect. He had been around a bit, seemed so worldly-wise and knew all about suffering, although not in the same way as I did. He listened with interest as I opened up to him about my painful childhood in the orphanage, and how I longed to know who my mother was. My lack of love as a child seemed not dissimilar to his own. Then it was my turn to hear about his life.

Growing up in poverty-stricken London during the depression of the 1920s had been tough. His father was a brute who regularly beat him and was egged on by his mother who never showed any sign of love. She'd tell him to give Eric a good thrashing for the least little thing whenever she worked herself up into a frenzy.

At 18 he signed up to fight in the Second World War. He couldn't wait for an excuse to leave home. Better to be blown up by Jerry than have to put up with his tyrannical father. He had tried to leave two years before, to make his own way in the world, but his father dragged him back and punched him in the face with such force that he nearly cracked his skull open against a brick wall. He was bullied because of his slight frame, a result of his ill health since he was a baby and which later on stopped him being selected for grammar school. That was something he deeply regretted. His life sounded such a sad, unloved, miserable story.

"Do you want to go home, Phyllis? Have you had enough for one night?" he asked, seeming to understand my needs.

"I can give you a lift back to the nurses' home in my motor-cycle sidecar…?"

"Oh, Eric that would be great. But what about Patsy and the others?"

"Don't worry," he said. "They'll be fine. I'm sure they're capable of finding their own way home. Here, put this spare helmet on."

Thankfully it wasn't far to ride. The icy air blistered against my face as we sped through the country lanes back to the nurses' home, where he dropped me off outside the main gates.

"Better not come any further. We don't want people getting the wrong idea, do we?" he teased.

"Ah, well… no," I agreed.

"Goodnight then, Phyllis."

"Goodnight, Eric."

"Yeah. See ya then." He started up the engine and while it was idling, he called out, "Hey, don't fancy coming to the pictures with me then – on Friday? There's a Norman Wisdom film on. *Follow that Star*, I think it's called… at the Gaumont. What d'ya say?"

"Norman who?"

"You mean you've never heard of laugh-a-minute Norman Wisdom?"

"No, I haven't now. I've not been to the films much before, only when I was a child once a year if I was lucky. But I'd love to. That'll be grand."

"Pick you up at seven then."

"Here at the main gates?"

"Er, no, better not. Might be a bit too risky. We don't want anyone to see us now, do we? What with your nursing career and all."

He had a think. "I'll tell you what… meet me at the bus stop on the main road by the crossroads. It'll be dark, so no one will see us there. Alright?"

"Yes, that will be fine," I said, agreeing to his plan, although not relishing the 20-minute walk on my own, in stilettos, down a dark country lane.

"Okay, see you then."

*

The doctor's surgery was packed out with an eclectic mix of people impatiently flicking through magazines, fiddling with their phones or, like me, staring into the middle distance without making eye contact. It was only a few days since our trip out, but Mum's health was deteriorating and I was growing worried.

"I shouldn't have taken you on that trip, should I?" I said. "I don't think you were really up to it, were you?"

"Oh Sal, Mammy's fine. You fret too much."

"Well, I was going to ask about you and Dad but I don't want to wear you out."

"Your father?"

"Yes, how you got together and ended up living with him."

"Him? Oh, don't talk to me about him, naw."

A man opposite, who sat with folded arms, crossed and uncrossed his legs as he fixed his eyes on my mother. He seemed to be taking an interest in our conversation. I could tell immediately what he was thinking and I wanted to laugh. Dressed in skin-tight leggings with her pink-crocheted peaked hat cocked at a jaunty angle, she looked like a member of a geriatric all-girl pop band.

"Shush!" I said. "Don't talk so loud. People are listening."

"Sorry Pet, I'll try and talk quieter."

"Mum I know you're not keen to talk about the past, but please can you just tell me about what happened?" I said, leaning into her and lowering my voice.

"What happened?"

"Yes, you know… about you and Dad, your courting days… and what made you want to be with him."

"Oh Sal, I was so taken in by him. If I had known what I know now I'd never have let him into my life. I was just a young girl not long over from Ireland and I thought I could change him. But darling, you could never change a man like that."

"So, what happened then?"

"Well, you know what happened don't you? That was when I found out the truth, Sal."

Chapter 6

Dashed Expectations

Phyllis

Bang! Bang! Bang!

"Phyllis, are yous alright in there?" yelled Patsy as she hammered on the door.

She could hear my muffled sobs as I lay curled up in a ball on my bed clutching at my pillow.

"Phyllis, open the door, please. It's Patsy."

I ignored her. I just wanted to be left alone, but she persisted.

"Phyllis, open the door. I know you're in there. I can hear your crying and I just can't bear it."

"Just go away!"

"Please, Phyllis, please."

"Leave me alone."

"Look, are you going to open this feckin' door naw, or do I have to break it down?"

There was a long pause, then, reluctantly, I opened the door a crack. "What do you want?" I said, choking back tears.

"What in the name of God has happened to yous?" exclaimed Patsy. "You look like a drowned rat. And what's all that mud on your legs?"

"Sure, it's nothing. I'm fine."

"Well, you don't look fine to me. Are's you goin' to let me come in or what?"

I finally relented and let her in. Then sniffed and blew my nose.

"Well?" she urged, as she sat on my bed.

"Really, Pats, you don't need to fuss. I was meeting someone and they didn't turn up. I waited and waited and got wet in the rain. That's it."

I sneezed.

"Wet? More like soaked through. And who didn't turn up?"

"I can't tell you."

"Why?"

"Because it was only a date and we wanted to keep it quiet."

"We? Who's we?"

She scanned my crumpled face for an answer, but she could see I was not going to give anything away.

"Ah, Phyllis, cam here," she sighed, and put her arms around me. "Whoever himself is, that is no way to treat yous and he's not worth it."

"It's because I'm not good enough for him, isn't it?" I blurted out. "I'm not sophisticated. I don't even know who Norman Wisdom is. I think he must have changed his mind."

"Norman Wisdom? Who's he and what's he got to do with it?"

"He's a film star."

"A filum star? Never did I hear of him. And that's a load of baloney about not being good enough. Who's he? The Lord Mayor of London, or someone? You're gorgeous Phyllis. What fellow wouldn't want yous? Naw, tell me... who was it?"

I couldn't tell her, because if she knew it was Eric she'd be blazing mad and give him hell. But why did he stand me up? I felt nothing but humiliated, wet and cold. I had waited over two hours with the rain slanting down, without shelter, in the black of night, the cold wind stinging my face and cars spraying my legs from the puddles. I really believed he would come and I was so looking forward to being with him again. Now my heart ached and I just felt miserable.

A few days later, when I was busy on the ward, Eric finally appeared. There was definitely a sheepishness about him as he wheeled in a chair to collect a patient and deliberately avoided my gaze. Even though I felt plagued with hurt when he didn't look my way, I conceded that it was probably for the best. Maybe Patsy was right, he was just too old for me. I was out of my depth and didn't understand about men. So, I carried on with my duties and acted as though he wasn't in the room.

Later on, when I got back to my room, there was a note written on an unravelled cigarette packet and pushed under the door. I picked it up:

> *Dear Phyllis*
> *I'm sorry about the other night, but something came up and I couldn't make it, even though I wanted to. I hope we can still be friends. Please can we talk?*
> *Eric*

My eyes widened as I read the words. He still wanted to see me and he sounded sincere. My stomach was all fluttery with excitement. Perhaps there was a good reason why he hadn't turned up? The reason he let me down didn't matter anymore because he still wanted to see me.

Christmas was upon us before we knew it. The staff room was decked out in paperchains and lines of Christmas cards adorned the walls along with bunches of mistletoe strategically placed over the door, threatening a stolen kiss for anyone who was single. The doctors delighted in telling saucy jokes and even matron had a smile on her face for a change.

We rounded up the patients in wheelchairs to take them down to the carol concert organised by a local school. I wheeled my patient to the back of a packed-out room. The singing was in full flow as the children belted out *Good King Wenceslas...*

I was joining in with my patient when I sensed a presence trying to share my hymn book. To my surprise it was Eric, who gave me a reassuring smile, gazed deep into my eyes and entwined his fingers around mine. My head swam in confusion and I felt so giddy with excitement that I stumbled over the words and wanted to laugh. The hospital chaplain wound up the concert with prayers and then we headed back to the ward. Eric brushed his arm deliberately against mine as we wheeled our patients through the corridors. He was greedy for my touch, as I was for his, but I looked straight ahead so as not to attract attention.

"Phyllis! Did you get my note?"

"Ah, sure, I did," I whispered, blushing.

"D'you forgive me then?"

"Shhh... people will hear." I lowered my voice. "Forgive you for what then, Eric?"

"Look," he whispered, "I'm really sorry. Really, *really* sorry. It couldn't be helped that night. Me old mother had a bad fall... and I had to go to hospital with her. There wasn't anyone else. She lives by herself, apart from my sister who is partially blind, so she couldn't help her, could she? Are we still friends... and can we try again?"

"Ah Eric, that's fine. Things happen. I do understand, you know. And yes, of course we're still friends."

So, a short time after that, we started going out. Sometimes it would be to a pub, although I didn't drink; other times for a walk down a country lane or a ride out in his motorcycle-sidecar. Anywhere where we could snatch a kiss in the dark without being seen. That's what I liked about him. He always had my best interests at heart. He said if anyone knew I was courting then I could lose my job and, of course, I didn't want that. In those days your choice was either a nursing career or marriage and a family.

Eric always seemed very chivalrous, opening doors and making me walk on the inside of the pavement when we were out together. He made me feel protected. I'd never, ever had anyone like that in my life before, so mature and dependable, that it was only a matter of time before I fell even deeper for his charms.

After four or five months, I still hadn't told Patsy. We had always confided everything in each other, but now I had changed. I never told her where I was going or what I was up to. I made excuses. Never the type to hold back, she confronted me with her suspicions one day and asked me outright.

"Is there something going on between you and Eric?"

"What makes you think that, Pats?"

"Because I've seen it in your eyes. The way you light up when he comes on the ward. The way he looks at you and the way you look at him. You can't be denying it, Phyllis. I know – I absolutely know something's going on."

"Ah no, I think you've got that wrong."

"Have I? You sure naw?"

"Of course."

"Well, don't say I didn't warn you. I overheard him bragging to Johnny Butters in the canteen the other day, how he can't make his mind up between dark-haired types or blondes. I mean, who in the name does he think he is? And the younger the better it would seem as well. Phyllis, I don't trust him as far as I could throw him."

"Pats, I don't know what you're talking about… and I find that hard to believe about Eric. He seems a good man to me. And I can assure you, there is nothing going on."

"I'm telling you straight. I have a bad feeling about himself, naw. I know you won't admit to it, but you would be better going out with someone of your own age if you wanna do that."

I continued to brush her off, but was secretly shocked by her accusations and didn't want to believe a word.

That evening Eric and I met up in our secret spot down a nearby country lane. Stolen moments in the dark were becoming increasingly frustrating. I wanted us to be together properly, and for the world to know.

"Oh Eric, could we not go somewhere else for a change? It's cold standing outside all the time," I said, exasperated.

"What's wrong with it? We get to see each other, don't we? Have a little kiss and a cuddle and all that. Going out costs money, Phyl, and you know I ain't loaded."

"I know Eric and I'm sorry. I don't want to be a burden to you because you're always so good to me, but perhaps we could go back to your place one day and spend some time together there?"

He looked as if he was about to choke.

"My place? You are kidding me, aren't you?"

"No. Why not? You said you lived alone, didn't you?"

"Yes – but it's not possible."

"Why isn't it?"

"Because… my old mum has moved in for a while and the place is a mess. There's all her stuff everywhere. She's very untidy you know."

"Your mother? But what about your sister who's partially blind? Who's looking after her?

He rubbed his nose and sniffed.

"What… my sister? Who, Maisy? Oh, the neighbours are keeping an eye on her. What do you want to know that for anyway?" he said.

"Well, I just wonder—"

"Now look Phyllis, it's not possible and that's it! Alright? Can we change the subject?"

"But I could help look after your mother if she's elderly. Tidy up the place. It's my job after all and what I do every day. Then at least we'd be together, even if she's there."

"No!"

"No?"

"No! And that's the end of it, Phyllis. What is it with you women? Why do you have to keep on and on and on? You're all the bleedin' same."

"I'm sorry Eric, I didn't—"

"Look! She wouldn't like you. She's from the north of Ireland! You're from the south! She will never accept you. Understand?"

I backed away feeling anxious and rejected, but I didn't know why.

"Yes, I understand," I said, beginning to quiver. "I didn't mean to upset you. Please don't be cross with me. I won't mention it again."

"Right!" he said, putting his helmet on, impatient to go. "Well I'm off now. See you tomorrow."

"Don't I even get a kiss first?" I stretched out my arms.

"Sorry, no time. Gotta go. Bye."

Then, before I knew it, he had revved up his engine and sped off.

I felt as if I'd been punched in the heart. I stood there, dazed, and watched him disappear out of sight. The smoke from his engine left a long plume where he once had been. I pulled my cardigan around me as it was starting to get chilly. Slowly, I followed, back along the path where the light of the moon guided my way and an owl hooted at me from the trees above.

The next day came and went, but there was no Eric. I wanted to apologise for upsetting him, but it was several agonising days before I saw him again.

Then, after finishing my late shift, I said my goodbyes to the night staff and started walking back to my staff quarters. It was good to escape the busy routine of the hospital after a tiring day on my feet. I lit a cigarette and relaxed. Outside it felt calm and peaceful. I could smell the sweetness of freshly cut grass and all I heard was the birds singing their evening songs as their silhouettes flitted in and out of a dusky sky.

My thoughts began to unwind. The green smells evoked memories of Ireland and times spent in the orchard back at the orphanage. I thought of Auntie Bea. I hadn't seen her for a few years now, since I left, although we were in regular contact. In her most recent letter, she said she had booked a boat ticket and would be over to visit in a few months' time, when I was due to qualify as a State Enrolled Nurse. I couldn't wait. I was so looking forward to seeing her.

"Psst!... psssst!" I heard a voice coming from the bushes.

Eric's gaunt shadowy figure was beckoning me.

"Phyl! Quick – over 'ere! And shush," he added.

"Eric, what on earth are you doing here?" I whispered.

"Can't be long. Parked the bike down the lane and walked up. Had to see you. I couldn't stop thinking about you after the other night. I'm sorry if I was a bit off, but I've been under a lot of stress recently, with one thing or the other – you have no idea. Are we still okay?"

"Of course, we are!" I said, flinging my arms around him. "I guessed you might have things on your mind. We all say things in haste sometimes and then regret them. All that matters is that you're here now."

He held me tightly, then looked intently at my face and caressed my hair. "You're beautiful Phyllis. D'you know that?"

"Ah, go on with ya naw. That's a silly thing to say."

"No, it's not," he continued. "You, and you alone, are the best thing that has ever happened to me. You must believe me. You're so fun-loving and full of life – different from all the other women I've ever met."

I shook my head.

"Yes, you are… and I am gonna make it up to you, I promise. Just give me a bit longer and I'll invite you back to my place. The time has to be right because I don't want to spoil anything. D'you understand what I mean?"

"Ah no, Eric. What do you mean?"

"Well, don't worry about it now. Just remember we'll be together soon. Just be patient."

Sure enough, several weeks later he kept his word, and I was delighted. We both had the afternoon off work and he picked me up in our usual spot and drove the four miles home to his prefab. It was a single storey building, one of many built *en masse*, after the bombing raids of the Second World War.

The rooms were small and cosy, although the construction was pretty basic with a corrugated iron roof and a design like the chalets at a holiday camp. Although he lived alone, he had a woman's touch when it came to making it feel homely. There were floor-standing lamps with frilly lampshades, floral-patterned furniture and greying net curtains that diffused the light flooding into the living room. Over the mantelpiece hung an art deco mirror. Strangely though, I remember noticing there were no photographs or ornaments apart from a clock and an old brown Bakelite radio set that sat proudly on the sideboard. I was really surprised, as it was not what I expected of a man living by himself. Perhaps it was his mother's taste, I told myself, and she'd helped put it all together.

He invited me in, made me a cup of tea and put some music on the radio. I kicked off my stilettos, flopped on the sofa with my legs up and flicked through a magazine. We got chatting and he told me more stories of his time in the war, driving big army trucks across France and Holland, and how he'd suffered injuries when the truck in front was blown up. I was fascinated and thought how brave he was to survive that. Before I knew it, I was nestling back into his arms and feeling very contented as we relaxed in each other's company.

He started rubbing the balls of my feet and massaging my aching toes. I wasn't used to being looked after like this; my life was always on the go looking after other people. It seemed perfectly natural at the time, me not being able to resist him.

For the next few weeks, he brought me over in his motorcycle-sidecar whenever I wasn't on an early or had the weekend free. Sometimes I stayed the night. It was bliss, and soon I was treating his prefab like my own home. Then, out of the blue, he offered me a key so I could let myself in when I had finished for the afternoon.

Everything was working out fine and we soon fell into a little routine, until that day in the school summer holidays. An ice-cream van had turned the corner as I neared the prefab, and children were riding up and down on their bicycles. A lad rushing to buy ice cream had left his scooter lying sideways on the path and I stepped over it to open the gate.

I let myself in. The prefab smelt stuffy from cooking; it was lingering from the night before and from being locked up all day. Without hesitation, I threw open the kitchen window to let in some air. I filled the kettle and put an egg on to boil. I'd been on my feet since early that morning and hadn't eaten anything so I was ravenous and dying for a rest.

I heard the front door rattling. The clock said quarter to two – too early for Eric, so who was this, I wondered? My eyes were drawn down the narrow, dimly lit hallway, and through the frosted glass panel I saw the reflection of a woman scrabbling with a key, trying to get in. I remember an instant feeling of dread as I held my breath and heard her voice. She sounded stern, with a London accent, but I couldn't tell who she was talking to.

I stood there, paralysed with fear as my eyes darted around for an exit or somewhere to hide, but there was none. I was in a complete panic. I could hear every thud of my heart throbbing out of my chest. What should I do?

Before I knew it, the woman was in the kitchen. She was tall and slightly stooped. A large kiss-curl of bleached blonde peaked out from beneath her headscarf, which matched the shade of red on her tightly pursed lips. By her side was a suitcase that she plonked determinedly on the floor. She narrowed her eyes and looked me up and then down.

"Who the bleedin' hell are you?" she shouted. "And what're you doing in my house?"

"I…I-I'm Phyllis. Y…y-your house?"

"That's right. *My* house. And I bloody well live 'ere!"

I folded my arms around me for protection and shivered with fear.

"Well, are you going to explain yourself?"

"I… I-I let myself in… with a key door. I-I mean… door key. Eric gave…"

"Eric? Eric! Why, the filthy dirty bastard! So, it's his idea, is it? This is what he gets up to when my back's turned and I spend a few weeks at my mother's? Moves his floozy in does he? Didn't he tell you he had *a wife*?"

"A wife? Are you his w…w-wife? N-no, sure he did not."

A little boy with yellow hair emerged from the hallway. He stood shyly behind the woman and clutched at her coat, looking bemused. Eric's wife ushered him into the living room.

"Mum…"

"Be a good boy, Derek. Now, go and find your toys and Mummy'll be with you in a minute."

I heard her shrill voice from the living room: "And where's all my pictures gone? What's he bleedin' well done with them then?"

She stomped back, more agitated and aggressive than before. I felt my legs go weak, but I couldn't make them move.

"Oh yes… and a son! Did he mention a son?" she continued.

My stomach turned over.

"A son? That little boy…"

I thought my legs would give way. I was stunned and couldn't take it in. I thought I was going to be sick, so I bent over the sink and gripped the sides for dear life.

"Yes! A bleedin' son! *His* son. Eric's son."

"I…I-I can't believe it. I never knew any of this. How could he be doing this to me?" I sobbed. "He told me he was looking after his old mother from time to time… but he said he lived on his own."

"Lived on his own! What, him lookin' after Tilly — that old bag? That's a laugh, ain't it?"

Now I was crying. "That's what he told me, honest. Please, listen. I'm so sorry… I never knew. You have to believe me," I begged.

"My arse, you didn't know! If you think I'm falling for that one, you must think I'm away with the fairies."

"But it's true…" My tears stuck in my throat and I could hardly speak.

The woman moved menacingly towards me.

"You know he likes em young, don't ya? I was one of those once, until I knew what he was all about."

"I don't want to know," I bleated back.

"It's the innocence he finds appealing."

"Stop!" I put my hands over my ears.

She looked me up and down again with a venomous gleam.

"Yeah – that's probably what he sees in you."

"No! I don't want to hear it."

"But then I discovered his little secrets and it changed everything. Ask him about the railway and what went on there. He got the sack, you know. Not many people know about that. He was lucky he got away with what he did. Go on, I dare you… ask him. Mark my words, you'll soon wish you'd never clapped eyes on our Eric once you know the truth."

By now I had completely broken down and was sobbing uncontrollably. The egg had boiled and was rattling around fiercely in the pan and the kettle whistled its high-pitched scream. The sound was deafening. It seemed to go on and on. It was piercing my brain. Someone needed to turn it off but I stood there helpless looking across at Eric's wife through blurry eyes. She seemed to be relishing these moments of torture. Everything grew louder and louder – the whistling higher and higher. I couldn't stand it anymore and at last I reached to turn off the gas knob.

"Leave it!" shrieked the woman.

I cowered in terror as she lunged towards me with her hand in the air. I ducked out of its way but, instead, slipped on the greasy floor and hit my head with a bang on the heavy stone sink that jutted out. The shock and the pain shot through me like a steam train but there was no time to fuss. I had to run. Tears were streaming down my face in a torrent.

"Dirty little tramp! Get up and get out of my house. And take your trash with you," she said, throwing my handbag and coat at me.

"I'm sorry…" I mumbled. I'm so… so sorry…"

"Whore!" she shouted back. "Slag!"

Frantic with fear and shame, I ran in blind panic down the hallway and grappled with the latch on the front door, which wouldn't open.

"Open – for God's sake – open!" I screamed, my hands fumbling and shaking all the while, as I pulled at the door, with her right behind me.

"Get out of my house… before I bleedin' kill you!"

She grabbed me roughly by the arm, her painted fingernails piercing my skin as she man-handled me outside with a rough yank. She hurled me with such force that I fell onto my side on the path, bloodying my knees and tearing my stockings on the way. I could feel a stinging sensation in my grazed hands as I picked myself up, but I was in such shock that I couldn't feel the pain.

The door slammed, leaving me quaking and so distraught that I couldn't stand up straight. The children in the street skidded to a halt on their bikes and stared with concern as I controlled my breath. The ice-cream van was still playing its song.

"You alright, Mrs?" called out one of the older children.

I couldn't speak or look them in the eye. I waved my arm to say, "Don't worry, I'm alright," and limped off down the street towards the bus stop.

The shock discovery of Eric's wife and a child I knew nothing about was so devastating that as soon as I reached my nurses' quarters I rushed to the bathroom and threw up. I had been deceived and betrayed. How could he give me the key to his house when his wife and child lived there? And how could he lie to them and about them? The rollercoaster ride had ended with a jolt; I felt dizzy with bewilderment and pain and I wanted to get off. Everything was spinning around, but I was standing still, small and alone, trying to take it all in.

I threw myself into bed and lay there sobbing until the next day. *If only someone would shoot me and put me out of this misery,* I thought, but only the walls heard me. When I got up, I looked in the mirror. My eyes were bloodshot and my face raw. The thought of facing everyone crippled me with shame. What would people think of me now? A brazen hussy! I couldn't look anyone in the face. I had to get as far away from Eric as I possibly could.

Auntie was delighted when I rang to ask if I could come and stay for a couple of weeks. I still had unused annual leave from work, so I booked my tickets and headed to Holyhead for the boat to Dún Laoghaire.

Although she was happy to see me, at first, the conversation was stilted and awkward. Auntie was living with her widowed sister. It was Edna's house and I sensed she didn't want me there.

Knowing her as I did, I think she sensed something was wrong, even though I tried to hide the truth, but she never asked any questions. Especially when I took myself off for solitary walks down to the harbour, watching the ships coming and going and thinking about my life. I was glad to have breathing space, but no way was I going to burden her with my troubles. She would have been shocked and horrified to say the least, and doubtless very disappointed in me, being such a Christian woman as she was.

By the time I returned to work it was nearly time to qualify as a nurse. Several of us were passing out at the same time and there was a buzz of excitement about the place. Patsy still had a way to go as she had started her course after me, but she was nonetheless excited for me.

"Where've you been? I've missed yer," she asked, as we washed out bedpans together in the sluice room. "I've been frantic with worry, and it's passing-out day next week. I hope we're still goin' out to celebrate? I'm really looking forward to going to the pub again with yous."

"Sorry Pats, I know I didn't tell you, but I had to get away for a while – to Auntie's."

"Why Phyllis? What's wrong? Why did you have to get away?"

My voice croaked, "Because... becau..." And I burst into tears.

"Phyllis! Oh Phyl, don't cry. What's the matter?"

"Can't tell you... I'm too ashamed."

"You can, you know you can. Ah, Phyllis, cam on naw. Tell your old Pats. Whatever it is, I won't judge yous," she said, putting her arm around me.

"Oh Pats, you were right. It's Eric... he lied to me. He's not single at all. He has a wife... and a s...s-son. A son would you believe? How could he, Pats... how could he do that to me?"

"Why the dirty dog!" exclaimed Patsy." He did what? So, you were seeing each other. I knew it."

I leant my head on her shoulder.

"His wife came home... and she went for me. It was awful. But I never knew, Pats. I swear to God, I never knew."

"Oh Phyllis, I told yer he was no good. How could a man of that age still be single anyways? Oh dear, what a way to find out. Does your auntie know?"

"No. I couldn't be telling her. It would be too much – I think it would kill her."

"But Phyllis, it's not your fault. I saw what he was like but you were taken in by him. I did try to warn you."

"I know you did Pats, and you were right all along. I should have listened. I should have been wiser."

"Phyllis, we all make mistakes. You are going to have to put this behind yous. Listen, dry yer eyes, we don't want to let people see you've been crying. Go and get yourself a cup of tea in the canteen. I'll cover for you and say you needed your tea break early."

A week later a large group of us were lined up for our official photo after passing our exams and qualifying as State Enrolled Nurses. Among the crowd of family, friends and well-wishers were Patsy and Auntie Bea. Patsy was waving and Auntie took a picture with her Brownie box camera. I felt so proud I could burst. I smiled, waved back and rushed up to greet them both as soon as I could get away. We sat with the other visitors, having tea and cake, and then I showed Auntie Bea my room in the nurses' quarters. Patsy seemed to get on very well with Auntie that day and when someone else wanted my attention, they were happy to carry on chatting away together without me being there. It was a flying visit for Auntie as she had decided to combine her stay with visiting her niece, Bunty, who was working as a nursing home matron near Hampton Court.

It was more than a surprise when two days later I was called into matron's office unexpectedly.

"Sit down, Phyllis," was all she said. "I have something of deep concern to discuss with you."

I sat with a wavering apprehension. What could matron be talking about, I wondered? She seemed even more formal than usual and something was seriously wrong.

"I'm afraid there is no easy way of saying what I am about to say. It has been brought to my attention that you have been having an affair with a married man. Is this correct?"

I thought I was going to fall through the floor. I cleared my throat.

"An affair? Yes, matron, I can't deny it. I'm afraid it's true… but I didn't know he was married. I promise you, I didn't."

"I am aware of all the facts," she continued, "and I can only say how very disappointed I am in you."

I placed my hands in my lap and looked down at them. I felt too humiliated to look matron in the face.

"You know, this sort of behaviour cannot be tolerated when you become a nurse. We do not want the hospital name brought into disrepute. I should terminate your employment forthwith, but your aunt, a Miss Davidson, has intervened on your behalf and explained your situation. I have, though, spoken to our hospital secretary and Mr Eric Herbert, the man you were seeing, has already been dismissed."

I was stunned. My aunt knew! How though? And Eric had been sacked? I was shaken to say the least.

"Have you anything to say?"

"No, matron. Well, apart from that I am truly sorry and wish it had never happened."

"Yes, I'm sure. We will now be keeping a close eye on your behaviour, so let this be a warning to you."

I left her office, reeling from the news that Eric had been sacked and I had only been kept on because of my aunt's intervention. It must have been Patsy who told her, on the day I got my SEN badge. Although they both had my best future at heart it didn't stop me feeling how I did about Eric. I missed him terribly, even after what he'd done. It was like walking around with a permanent pain in my side, though I knew there was no hope for us anymore. He must have felt the same because, not long after, I started receiving pleading letters from him, one after the other, begging for forgiveness. His wife had left him, they said, taking Derek to her mother's, and now he really was alone in the prefab.

I tried to ignore them at first but, despite my better judgement, I gave in and met him for a drink. Within a few months I was back at the prefab; only this time I was living with him.

I didn't tell my aunt as she would have been mortified. As far as she was concerned Eric could not be trusted and had already proved as much.

"Phyllis," she told me, "I want you to have nothing to do with that man. He will never be any good to you if he can deceive both you and his wife like he did. He will only make your life unhappy."

How prophetic her words turned out to be.

*

"Well come in Mrs Herbert," said the doctor. "Please take a seat."

It was two weeks later and we were back in the doctor's surgery awaiting the results of Mum's X-ray. He swivelled his chair away from his computer screen and bent forward to speak to Mum, his hands clasped.

"I've had results back from the chest consultant at Downsview. I'm afraid there's a query on the X-ray, Mrs Herbert."

I gripped Mum's hand and felt her fingers trembling as we hung on to his every word.

"Oh yes?" Mum cleared her throat and her voice sounded scratchy.

The room was silent except for his desk fan whirring as it oscillated. All I could hear was the click, click, clicking as it kept catching on a book on his desk. He studied our faces for a reaction. Mum and I looked at each other, both thinking the same thing. I closed my eyes and took a deep breath, trying to calm myself.

"I'm going to send you for a CT scan, Mrs Herbert. Do you know what that involves?"

"No, not exactly. Will it hurt?"

"No. It just means they will put a needle in your vein and a yellow dye will be pumped through it, so they can see more clearly what is going on inside you."

Mum looked at me for reassurance. "Aah, naw, I'm not sure about that. Do I have to have it done?"

"Yes, I strongly advise you do."

"Sorry, doctor," I interrupted. "I have to ask. Do you suspect cancer or something?"

The doctor's face was expressionless as he inspected me over the top of his spectacles.

"Well, we can't say for certain at this stage, but it might be a possibility."

My stomach dropped. "But only six months ago you said there were no signs of lung cancer."

"That was six months ago. A lot can change in that time."

I flushed with embarrassment. Didn't I have the right to query anything? She was my mother after all.

"Don't worry, Mum, I'll come with you," I said, sensing her fear. "It'll be alright."

The doctor checked his computer and tapped away furiously.

"You'll receive a letter within two weeks. The scan will be at the Devonshire, a private hospital that accepts NHS patients when no other appointments are available."

As we got up to go, worst-scenario thoughts began spinning around my head. I put my arm around Mum and led her to the door. She was the frailest I'd ever seen her, still trembling and hunched over. The news was not what she'd been expecting.

I tried to hold everything back and be strong, but as we walked over to the car I felt my legs turn to jelly, as if they were going to give way.

She looked at me meekly, her face pale and gaunt. "Are we going home now, Sal?"

I wiped my eyes with a tissue and pulled myself together.

"Yes," I said, swallowing hard. "We're going home now."

"You're not crying now, Pet, are you?"

"No, course not. It's just a bit of hay fever."

"Mammy's cold darling. I just want to get in the warm."

"But it's a hot day, Mum, and look at all the clothes you've got on."

"I know, but I'm not feeling well. I feel a bit sick and just want to lie down."

"Oh, Mum."

As I drove, the warmth from the sun and the motion of the car soon caused her to nod off. My brain was scrambling to find a logical solution. How could this be happening? Perhaps it wasn't cancer, but something else... some sort of virus. I didn't want to think the unthinkable. It wasn't fair, not after the life she'd had: given up at birth, never knowing where she came from, and now this, cutting short my chances of ever finding her family. I thought back to spells when my brother and I were without our mother; I knew those devastating feelings of abandonment too well. Memories, painful memories, came flooding back, transporting me to a time when I was six years old and the trauma my brother and I experienced when we were separated from her. It was right after she left my dad and ran away to Ireland – a time I can never forget.

Chapter 7

Running Away

Sally

It was 1969 and a bitterly cold start to the year. Dad had not really been very well since just after Christmas. But he often suffered from ill health. He was nearly 13 years older than my mother, and their marriage was not a happy one. They had been together for about 10 years, marrying five years earlier at the insistence of Auntie Bea who was horrified at the thought of Mum and Dad living in sin with one child born out of wedlock (me) and another on the way. My father had no desire to marry again but, as Auntie Bea had paid for his divorce, he eventually gave in. From what I can gather, the few years they had together before any children came along were happy. They spent their summers down on Brighton beach or caravan-holidaying in nudist camps. Dad said that my Mum was "the life and soul of the party", when they used to go out. I can well imagine, but the novelty must have worn off because by the time my brother came along they were sleeping in separate bedrooms.

We lived in a small, terraced council house; lino on the floor, offset by a large threadbare mat and an old 1940s circular mirror from his first marriage that overhung a beige tiled mantel. The ceiling was a dirty yellow and the walls receded into a grey retro wallpaper that looked tired and faded. In the far corner sat a brown television set, its screen covered in a thin film of nicotine. All the furniture came from the local Mission Mart charity shop, apart from a makeshift sideboard that my dad had built after taking up carpentry lessons. He could turn his hand to anything, and would, if he thought it would save money. It was a hideous thing, designed to look modern, with a shiny Formica top and metal rods for legs that were crudely bolted together like a Meccano toy for stability and made it look permanently about to collapse.

This particular abode was one of many we had exchanged in recent years as it seemed that Mum just couldn't get on with the neighbours – or that's what Dad said, but it was probably because he didn't like her talking to them.

"Have nothing to do with neighbours and keep yourself to yourself," he would warn her.

My father was no saint, and I know there were other reasons why we moved house so often in those days. He had a side that not many knew about.

A year earlier, at a previous house, there'd been an angry confrontation on the doorstep. A man punched Dad straight in the face as he opened the front door, while my mother, witnessing it, stood helplessly screaming at the top of the stairs. After this incident, an older girl from down the road who used to come in to play was forbidden to come anywhere near our house. Dad used to encourage my friends to sit next to him on the sofa. Sometimes he played tickling games with them, which always made my mum so edgy that she'd encourage them to go home. I rarely saw them again after such incidents.

Mum tried to leave him several times, but always ended up going back because she had no family to go to, nor anyone else to turn to. She daren't tell Auntie Bea because she would have been mortified at my father's behaviour. After all, she had warned Mum years ago that he was not trustworthy. She told me how it hit home just how alone she was at those times. One dreadful day she left without any money and walked 30 miles to a nursing home where she knew the matron, and promptly collapsed with pneumonia and exhaustion. The matron, I later discovered, was Bunty, Auntie Bea's niece, now living permanently in the UK, who had never had any time for Mum since childhood. It was three long months before I saw her again. She needed someone to understand the turmoil of being rejected by my father and the suffering she went through in his ill treatment of her. She felt trapped and desperately unloved, but in those days unhappy marriages were not openly discussed. Those sayings, *You make your bed, you lie in it,* and *Don't wash your dirty linen in public,* certainly applied if you came from an Irish background like Mum's, where the culture was never to bring shame upon your family.

My father was not the loving man she had imagined and longed for. He was emotionless, distant and rejected her on every level, preferring pornography to a physical relationship, which greatly upset her given her strict religious upbringing. As their lives grew more separate she became powerless to stop him doing anything and everything he wanted.

He even had his own dark room where he developed photos. I remember him showing me once. The room was blacked out apart from a single red lightbulb. A washing line was pegged with photos of naked women and underneath were trays filled with strong-smelling chemicals.

"Look at that, Sally," he said as he showed me. "See what Daddy can do. It's magic!"

And before my eyes, what looked like plain white glossy paper would turn, after a minute in his tray of liquid, into a coloured photo of naked women with heavy eye make-up and their legs spread wide apart.

But despite that, Dad wasn't a bad dad on the whole. He did try to show us love when we were young.

"Who loves their dad?" he would call as he opened the front door on his return from work.

"We love our dad!" we'd cry, rushing up for a big hug.

We didn't have much in those days, with Dad on a limited income, but he did the best he could. He made me dolls' furniture out of marine plywood in his spare time at work because we couldn't buy expensive toys. They were larger than I expected and a bit clumsy, but I was delighted nonetheless.

For my brother, he'd put together Airfix models of Second World War fighter planes or balsawood boats that we sailed on the big pond on Clapham Common. We never went away but Dad took us for car trips to the countryside in the summer holidays, stopping off at as many pubs with beer gardens as possible. Along the way we stuck our heads out of the car window and sang songs he'd taught us from his time in the war: *Maybe it's because I'm a Londoner* and *Pack up Your Troubles in Your Old Kit Bag*.

Everything was on tick. Goods from the milkman, the corner shop and even the ironmongers were all on a tab that Mum was meant to pay at the end of the week but, more often than not, forgot about. The problem was, she liked to spend. I don't think she ever understood the value of money. Being institutionalised as a child had not taught her many life skills, so it didn't take much persuasion for a travelling salesman to call at the door and sell her something. She would let anyone in if they were friendly enough and was often taken in by their charm. I remember the ghastly peach-coloured glass tea set that never got used and sat in a display cabinet for 20 years. Dad nearly hit the roof when he saw it.

One day, when I was using their double bed as a trampoline, my mother rushed into the bedroom. She was barefooted, her hair in pig tails, wearing skimpy red shorts, and looked petrified. Scanning the room for a place to hide, she dived into the old Victorian wardrobe, which was ajar. Next, the bedroom door flew open with such force that the door handle bashed against the wall leaving a dent in the plaster. My enraged father was in hot pursuit, swearing and cursing.

"You stupid cow! You stupid, stupid cow! How many times must I tell you that money is for paying the bills, not to squander as you wish."

Realising she was in the wardrobe, and oblivious to my presence, he dragged her out by the wrists, with her screaming and begging.

"No Eric, no! I'm so sorry, I didn't mean it. Don't hurt me, please. I'm sorry, I'm so sorry. Don't hurt me."

She said he used to hit her, but I only have a vague recollection. Maybe he didn't do it in front of me or perhaps I blanked it out, but I feared deeply for my mum when my father was angry because I knew he could lose control.

"Your daddy doesn't love me. He doesn't love me," she would say, breaking down as if she were a child herself.

"Don't cry, Mummy. I love you! Don't be sad," I would say, trying to console her as I wrapped my little chubby arms around her.

She used to stare longingly into the garden from the kitchen sink; I imagine she was despairing about how to escape from the misery. Her limp posture, black hair untidily scraped back and her silent tears – they all pulled at my heart.

As the arguing got worse Mum grew more agitated than ever and was permanently neurotic. Dad later said it was due to the pills. But she later confided that she reached for pill bottles after a row, as if they could relieve the pain of him making her so unhappy. He never considered for one moment that he might be responsible for her being so dependent upon them. That's probably why she never slept. She was always going to the doctor and requesting tablets for her breathing, which she said she found difficult. I wonder now if that wasn't stress. Eventually they refused her requests because she became so dependent; then she would argue and cross herself off their lists.

In the early days she did private nursing and worked night shifts, but she rarely slept through the day; she just kept on going. One morning she came home earlier than expected, to find my father peering down watching me in my bed. I always remember it by the cream Aran jumper he was wearing and how, for a reason I couldn't understand then, I felt afraid.

"What are you doing in Sally's bedroom?" she snapped.

He turned around, surprised to see her standing in the doorway.

"I'm not doing anything, okay? I was about to wake her and see if she'd like a little trip today – get that present she wanted for her birthday."

She narrowed her eyes and inhaled deeply on her cigarette.

"Well come out, you've no business being in there," she hissed. "I can get her up and dressed now I'm home."

She was fiercely protective of me when I was a child; as it turned out, with good reason.

I was five years old when it happened, at the beginning of a traumatic year that affected all our lives forever.

It was morning and Mum had just arrived home after a night nursing a private client. I saw her shadowy figure through the patterned net curtain on the glass-panelled front door. I stood in the entrance to the front room, listening intently as her key turned in the lock. She was in a good mood that morning, to begin with.

"Sally! Will darling! Mammy's home…" she called out.

Carefully stepping over a roll of red and black-flecked carpet still waiting to be laid in the narrow hallway, I could already smell her smoky breath and the damp coming in from outside.

"About time!" snapped my dad, impatiently fiddling with his tie in the hall mirror. "I've got to get to work. Where've you been for fuck's sake?"

"Got delayed. I can't help the trains, can I?"

"Yeah, right." He glanced at his watch. "Look, I haven't got time for this now. I've got the kids up and dressed. Will's in his pushchair and Sally's waiting for you to take her to school. You'd better get a move on or you'll make her late too."

"Why have you done that? I told you to leave Sally to me."

"Because someone has to take responsibility in the mornings. I can't wait all day for you to get your act together. Right, I'm off!"

The front door slammed, shaking the house with its echoing bang. Rebuffed by his remarks, she waited until he had gone, then angrily clip-clopped her way up the bare-boarded stairs in her kitten heels. Perhaps it was something I had done? Whatever it was, she was now in an angry mood, which meant she'd probably take it out on me even if she didn't mean it. I clutched my school satchel tightly in front of me.

"Sally… Sally!" she shouted over the bannister.

"Yes, Mummy?"

"Stay exactly where you are. I need to ask you something."

A wave of butterflies engulfed my stomach.

She flew down the stairs, barely able to catch her breath as she burst into the front room.

"Where did you sleep last night?"

"Where, Mummy?"

I shook and felt my knees buckle inwards.

"Yes, where?"

"In bed."

"Yes, yes. But whose bed? Your bed hasn't been slept in."

I lowered my eyes to the floor. My cheeks were ablaze. I felt torn and confused. I could still hear Daddy whispering into my brain.

Remember, don't say anything to yer mother now. This is our secret. Just Sally's and Daddy's.

"Look at me, Sally. Come here and look me in the face," she said, roughly fingering the hair out of my eyes. "Just tell me the truth, naw."

I nodded but kept my chin down. I didn't dare look at her. She bent to my level and grabbed me by the arms.

"I said LOOK – AT – ME!"

"You're hurting me Mummy."

"Sally, this is important, do you understand? I didn't bring you up to lie, did I?"

"No, Mummy, no."

"You know that to lie is a sin, don't you?"

"Yes, Mummy."

"Well then, be a good girl for Mammy and tell me where you slept last night. I promise you won't get into any trouble."

I continued to stare at the floor. I remembered the night before when Daddy snuggled up to me making me feel warm and cosy. And how he made a little laugh and rubbed up against me closer when I told him that I loved him and one day, when I was grown up, I would marry him. I think he thought that was cute. Why I said it, I don't know, but it just seemed to come out.

Her eyes focused on me intently and I wanted to flee, but there was no escape.

"Are you listening to me?"

I kept my head bowed.

"TELL ME!" she screamed, violently shaking me and making my head bob backwards and forwards.

I had blanked out most of the night before, but now the memory of sleeping with Daddy returned at a quickened pace, like a bad dream. I could recall him making a grunting sound as he stroked my hair then ran his hands down my body, but I had no inkling that it was wrong. I felt protected and content to be with him. I felt safe. Then he asked me to lie on my back and, suddenly, it didn't feel right. I felt scared. I wriggled about. I didn't like it. His body was naked and heavy when he lay on top of me. I felt overwhelmed and claustrophobic. I felt as if I couldn't breathe. I could smell his body odour, which smelt of dinner from the night before and I wanted him to get off but he wasn't paying any attention to me. I could sense his heart beating faster and I wanted him to stop. I begged him to stop… but he wasn't listening.

"No, Daddy! Stop it. Please stop! No. You're hurting me! You're hurting me, Daddy," I yelled, as he pushed himself into me.

My high-pitched childish voice must have screamed at him like a siren, dragging him back into reality from whatever place he'd been in, because he jumped up in a flash.

Like an erupting dam, a torrent of big fat sobs burst forth from my eyes, blurring my vision and making the room spin around me. The words stuck in my throat but spluttered out between sobs. "I'm sorry, Mummy, I didn't mean it. I didn't mean it."

I remember her eyes widening with anguish, and her voice softened.

"What are you sorry for, Sally? Is this something to do with your father? Did he do something to you? Did he?"

Reluctantly, I nodded, wracked with guilt for betraying my father and withholding the truth from my mother. Now I was certain that what he asked me to do was wrong. Now everything was my fault.

Mum stared at me blankly, her mind seemed to be racing, attempting to catch up and trying to comprehend the full horror of the situation.

"M...m-mummy..."

I sobbed wretchedly and stretched out my arms, longing to be comforted by her, but she wasn't listening.

"P...p-please Mummy..."

She gazed blankly around the room as though examining the alien world she now lived in. I was still calling her, but she was too far away to hear my voice.

"Mummy! I'm sorry Mummy..."

"Your – father – wouldn't – no. No – not this."

Her face began to crumple, twisting and contorting in pain, as she seemed to visualise the monstrosity of what my father may have done.

She shook her head. "No, no, this can't be happening..."

Then she dropped to the floor on both knees with her head in her hands and wailed, "You're just a CHILD!"

We sat on the floor, broken, our lives ruptured and torn apart. We held on tight, clinging to each other for dear life; she stroked my head and rocked me back and forth, her wet face soaking mine as we tried to make sense of it in our different ways.

"I'm so sorry, darling. I'm sorry Mammy wasn't here to protect you. I will never forgive him for this. Never."

She hadn't wanted to believe my father capable of such an act, even though she suspected for years, having rejected her, that his sexual appetite was unhealthy and becoming increasingly so. But his own daughter? This, for her, was the most horrendous crime he could ever commit.

Being so young I can't remember the exact timescale, but one evening very soon after this incident a policeman and policewoman knocked on the door. My mother had been out of her mind with grief, and in the panic and upset had fled to the next-door neighbours, feeling she had to tell someone. They, in turn, had written a letter to the police.

My father's face was ashen with shock when he came home from work to find two police constables standing in the hallway waiting to speak to him. He was taken into the kitchen to talk to the policeman, while I stayed in the front room with Mum and was questioned by the female officer. As he stood in the doorway, unable to acknowledge his fate, I saw his face begin to bleed. He often suffered with eczema brought on by stress or nerves, which would make him scratch. He looked frightened and I was scared for him because I didn't want him to be in trouble, but my moral conscience as a child was strong and in my head all I could think was *God wants you to tell the truth*. The policewoman sat me on her knee. Her voice was kind and friendly.

"Now, Sally, I have a letter here that I would like to ask you about. Is that alright?" she asked.

Mum perched herself on the edge of the put-me-up settee, nervously watching my reactions and inhaling deeply on her cigarette. I didn't know the content of the letter, but I guessed it was to do with what had happened between me and Dad. With all the rows and goings-on in the house I was learning to be perceptive, and anticipated what the policewoman was going to ask.

"I know what it's about," I said. "And it's true."

The policewoman looked surprised at how I could know so much at such a young age. "True?" she asked.

"Yes – true."

Shortly after questioning, I was sent to the hospital to be examined. It was a painful and shameful experience that I will never forget. I was placed, bare-bottomed, high up on a cold slippery leather couch, which I slid around on as the doctors manoeuvred me into position for an internal examination. The room was painted *eau de nil* and felt as cold and sterile as its antiseptic smells. Without my mother present, and not understanding what was going on, I began to cry. The doctors treated me like an object, talking among themselves, but not to me, as they prodded and poked me with their rubber gloves, oblivious to the fact that I was a frightened little girl. I was sure I must have been very bad to end up here but had no idea what I had done to deserve it. After all that humiliation nothing could be proven, so my father escaped prosecution. This was the late 1960s when DNA hadn't yet been discovered, but today he would have gone to prison. So, we went back to our everyday lives and continued as normal.

Well, for a while anyway, until one day when my mother took Will and me to the social workers' main office at Mill House. We waited in a long corridor, next to tall grey filing cabinets, until Mum was invited in to speak to a social worker. I don't remember the discussion, but I do remember after the meeting that she got into the back seat of a car, shaking uncontrollably, with tears streaming down her face.

"Mammy's just going to the chemist to buy you some sweets and will be back soon," she said, winding down the window.

I may have only been five years old, but I knew it was a lie and that she was not coming back. If she had said "the sweet shop" I might have believed her, but "the chemist" did not ring true. My brother and I stood helplessly on the stone steps of the Georgian building, either side of a social worker who was holding our hands. We gasped in unprepared disbelief as the car containing our mummy sped off briskly through a haze of greenery and into the distance. How could our mother leave us this way?

Will and I were taken into the care of social services and placed in a children's home for several months without seeing either of our parents. To this day I have no idea why it happened because the records have been destroyed, but I can only assume that Mum was trying to protect me from my dad and couldn't cope, because she was never able to talk of that incident again. The psychological trauma it caused me was insurmountable, causing me to dirty the bed at night in the children's home and develop a fear of the dark, which I still have to this day. The pain of separation was too great and I needed to get back to Mum. But how? I wanted to take my baby brother too, but it was going to be difficult because he was so young and we had been separated into different bedrooms. One day, after infants' school, I decided I would try to get home. I was meant to wait for an official-looking man in a suit, wearing a white carnation, to collect me in his car and take me back to the children's home, but when I saw the crowds of mothers gathered outside the school gates, I saw my chance, mingled with them and ran. I had no idea exactly where I lived and there were several dangerous main roads to cross in between. I knew the direction to walk in, but began to panic when I realised that I didn't know where to turn off. Very soon I was lost. Luckily, a couple of young teachers from my school spotted me tottering along the main road crying my eyes out with snot dribbling down my chin and looking extremely distressed. They slowed down in their Mini and pulled over.

"Where are you going, Sally?" one of them asked.

"I don't know, but I want my Mummy."

"Here, get in the car with me and we'll try to see if we can find your Mummy."

Her voice was kind and friendly, although I wasn't totally sure if I could trust her. But eventually she managed to coax me onto her lap and they drove back to my house. When we turned up on the doorstep my mother was astonished to see me.

"What are you doing here, Sally?" she asked.

"I'm not going back to that place! I want to stay with you, Mummy."

Social services turned up to collect me, but there was no way I was going to be separated from her again. Struggling to fight them off, I became hysterical and threatened that if they didn't let me be with my mum I would kill myself. So, by some miracle, they agreed I could come back home. But it was several more months before my brother, who was barely three years old, was allowed to return too. My mother gave up work completely and stayed at home. It meant she lost her independence and had less money to spend on us, but I guess she didn't have any choice as she couldn't trust my father with me. From then on her mental health deteriorated progressively, although I didn't notice straight away.

If only there had been family to help us, but of course there was no one on Mum's side and, oddly, no one on Dad's either. I often wondered why Dad's family didn't help because support may have changed the course of events and saved us so much pain. It took over 50 years before I discovered the reasons why. Apparently, I was not the first child that Dad had been in trouble over. Before he knew my Mum there had been other incidents that caused his family to disown him. Mum couldn't possibly have known this when she met him, it was only later, and to her horror, that she learnt the truth.

Sometimes I find myself back in the dull brown living room, remembering the day before we set out on the journey that shattered our family life for good. Dad was clutching his stomach in pain, and trying to stand up from his dog-eared armchair that was perched beside the old gas fire. He looked paler and more emaciated than usual.

Top of the Pops was on television and they were playing the week's number one record, *Lily the Pink*, by the Scaffolds, as I sat cross-legged on the floor ignoring Dad's ranting and making my Barbie doll dance in time to the music.

"Turn that load of rubbish off! They don't know how to play music like we had in the 50s," he barked.

He hobbled over to the television and turned the sound down till it was barely audible.

"It's all plonker boys. Baby – baby – yeah– yeah! In my day, they'd've thought you had St Vitus' dance if you carried on jiggling about like that. Now you can't even hear the words. Why d'you kids wanna listen to that stuff?"

I put my hands over my ears. I wanted him to stop moaning so I could enjoy the record, but I didn't dare say so.

Mum was in the kitchen preparing Dad's evening meal, a chore she always hated. Her idea of cooking was to heat a tin of something in a pan of boiling water. Whatever was quickest and easiest; anything else was too much effort.

On this occasion, she had gone to the trouble of preparing a proper dinner for him. She brought it in on a tray and placed it proudly on his lap.

A smell of charred remains wafted in from the hallway.

"Ugh!" he groaned as he shovelled in a few mouthfuls. "What the bleedin' hell have you put in it this time?"

My mother appeared at the door, anxiously fiddling with a box of matches in her apron.

"What do you mean... 'what have you put in it?' You're always saying something's wrong with my cooking."

"Well nothing's right with it, that's for sure."

"Ah, go and do it yourself then!"

Dad pushed the food around with his fork. "It's disgusting, woman! Are you trying to bleedin' poison me?"

"Of course not, you eejit. Although, come to think of it, who could blame me with the way you treat me? Nothing I ever do is right."

"Well that's because you're fuckin' useless! You can't cook. You squander all my money on the kids and get me into debt. You're no fuckin' good. D'you hear me? No fuckin' good!"

"And what about you!" Mum screamed. "Are you so perfect then? Your ex-wife was right. What woman would put up with what I have to?"

"What you 'put up with'? That's a joke!"

Mum walked defiantly into the middle of the room, fists tightly clenched in her apron pocket and her eyes glazed with anger.

"I never did find out why you got the sack from the railway when you were a guard, but I can guess. No doubt it's something you should have been put away for."

"Oh, shut your mouth! You know nothing."

"My aunt warned me, Patsy warned me. I should have listened. Look what you have done. You've ruined my life with your filth and dirt."

"Don't talk to me about your 'auntie'! Her, with all her religious claptrap, never did you any good did she? You're no good to anybody."

Mum couldn't take any more. She undid her apron, threw it on the floor and ran out of the room slamming the door behind her as we all looked on. Dad's constant undermining clearly made her feel worthless and perhaps reminded her of her childhood in the orphanage. Alongside his progressive rejections she had lost any slight confidence and self-esteem.

My brother and I had frozen. We were frightened and confused and didn't know what to do.

"Get out of my way!" Dad yelled at us. "I need to get to the khazi!"

"Ouch!" he said, stepping on one of Will's Matchbox cars. "Who put that bleedin' thing there?"

Will looked up at him nervously. "Sorry, Daddy."

He stormed out, leaving a vacuum of emotional turmoil, the sound of the bed creaking upstairs, and my mother's heart-rending sobs that we heard echoing through the ceiling.

*

Mum, Will and I arrived after midnight at the shipping port having made the day-long train journey from London to Holyhead. A massive boat, adorned in brilliant white lights, shone out like a beacon against a curtain of pitch black. Alongside it, a bridge guided us from the shore to the ferry, and Mum was urging me to cross it. Will had fallen asleep over her shoulder and I frantically tried to keep up with them.

I awoke next morning to a sharp rat-tat-tat on the cabin door.

"Excuse me, madam, you need to wake up. You've 10 minutes to vacate the cabin." A tall, uniformed man walked in and hammered his palm on the end of our bunk to attract Mum's attention.

"You've already missed breakfast – it was two hours ago. It's nearly half past nine, and we need to depart soon." He was brooking no nonsense.

I lifted my head, startled by his abrupt presence, and my little brother, who was curled up beside me in the warm and cosy lower bunk, shifted about, disturbed by the noise.

Where are we, I wondered? A bright light dazzled me from the fluorescent strip above, making me blink and screw up my eyes to make out where we were. Everyone had gone. Only a few blankets were left, tossed in disarray on the bunkbeds opposite. There were no windows to let in natural light. Instead there was a washbasin with a small mirror directly above. I urgently sought my mother's reassuring voice as I adjusted to the light.

"Mummy, where are you?" I called out.

She peered over from the top bunk, looking dazed, and squinting in the strong light. She looked as if she hadn't slept in years. Her complexion was tired and sallow with dark circles engulfing her once beautiful green eyes. She leant exhaustedly over the side of her bunk and I could smell her sweet, sickly body odour.

Her stale smoky breath clouded over me as she spoke.

"Sally, darling… Will, darling. Petsies, are you alright?"

"Mummy, you've got to wake up. The man wants us to go," I urged, tugging at her arm which was half hanging down over our bed.

She pulled the blanket up around her shoulders, ignoring my pleas.

"Mammy will get up in a minute. Don't be worrying – we've got plenty of time."

"Mummy, don't go back to sleep. Please don't."

She made a half-hearted attempt to shake off the bedclothes and heaved a reluctant sigh.

"Oh, alright then."

Even now I can see her sitting up, slumping her shoulders forward and burying her head in her hands. Then, as the official turned to leave, she rummaged through her handbag for her first cigarette of the day. I saw a look of relief ease across her face with the first deep intake of nicotine as she blew caliginous grey plumes high into the air. Then, another quick rummage and she pulled out a bottle of pills and popped a couple in her mouth, cupping water from the cold tap in her hands to swallow them. She checked her reflection in the mirror, and looked dazed as if she didn't recognise herself. Will and I, young as we were, sensed that this was it. She had finally left him.

Mum collected up our possessions from the tiny cabin space and chivvied us into our coats and shoes. I don't remember suitcases, just a few carrier bags, one of which was filled to the brim with my Barbie and Sindy dolls, their legs and arms poking out through the plastic.

As we left the warmth of our tiny cabin and ventured out into the world, we were hit by the chill of an Arctic blast. All I heard were loud noises of the engines humming, vibrating below us. Mum carried Will on her hips and juggled bulging carriers on her other arm as she carefully footed it down the iron steps. I clutched her coat, hanging there for dear life, and gripped tightly at the slippery handrail to keep my balance.

It was a relief to land on firm ground again. A sharp frost had turned everything white and it was slippery underfoot, but the whole scene sparkled in the bright day. Seagulls were crying loudly overhead, and I noticed the constant purr of small fishing vessels moored against the quay, bobbing up and down as if they were eager to head off.

"Mummy, where are we?" I asked.

"Dún Laoghaire, Ireland. You know – where Mammy comes from," she replied. "Quick, we need to get going. Hurry along now."

Her mood had changed. From being barely conscious, I could tell she was now wide awake and very agitated. She inhaled deeply on her cigarette, reams of smoke snorting from her nostrils and her breath disappearing into the fresh morning air. She had a faraway, lost look in her eyes.

Will's nose had started to run. He was the cutest brother a girl could ever wish for. He had a little dumpling face, with my mother's huge eyes, dark hair and dimples. In fact, he was the absolute image of her. He toddled along, wrapped in his chequered brown and white duffle coat, on a pair of matchstick-thin legs. Some of his front teeth were missing and he sported large gaps. Being born prematurely, at seven months, his health had not been good to start with. He didn't walk properly until he was two and a half years old and sometimes he still looked unsteady on his feet.

Mum bent down to fasten his toggles, balancing her cigarette precariously to one side of her mouth, then took out a large white hankie from her pocket and wiped his nose for him, before passing another one to me.

"There, that's better," she said. "Now, we're going to Auntie Bea's and I want you both to be very well behaved for Mammy."

"Will we be there long? And will we get breakfast, Mummy?" I asked, my tummy starting to rumble because we had missed our only chance of food that morning. "I'm hungry."

"I'm sure Auntie Bea will give us something. And I don't know how long we will be there. We'll just have to see."

"Mummy, why do we have to be here? Will we see Daddy soon?"

She turned her head away.

"Daddy wasn't very well… and I'm worried if he'll be alright."

"Put your mittens on, Sally, it's freezing," she replied.

"But, what about Da?"

"Sally, did you hear me?"

"Da wasn't…"

"Now look! I'm getting annoyed with you. I said put your mittens on! Do you want a slap?"

"Alright Mummy. I'm sorry. Don't shout at me."

Her toned softened. "Look, darling… your Daddy's…" Her voice faltered, broke off and started to crack; I thought it was almost breaking into a squeak. "Mammy has to get away for a while…" She hesitated. "…with you and Will. You don't have to worry. We're having a little holiday and your Daddy needs a rest too because he's not been feeling well. It's for the best."

Still bent down, she pulled us close, wrapping her arms around us both and giving us the biggest bear hug ever. I could feel her whole body silently trembling against mine. Giant teardrops fell from her cheeks like cold rain onto my freezing hands| before she buried her face in the collar of my coat. A flowery pink Capodimonte brooch on her lapel pinched my cheek; it was the first time I ever noticed it.

Her voice choked with emotion. "Mammy loves you, darlings. Never forget that. Mammy will always look after you, no matter what," she sobbed.

I wiped the back of my chubby hands across her eyes, clumsily trying to dry her tears. I didn't understand why she was upset, but seeing her so unhappy was tugging at my heart strings and made me tearful too.

"Please don't cry Mummy," I said. "I love you. I don't want you to be upset."

I studied her gaunt figure as she stood up. I remember how her sunken cheekbones and untidy mass of unruly dark locks made her a shadow of herself. Her short olive coat was half undone, despite the freezing weather, revealing a loosely fitting jumper and her bony neck with the cross and chain she always wore. She still wore her ever-faithful kitten heels but sported goose-pimply unshaven legs.

We trekked along the concrete path alongside a granite wall and I turned to take a last look at the ship. I could still hear the huge engines whirring and rumbling in its bows, and a faint smell of diesel infiltrated the cold air. A dog barked fiercely in the distance as we headed along the frosty path to an unknown destination.

Chapter 8

The Children's Home

Sally

We seemed to walk for miles. The temperature was raw and a bitter wind gnawed at my face and pinched the inside of my thighs.

"Mummy, I'm cold. Will we be there soon?" I asked for the umpteenth time.

"For God's sake, will you stop whining Sally. I've already told you; it won't be much longer."

She stopped abruptly in the middle of the pavement and seemed to be in a panic.

"Wait a moment, I might need to get cigarettes."

She dived into her handbag, rifled about and pulled out a half an empty packet.

"Damn, I'm nearly out. We'll have to find a newsagent."

"They look like shops, Mummy," I said, pointing to a parade of different-coloured buildings, across a busy main road.

"Yes, they do. Good girl. Quick, let's cross here," she said, gripping my hand tightly.

"Mummy, you're hurting me."

"Ah, come on, Sally, we need to get across this road."

I hesitated and pulled back as she stepped off the pavement.

"What are you doing? Just stop it!" she shouted, and shook my arm. "Cross the road now!"

BEE–EE–EEP!

An oncoming car sped past nearly mowing us down.

"No, Mummy – it's too scary." I started to cry.

"I've had enough of this!" she screeched at me.

And with that, she dragged Will and me through the traffic to the centre of the road, dodging cars before making a dash to the other side. The experience was traumatic and I thought we'd be killed, but a newsagent was in sight.

"Three shillings, please," said the shopkeeper, as he picked the cigarettes off the shelf and held out his hand.

"Ah, just a minute naw…" Mum spilled out the contents of her handbag onto the counter. "I know I've got some… it'll be lurking at the bottom here somewhere."

A lighter emerged, the half empty cigarette packet, a hairbrush covered in a mass of black hair, a pan stick, a bottle of pills and an unpaid gas bill – but there was no money. Then she pulled out my father's leather wallet.

"Aha! Naw wait, here we are. I bet there'll be some coins in here."

She prised the compartments apart one by one and then checked them again… and again; but they were empty. Her face dropped.

A queue of people had started to form behind Mum.

"Do you mind if I serve these other folks while you're looking?" said the shopkeeper, betraying his impatience.

Her voice weakened. "No, you carry on. I'm sure I've got some change somewhere."

She continued, pulling out the insides of her coat pockets in desperation. Some dirty tissue and hair clips materialised, along with a few pennies and a couple of sixpences, but not enough to pay for her cigarettes.

"Any luck?" enquired the shopkeeper.

She lowered her head, avoiding eye contact with him as she shoved everything back in her bag and pockets.

"No, I'm sorry. I must have left my money in my other coat. Come, we'd better be going," she said to Will and me.

The door bells chimed as a paying customer came in. A few paces away from the shop she stopped in her tracks and her head and shoulders drooped.

"No, Mummy − no! Don't get upset again," I said as I wrapped my arms around her waist. The shaking started again as I held her tight and felt the vibrations of the traffic thundering past through the soles of my shoes.

We walked on in a doleful silence until we eventually reached a white-washed 1930s semi-detached on the corner of a smaller road. She lifted the latch and the gate squeaked open.

"At last," she said. "Thank God."

"Whose house is this?" I asked.

"This is where Auntie Bea lives, but the house belongs to her sister, Mrs Carter. She's a widow so they live together."

"What's a widow? Doesn't she have a first name?"

"A widow is someone whose husband has died. And it's Edna, but don't you ever call her that. She's Mrs Carter to you."

Two grey, crimped-haired elderly ladies appeared at the door.

"Phyllis! What a surprise... come in," welcomed one, in a kindly voice.

Mum heaved a sigh and dropped her bags on the stone-tiled floor.

"Auntie! I can't be telling you how good it is to be here at last."

"Phyllis," nodded the other one, acknowledging her with a nervous smile before backing away into the sitting room.

"You must be freezing!" observed Auntie Bea. "How are you, my dear? And you've brought the children, how lovely. Haven't they grown since I saw them last?"

We stood in the hallway where it didn't feel much warmer than outside, and there was a distinct smell of coal dust in the air.

Auntie Bea rubbed her arms nervously. "What are you doing here? Has something happened?" she asked.

My mother crumpled; she didn't need to hold it back any longer.

"I've left him!" she blurted out.

"Oh, Phyllis dear, no..."

She rested her shaky hand on my mother's shoulder. "I'm so sorry, Phyllis. You had better come in and tell me all about it."

She took a sideways glance through the crack in the sitting room door, catching the eye of her sister Edna who was uneasily knitting away next to the fire.

"But what are you going to do, Phyllis? And what about the children?"

I looked up at my mother, her shoulders now quaking as a cascade of tears ran down her cheekbones like a winding river, finding the corners of her mouth. She took a large gulp to speak, but no words came out.

"Come Phyllis, come in," said Auntie, handing her a white handkerchief and guiding us into the sitting room. "Let the children warm up by the fire and you can explain what happened while we have some tea. There, there, dear."

My mother slumped into a floral-patterned comfy chair. Edna looked over and forced a smile.

"This is a surprise Phyllis," she managed. "We haven't seen you in Ireland for a few years now, have we?"

Mum only managed a one-word answer. "No."

The home seemed warm and inviting as my brother and I plonked ourselves cross-legged on the hearth mat. The flames hypnotised us as they flickered away, warming us up and illuminating the gloomy room.

Over the fire rested a kettle on a metal grill. Either side of the fireplace were well-stocked mahogany bookshelves that climbed to the ceiling. On the settee sat a large cloth bag, brimming with balls of different-coloured wool, punctured by several pairs of knitting needles.

I took some of my dolls out of the plastic carrier and started to play with them on the floor while Will pushed his metal cars along in the thick carpet pile.

"Would you like a cup of tea, children?" offered Edna.

We shook our heads.

"Some cold milk then?"

I shrugged and then nodded and continued playing with my dolls. I didn't like milk, but I was thirsty.

"Phyllis, what about you?"

She nodded. "Thank you."

From the other side of the room, I could only hear snatches of hushed conversation, which made me uncomfortable because I sensed something was going on that would ultimately affect me and Will. Mum had a habit of veering from one disastrous situation to another. I had a strong sense of intuition as a child and wanted to protect her from herself because she could never see ahead. My partner Philip once said that I'd only been born so I could be a mother to her.

Auntie Bea looked tense and strained, wringing her hands and listening attentively as Mum poured her heart out.

"Mummy," I called over, "are you alright?"

"Yes, Petsey. Mammy's fine, just not quite herself today," she said, wiping her nose.

After a while Edna got up and suggested she made another pot of tea.

"I'll give you a hand," said Auntie Bea, seizing the excuse to follow her out.

They seemed gone a long time, but finally re-emerged with Edna carrying a tray of Royal Albert bone china and a plate laden with slices of fruit cake. She placed it carefully on an ornate tea trolley with a lace doily on top of it.

"Well now, would you look at that," said Edna. "Will you not be helping yourselves before you head off?"

"Head off?" asked Mum, sounding surprised. She took a gulp.

"Well, I take it you've made plans? We'd love to have you here, Phyllis, but I've got my cousin coming to stay tomorrow for a short while. Her husband died only a month ago and she's finding it very hard on her own. You do understand, don't you?"

"P-plans…? Yes… of course I've got plans," said Mum, holding onto her cross and chain for reassurance. "Sure, I'd never want to impose myself on you."

"If it hadn't been for my cousin… but she's had a terrible time and all…"

"Honestly, we'll be fine, won't we children?"

"I'm sorry Phyllis, truly I am," said Auntie Bea, hovering sheepishly in the background.

"That's alright, Auntie. There's no need to apologise."

"If there was any other way…"

"It's fine, Auntie, really it is."

"You'll have something to eat and drink before you go, won't you? There's no hurry to go this minute, is there?"

I stared at my mother. She looked washed out, tiredness hanging like a veil as she struggled to put on a brave face, but realising that all three of us were effectively homeless with nowhere to go.

"Actually, I think we'll be getting off before it gets too late," she said. "Come children, it's time to go."

Then, politely, she gathered up our toys from the floor and hurriedly shoved them into the bags. I could see her hands were shaking.

"Can't we stay here Mummy?" I asked, now warm and comfortable.

"No darling, we have to go. Auntie Bea and Mrs Carter haven't got room for us and it's not fair on them."

"But Mummy, where will we go?"

She tried to raise a reassuring smile. "Don't worry, Pet. Ah, sure, Mammy knows somewhere." But I knew she didn't.

There was a long silence, apart from the sound of the crackling fire.

Auntie Bea guided us out of the sitting room with her hand on Mum's back. "Have you got enough money, Phyllis?" she asked.

"Oh yes! You don't have to worry about me, now. I've got plenty," Mum replied.

"Are you sure, now?"

"Of course, Auntie. I'm grand."

"Well, take this just in case," she said, pushing a five-pound note into her hand."

But my mother pushed it back.

"No, no. Now look, I told you, I don't need it. The children and I will be fine."

"But Phyllis, just in case…"

"No, naw. I swear to you, we'll be okay."

"Promise me, then, to ring me when you find something. You've got my number, haven't you?"

"You don't have to explain, Auntie. I understand. And yes, I'll let you know where we are staying. Say goodbye to Auntie Bea," she told us firmly, before kissing her on the cheek.

Edna called after us as we heard her pouring herself a cup of tea, "Goodbye Phyllis. Bye, children!" but she did not get up from her chair to see us off.

As we left Auntie Bea's house and waved her farewell, I was puzzled. Why was she sending us away? I thought she liked Mummy. It was only later that I discovered that it was not her house and she had little say in anything.

Back in the cold midday, we trudged on past a few more houses until, without warning, Mum needed to stop and leaned on a gatepost. She was clutching at her chest and gasping for breath, then bent double and rested her hands on her knees. I didn't know what to do to help her.

"Mummy, what's happening?" I cried, grabbing her coat sleeve.

There was no answer for me because she was struggling for air. I felt gripped by fear. Dear God, what should I be doing? My eyes pleaded at the passing traffic. Please someone... anyone... stop your car and help me save our Mummy, I thought. But no one did.

"M...m-mammy will be fi-fine. Ju-st give me a little m... m-in...minute," she said, struggling to inhale and sporadically taking large gasps of air. She reached for a bottle of pills in her bag and popped two in her mouth, grimaced as she swallowed and gulped. After a few tense minutes, her breathing calmed down and she pulled herself straight again.

My little brother started tugging at her hand.

"Wee-wee, Mummy, wee-wee," he said.

Mum stroked his head and pulled him in close while he looked up at her with his huge innocent eyes.

"Alright darling, Mammy will find a toilet. Don't be scared, my little pet."

After another endless time walking, we arrived at the corner of two roads in front of an imposing Victorian building that had a prodigious storm porch fronted by black and white painted gables. Outside was an old-fashioned bell on a pulley that would have rung back at the turn of the century, only now it looked dilapidated and rusty. Beside it was an electric bell, which Mum pressed.

A friendly young woman with a mop of black hair tied loosely in a bun answered the door and smiled at us.

"Hallo, can I help you?"

My mother moved forward, pushing us in front of her.

"Ah, hello there. I was wondering if my two children could possibly use your toilet as they are both bursting to go. I wouldn't normally ask, but we're here on a visit from England and I don't know where the public ones are."

The girl hesitated, looking indecisive as to what she should say, but was interrupted by a voice behind her.

"Phyllis? Sure, it's Phyllis Little! How the devil are yous?"

The voluptuous middle-aged woman with expressive eyes and boisterous charm rushed up to the door, threw her arms around Mum and gave her a big hug.

"Oh, Mary... hello! Ooh, I can't tell you how good it is to see you again," said my mother, raising a feeble smile. "I see you're still working here, then – after all this time?"

"Well, you know how it is, Phyllis: no one else would have me!" she teased. "But I must have done something right though, as I'm in charge of the place now, so I am."

"Really? You are?" Mum looked relieved.

"I am so, Phyllis. Come in yous two. Noleen will take the pair of yous upstairs and show yous where the toilet is."

"What's this place, Mummy?" I asked.

"Oh, Mammy used to work here a long time ago. It's a children's home."

As we entered, I observed a long hallway with a dozen tiny Wellington boots all lined up in a row on a timber-laid floor. There seemed to be a warming glow coming from inside and the smell of stew hung high in the air, reminding me of school dinners. A shower of children's voices echoed around the place, although I couldn't see any at first, only heard the sound of them clattering about and laughing.

The kindly girl with the black hair held our hands and led us up a tall wooden staircase that turned in two places, past a large cupboard, before we got to the top.

She waited until we'd finished then took us down to where my mother was sitting at a long table covered in a white tablecloth on which place settings were laid out.

Mary handed my mother a cup of tea and offered her a cigarette, while she sat there unburdening herself of her woes. Then she reached into her handbag, and discreetly pushed some pound notes into my mother's hand.

"No. No, I couldn't take it, Mary," I heard her say.

"Yes, you will. Now go on, Phyllis, I won't take no for an answer."

My mother looked up to see us holding Noleen's hand in the doorway.

"Hello, my little Petsies. Come and sit next to Mammy and have something to eat." It seemed as if she had cheered up a bit. She picked up my baby brother and sat him on her knee.

We were handed buttered Irish soda bread, which I just loved, and a small bowl of the stew. Suddenly everything felt so much better. Mum continued chatting away to Mary for a long time and as we tucked into the much-needed food I somehow felt safe at last; well for the time being, anyway.

Having taken pity on my mother's plight, Mary offered us a temporary place to stay and led us back up the wooden staircase, this time to a small attic bedroom. There was a cast-iron double bed draped in a knitted patchwork quilt, and a bedside table with a wonky lamp. Painted on the wall opposite was a harbour scene, with the name Mary D scratched below it.

After an already over-long day, Mum tucked us both in and knelt down beside us so we could all say our prayers together before we sang the songs that she had learnt when she was a child. We always did that when we went to bed.

The best book to read is the Bible,
The best book to read is the Bible.
If you read it every day, it will help you on your way,
Oh, the best book to read is the Bible.
The best friend to have is Jesus,
The best friend to have is Jesus.
If you seek him every day, he will help you on your way,
Oh, the best friend to have is Jesus.

Then she kissed each of us on the forehead before going downstairs, leaving the side light on as I always had a fear of the dark. Next morning, we had a good breakfast at the staff table in their dining room. I could smell the comforting odour of the Irish soda bread even before it was brought into the room. Other staff joined us this time: a few younger girls in their 20s or early 30s, and an older lady called Mrs Gold, who seemed slightly abrupt. It seemed she was Mary's counterpart and ran the home in her absence.

"Hello Phyllis, do you remember me?" asked Mrs Gold, brusquely, as she poured her tea.

Mum lit herself a cigarette and shook the matchstick vigorously, leaving the smell of sulphur hanging in the air.

"Ah, no, I don't think so. Well, I'm not sure. Perhaps I do so. It was a long time ago – wasn't it, now?"

"Well, I've been here 30-odd years on and off and seen lots of staff and children come and go in that time. But I had a spell about 16 years ago, when I wasn't here so much – when my Bernard had his accident and I had time off to take care of him, so you would have seen less of me then. But I remember you."

"Do you?" said my mother, fidgeting in her seat.

"Yes, you came from that orphanage in North Dublin, didn't you? A lot came from there. You replaced me for that six months, while I was off with Bernard."

"Oh, yes, that's right."

"And what have you been doing since?"

Mum picked at her lips.

"Well, I left Ireland, trained to be a nurse and then got marr—"

"You trained to be a nurse?"

"Yes, I did," said Mum, sucking hard on her cigarette and blowing smoke high in the air. "You sound surprised?"

"I thought that all you orphanage girls were only trained to be domestics, and that's all you did."

"That's true, but that's not to say some of us didn't have other ambitions."

"So, what brings you here now, after all these years?"

The others kept their heads down and carried on pouring or drinking their tea, hoping not to be drawn into the conversation.

Mum blew out through her nostrils.

"Well… I thought maybe I would come and visit my great aunt – but unfortunately she's not well at the moment."

"Is that so?" said Mrs Gold, raising her eyebrows.

I could tell Mum was starting to feel uncomfortable with all these questions, as she was talking very quickly and seemed short of breath. She reached into her handbag and fumbled with her tablets.

"She lives with her sister now and it's just the two of them. I didn't realise until we arrived, and I won't be a burden to them. So, Mary said we could stay here, just temporarily, while I sort something out."

"Yes, I heard that," Mrs Gold said, confidently. "That's a kind gesture of Mary, indeed it is. You know she's off to Australia for six weeks on Tuesday, don't you?"

My mother shrank back in her chair and looked stunned. "No?"

"She's going to visit her niece who emigrated out there some time ago. I'll be in charge while she's gone."

Mum's eyes glazed over as she worked out the situation.

Mrs Gold poured hot water into the teapot and gave it a careful stir.

"Another cup of tea, Phyllis? Or have you had enough?"

"No, I'm fine thanks. I'm going to go and get the children ready for church now. We don't want to be missing the bus."

"Right so, then. We'll see you later."

Even I sensed we weren't welcome and that Mrs Gold didn't approve of us being allowed to stay. I didn't like her tone, nor the way she spoke to my mother.

The days flew past quickly as we settled into the routine. Our time mainly consisted of playing with the other children, although we had our meals with Mum in the staff dining room, walks into town and rainy bus rides to boring church services. Auntie Bea came to visit us once in those first two weeks. Somehow, I missed her visit and discovered, on their return, that she had taken Will out and bought him a toy helicopter. I met them, looking for me, halfway up the wooden staircase.

"Look, Gaggy!" (He always called me that as he couldn't say my name.) "Look! Hel-i-cop-ter," he said, gleaming a big smile as he proudly lifted his prized new toy in the air.

"Sorry, Sally dear, I didn't get you anything, I'm afraid. But here, you have a toffee," said Auntie Bea.

I stared at the floor.

Realising her error, she continued, "But I will make some new clothes for your dollies and bring them next time I come."

I nodded shyly, but still felt hurt that I'd been left out.

Then, without explanation, one night we were put to bed by one of the carers, which seemed strange, but with a reassurance that Mummy would be up to bed soon. I hadn't seen her that afternoon and wondered where she had gone. I kept asking for her but nobody seemed to know where she was.

The room was dimly lit by the wonky table lamp. All was calm, but a nervous feeling kept pinching my stomach, wondering why she had not told us where she was going or when she'd be back. I was still waiting for her to follow us up, when the door opened wide and it was Mrs Gold. A long shaft of light from the corridor shot through the room. As soon as I saw the look on her face I knew something was not quite right. My heart raced as I pulled the blankets up close to my face.

"Where's Mummy?" I asked, my lips and chin starting to wobble.

"Mummy..." echoed Will.

I cuddled him close to me and held my breath.

"Your mammy's not been very well, I'm afraid," she said, in an unusually kind voice.

My heart screamed from within.

"What do you mean?" I demanded. "Where's my mummy? What do you mean not well? I want Mummy."

Mrs Gold stood there awkwardly, pinned to the spot as though she didn't know how to break the bad news to us. She twiddled her thumbs before heaving a big sigh.

"Now, now," she said, with compassion. "Your Mammy was taken to hospital this afternoon – in an ambulance. It's for her own good. To make her well."

The room started to spin as tears of disbelief trickled down my face and snotty remnants dribbled onto my chin. Will started crying too, and I squeezed him tight.

"Ambulance? Hospital? When is she coming back? Please, I need my mummy here! Please, bring her back... please," I pleaded.

The separation was terrifying and triggered memories of the last time. What would we do without her in this strange country? I thought of running away to try to get back home, but when I remembered that big boat that carried us across the sea I realised there was no hope of escape.

"I don't know, is the answer," replied Mrs Gold in a conciliatory voice. "Your mammy is not well and needs a rest, but as soon as we know, we'll tell you too. In the meantime, I'm afraid you can't sleep in here anymore. You'll have to be like the other children now and sleep in the dormitories with them. Come, I'll show you."

"No!" I wailed. "I want to stay here with my baby brother. I want us to stay together and I want my mummy! I... need... Mummy! Help Mummy!"

"You can't have her just now I'm afraid," she replied calmly. "And the girls and boys have to sleep in separate rooms. Those are the rules and that's how we do things here. You can't sleep in this room any longer. It will only be until your mammy returns."

"But please, Mrs Gold, can't we——"

"No, Sally, you can't."

With that, she forcibly prised us apart, but as much as she tried, we still clung to each other. I was near hysterical with this fresh pain of separation.

"Gaggy! Want Gaggy," sobbed my little brother as he hung onto my nightdress.

My face was a swollen mass of red blotches and Will had wet his winceyette pyjamas, but Mrs Gold had seen it all before and seemed unfazed by our reactions. Reluctantly, we padded behind her in our bare feet on the cold wooden floor towards the shaft of light.

Next thing I knew we were being separated into different rooms. There was a dormitory for girls and one for boys: both were dark, bare-boarded rooms with about 10 rows of metal-framed bunk beds, like the ones used in hospitals. And there were no lights. I was absolutely panic stricken. I don't remember what happened next because the trauma of that night has left it blank, but I do remember the weeks and months that followed.

Breakfasts were now taken in the children's dining room and, instead of my favourite bread, we were offered porridge. I simply refused to eat it and would push it away. At six o'clock every evening we queued up at a Belfast sink in the bathroom for a cold wash and to brush our teeth with pink toothpaste out of a tin. Our own clothes were replaced with those shared by other children from the large cupboard at the top of the stairs. I had to wear tights now instead of long white socks, and had a different-coloured pair for every day of the week.

We were well into late winter. Feeling lonely and disheartened I used to press my face against the cold window pane, wondering if I would ever see our mother or father again.

The snowflakes fell in a gentle hush on the back garden making everything look like an enchanted winter land, with icicles clinging by a thread from the climbing frame and the trees sprinkled in glittery frost. But not knowing if we would ever be reunited with Mum, or go home again, took the edge off such beautiful scenes. We had become like orphans ourselves, as Mum had once been, with only imaginary worlds to retreat into.

We did, however, make a couple of friends who were near enough our ages. Their names were Jonathan and Adam and they came from Northern Ireland and didn't have a mummy at all, which made me feel very sad and sorry for them. At least we knew our mummy and all the love and care she had given us, even if we didn't know if we would see her again.

Auntie Bea only came to see us once more in those three months. She kept her promise to me and crocheted and knitted some lovely clothes for Barbie and Sindy. But she had nothing to tell us about Mum, or when she was coming back. I've often asked myself why she wasn't more supportive, since we were without a mother or father, but I guess I will never know the answer.

Then one day, as we limped into March, weighed down with heavy hearts, a social worker came to the children's home to call for us. The day we left was my brother's fourth birthday and this kind lady was taking us to meet mother and then go to her house. I don't remember the car journey, or even how we met Mum again, but I do remember the social worker presenting Will with a chocolate cake topped with Cadbury's Buttons and candles. I was ecstatic to be going home at last. The lack of any communication from adults about how Mum was doing, or when and if we would see her, had left me despondent that we would be stuck in the children's home for ever. Despite the war zone between my parents that existed in our house, all I wanted was to go home and back to the only life I knew.

And there, waiting at the train station in London to greet us, was our dad.

"Daddy, Daddy!" we cried as we ran into his arms. He picked us up, one by one, and swung us round.

"Kids! Oh, it's so good to see you!"

Mum, stood back, stared at him coldly and lit a cigarette.

He gave her a cautious smile. "You alright, Phyl?" he asked.

"What do you care?" she replied.

We all climbed into Dad's Ford Anglia, which was parked down a side street away from the station. Mum and Dad didn't speak the whole way home. It was as though nothing had changed.

First thing when I got back to school, I was called to see the headmistress who wanted to know all about my time in Ireland, no doubt because I had missed three months of schooling.

She was a lovely lady, called Mrs Kara, probably in her 50s, who I think had a soft spot for me. She already knew about my unstable home life through social services, and gathered that I had been through tumultuous times in Ireland. In those days there were no offers of counselling or pastoral care, only concerns that a child had missed academic schooling for a long period of time.

Her office looked very neat. Behind her desk was a square window with a modern louvre blind and, as you came in, a tall avocado green metal filing cabinet with a spider plant on top. That was where the first aid box was kept, and the whole room reeked of TCP. I remember how she looked well dressed and sophisticated, and was peering over her large, tinted spectacles as I entered. She was calm and relaxed as she butted out her cigarette into a chunky glass ashtray, leaving a thin trail of smoke vaporising into the air.

"Come in Sally, love, and take a seat," she said, in a husky voice. "I understand you've been in Ireland for a while. Would you like to tell me all about it?"

I had to climb up onto the chair as it was so big. When I think back, it reminds me of the style Ronnie Corbett used in his monologues on telly, and which made him look really small. I began to tell her the whole story, reiterating my mother's version of events and how she was taken away.

"Mummy said she went to the doctor's and he wasn't very nice to her. He said she was demanding medicine... and she got very upset."

"Really?" said Mrs Kara, looking shocked at my explanation and how much I knew.

"Yes. Then the doctor sent an ambulance to the home where we were staying. It was a children's home where we'd gone because Mummy and me and Will had nowhere to stay. And then Mummy said these two ambulance men pushed her in and strapped her down and looked up her knickers. It upset her very much... and she cried because she wanted to see us, but they took no notice and wouldn't listen to her. I think she was frightened. Then we didn't see Mummy for a long time."

Mrs Kara coughed and tapped her chest with her fist.

"Oh, Sally, love, that must have been awful for you. How did you feel about your mummy being away for so long?"

"That woman told me that Mummy went to a hospital because she needed a rest. I didn't like her. She was horrible. She wouldn't let Will and me be together. Mummy said they put her in a mental hospital, but I don't really know what that means, and we didn't know if she was coming back. I cried for my mummy to come back... and... and... and I can't remember the rest."

The episode in Ireland, when Mum needed hospitalisation, was the first of several more that followed in England. Trapped in an unhappy abusive marriage where she was made to feel as worthless as she had in the orphanage, she slipped into a deep depression. Auntie Bea had been the only one she counted on to care about her, but as that relationship became distant and Auntie focused on her own family, Mum felt abandoned yet again. She was totally dependent on Dad for financial support and trying to protect her children from further pain, separation and assault, she stayed in the marriage; but by doing so her life broke apart under the strain. Knowing herself alone in the world, loveless and unsupported, her mental state deteriorated further and further. How I wish we'd been a normal family like everybody else appeared to be, that Mum had a mother and we'd had grandparents to turn to; but we didn't and we weren't 'normal'. We were dysfunctional, held together by the thinnest of threads. Even moving house again didn't help. In fact, all it did was make things much worse.

Chapter 9

Surviving the 1970s

Sally

The memories of my last day at our old house still stick in my mind. It was November 1970, the day before bonfire night, when we looked forward to waving fizzing sparklers in the frosty air and huddling around a blazing fire.

The removals' van had blocked off a large space on the road outside. Two men in brown coats and with thick sideburns sat rolling tobacco into cigarettes, while the sound of *Woodstock* drifted from the van radio.

Mum ushered us over the road to an elderly neighbour whom she was friendly with. She always seemed to get on better with people older than herself.

"Better keep out of your father's way for the time being, just until we've moved. You know what he's like," she said.

The elderly lady appeared at the top of her hand-railed steps and beckoned us over. She was frail-looking, with white frothy hair, and wore a yellow checked pinafore.

Dad appeared from the front door struggling with a large suitcase that had clothes poking out of its sides. He shouted over to my mother.

"Hey Phyl! Are you going to help me pack this bleedin' car or what?"

"Alright, alright, don't shout. I'm coming," she cried. "I'm just sorting the children out."

She turned to us. "See now. Quick, off you go to Mrs Jackson's; she'll look after you until this afternoon, when Mammy'll come back."

I didn't want to go to Mrs Jackson's. She looked really old and had a strangely humped back.

"Come and help me beat the dust from these rugs. It'll give you something to do while your mother's gone," she said, trying to entice me with a wicker carpet beater.

At the word "gone" I gave her a dubious look and tugged at my mother's coat.

"Can't I stay with you, Mummy?" I begged.

"No darling, it will be too much with everything else. It won't be for long, I promise you. And then you'll see our new house, and that'll be a fresh start for us all."

But moving only shifted their problems from one house to another, and this one, being so much smaller than the last, seemed to compound them. Why we had to move again after only two years I will never know.

Although the new house was an end of terrace and had a side entrance, it only had two bedrooms – one of which was divided into two tiny box rooms. The north-facing living room had a low ceiling, which made it dark and oppressive even during daylight hours, and the kitchen was tiny. It felt as if we were taking a step backwards.

Initially, Dad slept in the large back bedroom, while Mum, my brother and I shared the larger of the two box bedrooms. I slept with Mum and my brother in a camp bed. The smaller box room, which no one slept in at first, was so cramped that the tallboy had to be pushed up against the window, stopping natural light getting in. Condensation dripped down one wall causing black mould to seep through the blue flowery wallpaper, and everything smelt musty. As we grew older, that became Mum's bedroom.

Unlike the previous house, there was no bathroom at this place. It was built in the 1930s, when not everyone in council accommodation was fortunate enough to have one. Instead, a tin bath hung in a long kitchen cupboard and it was brought out and filled up with kettles from the gas stove. Until a prefabricated bathroom was added onto the back of the house, about a year later, we had to all share this bath once a week. Dad had first use. He was the breadwinner, as he often liked to remind us, so he always came first. By the time we got in, the water was lukewarm with a thick layer of scum floating on it and the smell of Wright's Coal Tar Soap still lingering in the air.

For most of the 1970s Mum spent her time alone in the isolation of her bedroom, while we watched TV programmes like *Benny Hill* or *Morecambe and Wise*; she had no interest at all in television. If she came down for any length of time it resulted in a row with Dad over something or the other.

"You're useless, utterly bloody useless! Explain this to me!" he shouted one day, waving a screwed-up envelope in his hand.

Mum kept her head bowed. She stood limp-wristed, her hands in the dirty water of the washing-up bowl, not caring how well she washed anything.

"Well?" he demanded.

She winced.

"I'm talking about the money I gave you to pay the electric bill!" he shouted. "They've sent me a red letter, so what did you do with the money I gave you to pay in at the Post Office?"

She blinked and took a gulp, knowing she had used the money to pay off the newsagent's where she had run up a debt. The newsagent said she couldn't have any more credit until she had settled her bill, which she hadn't paid for several weeks. As usual, she never spent the money on herself. It was always just on us; she was unable to resist bringing us back some little treat of sweets or toys every time she went to the shops.

Dad drew up close and rattled the envelope in front of her face. "D'you hear me, woman? Eh?"

She flinched.

"So, what did you spend the money on?"

"I needed some things for the children," she answered quietly.

"What – the kids? Haven't they got enough as it is? Not like when I was a kid, is it? When you had to earn yer keep."

"I…I-I'm sorry, but…" she tried to explain herself.

"Sorry? You're *sorry*? It's only my wage coming in and all you do is spend, fuckin' spend! If you were a normal wife I wouldn't have this problem, would I? But you're not fuckin' normal are yer? Everyone knows yer not fuckin' right in the head!"

"Leave me alone! Just leave me alone. And don't tell me I'm not normal. If anyone's not normal, it's you. If people only knew about the dirt and filth I've had to put up with all these years."

She started to cry.

Dad poked her in the arm and continued jabbing his finger as though to emphasise every word.

"Now, stop with – the – bleedin' – spending, or you – won't get – anything more – from me. Understand?"

"Y…y-yes."

She wiped her eyes with the tea-towel. Her life growing up had been so different from my father's. He was brought up during an era of food rationing, learning to scrimp and save. Mum's

146

institutionalised life had taught her none of that. She had no concept of the value of money or how to manage it. Living for the moment was all that mattered and she didn't really comprehend the importance of paying the bills or how to manage her financial responsibilities. All she learnt was to be subjected to others and do as she was told.

I knew this row would soon be forgotten, but it wouldn't be long before she'd be in trouble again and another would brew up in its place.

His aggressive outbursts forced her to retreat more and more. She rarely ate and stopped being interested in anything, becoming increasingly lethargic and taking to her bed during the day, with the curtains drawn. She got up to take us to school and popped down to the local shops when she had to, until we could walk to school by ourselves. It's as though she just wanted to shut out the outside world.

The only things that brought her satisfaction were standing in front of the mirror and pulling out her eyebrows until they were bald, or prising strands of hair from her head with her fingers, until eventually it resulted in her having to wear a wig.

Long gone were the days when she used to have a laugh with Patsy. It was harder to keep in contact with people then because we couldn't afford a telephone and people only wrote on the odd occasion. Patsy, who was more or less her only friend, had moved on with her life. She was happily married with a family and had three small children to keep her more than busy, so we saw her very rarely.

Auntie Bea, too, only wrote once a year at Christmas, when she sent a small parcel from Ireland for us. After a while her letters and the parcels stopped. Maybe it was because she was now quite elderly or even ill, but the lack of contact from the few people that Mum knew only added to her despair.

We had frequent power cuts that year due to the miners' strikes. We often sat by flickering candlelight, with fumes from paraffin oil heaters stifling the air, listening to my father droning on about the Second World War and how we didn't know how good we had it today compared to then. In between, during the silences when he nodded off, I used to think of Mum upstairs on her own and how lonely she must have felt. My heart ached with sadness; I wanted things to change but I didn't know how to make it better. Little did I realise there was nothing that I could have done.

Although she never watched television, except when she occasionally stood in the doorway and peeked at the news, Mum often listened to the radio. The big news of the day was the Watergate Scandal, involving President Nixon of the United States. I never understood a lot about it, apart from the fact it was something to do with dirty politics and bugging people's phones. Somehow though, the voices in Mum's head started to mix that scandal with reality.

"Sally, can you hear that?" she said one day, pointing to an old electric mantel clock that Dad had bought at a jumble sale.

I listened intently and noticed the loud electric current pulsating through it.

"What, Mummy, the ticking?"

"No, the voices. Can you hear what they're saying? They're listening in to us."

I drew closer to the clock, trying to hear what she could hear. Her eyes widened, manically searching the room; checking to see if anyone was watching.

"No Mum, I can't hear anything," I said with caution.

"Don't lie to me, Sally!" she snapped. "I know you can hear them."

"But Mum… I can't."

"You can, I know you can."

I felt frightened and confused, not knowing whether to run or to humour her when she was acting so strangely. I glanced at the clock, but it was still an hour or so before Dad came home. I didn't say anything to him when he finally arrived, as I didn't want to get her into trouble, but it wasn't long before her paranoia about the house being bugged had taken a dangerous turn and he found out.

At night, after we were in bed, she started disconnecting the electric light sockets and pulling all the wires out. In the morning she'd get up and reassemble them with a screwdriver. She was obsessed. Whether she knew what she was doing, I doubt very much, but by now other people, including my friends' mothers, had started to notice her strange behaviour too.

I would have been nine at the time. Jodie and I had been best friends for about a year. We got on well and had the same sense of humour. Jodie's mother was a single parent, which was a lot rarer in those days than it is now. However, apart from not having a dad, Jodie had a normal happy family life. Unlike me, she had other relatives including a devoted uncle who liked to make a fuss of her. Having a happy family life had filled Jodie with self-confidence, something I lacked. Maybe that's why I tended to stick to only one friend at a time; it felt safe and I preferred to be with someone I felt I could trust.

Making friends was difficult, being introverted, and not least because of my insecurities about being accepted, as well as the way I looked. Wearing jumble-sale clothes to school was a stigma then, unlike today with everyone recycling; but my choices were few. I didn't mind too much at first, but my Mum's eccentric idea of making me wear boys' jumpers and short dresses, which emphasised my plump figure, completely destroyed my self-esteem.

"Wear my nursing belt and hold your stomach in," she'd say. "It'll make you look slimmer."

I wore it once but it immediately drew questions about why was I wearing it, which made me more self-conscious than ever.

My father didn't help either.

"You got dropsy or something? Your legs – they look like tree trunks."

I was mortified and extremely hurt. I didn't even know what dropsy was, but I guessed it was some disease that fat people had and his comments just made me want to retreat into myself.

"With your mother like she is, I have to be a mother and father to you," he grumbled, as he roughly brushed out long strands of my hair.

He tried to make me look prettier by rolling my hair up in my mother's metal dinky curlers, but when he undid them they un-sprung into a mass of frizzy curls and I looked like a poodle, which was totally unflattering and did nothing for my face, only made me feel even fatter.

I was a disappointment to him, not living up to his image of what a daughter should look like: attractive, blonde and waif-like, like my friend up the road. My hair was mid-brown, flyaway and looked an untidy mass of rat's tails unless it was tied back in a bobble-tie. I'm sure he meant well, but staring at my image in the mirror all I could see was a fat, ugly child and I hated myself with a vengeance for the way I looked. I hated me.

One grey dismal Monday morning, I trudged to Jodie's house to call for her on the way to school. She answered the door as usual, while her mother hovered in the background unpinning the rollers in her hair with a cigarette dangling out of her mouth.

"I'm not coming with you today," she said, turning to check her mother's reaction.

"Oh, okay," I said. "I'll call for you tomorrow, then."

"No, I don't think so."

"What'd you mean?"

"Because – I can't."

"Why?"

"Because, becau—"

"Close the door please, Jodie," butted in her mum. "Tell her. Go on. We'll need to go in a minute."

Jodie looked embarrassed. Her hands were cupped protectively around the front door.

"Because... my mum said I can't play with you, or be your friend anymore. And she's going to take me to school."

I stepped back, shocked and confused.

"But why? What have I done?"

"Jodie!" shouted her mother again. "I won't tell you again. Shut the bloody door! You've told her now, so come inside."

"I'm sorry," was all she would say. "It's not you... it's your mum."

"My mum?"

The door banged shut. I turned and walked up the garden path in a daze, stung by her words and reeling from being rejected. She didn't want to know me anymore and it hurt like hell. I didn't understand and I felt so alone. As I plodded to school, I stared at the pavement and did not want to look up. Awful thoughts crept through my mind as I tried to work it out. I'd lost my friendship because of Mum. Was it because she looked a bit odd? But why? She couldn't help the way she was. They didn't know how unhappy her life was, and how could they? What if others didn't want to know me too? It wasn't long before I found out.

Nobody at school wanted to know me. My intuition had proved correct: I was completely ostracised. The mothers who hung outside the school gates, and who liked to gossip, realised there was something 'not quite right' about my mother and had warned their children to keep away from me. Perhaps it was because of how she walked; daintily tip-toeing along in her pointy heels as she'd been taught in deportment lessons, still dressed in miniskirts when they had long gone out of fashion. Or maybe it was the way she smoked like a Hollywood film star, blowing smoke evocatively to one side, holding her cigarette regally through yellowed fingers. Whatever it was, it filled me with embarrassment when I sensed them staring at Mum and ushering their children close when she came to meet us.

"Your mum's mental! Your mum's mental!" the children would chant in the playground.

I tried to retaliate by shouting back at them, "Leave me alone. She's not!"

I could feel myself being ripped apart inside. What did they know anyway? They didn't know anything about our lives. But trying feebly to stand up for her didn't help, and it hurt all the more when they laughed back at me. I hated myself for not being stronger, but there was nothing I could do.

Feeling isolated, I sought the refuge of the outside toilet block to get away from them. With its tiny opaque windows that let in very little light, and a permanently wet concrete floor, it felt more like a damp cave; a cold darkened space where I could retreat until the bell for the next lesson. I sat on a wooden toilet seat, the strong smell of pine disinfectant and urine penetrating my nostrils, and closed the door tight. It felt sad and miserable to be so alone. Sitting there I realised what loneliness was all about; I thought of Mum and my heart ached. Spending her time trapped in her bedroom, lying listlessly against a damp wall with no one to comfort her and nothing to look forward to, what life did she have? My father didn't care; all he ever did was shout and put her down. He told her she should be grateful to him for keeping her. Who would help her out of this situation? The answer was – no one. No family and no friends. Not a soul in the world. And as much as we children loved her, we were powerless. The only one who could make changes was Mum herself.

While all this was going on at school for me, Mum's tampering with the electrics had got worse. When Dad came home from work to discover she had cut the wires in the back of the television set and then the emersion heater, he decided to call our GP and ask for help.

We had just got home from school as the key turned in the lock. It was my father, pale and unshaven. He looked as if he was carrying the weight of the world on his shoulders.

"Eric, what are you doing back at this time?" asked my mother.

"I've come home early. We're expecting visitors shortly."

My mother looked at him suspiciously. "What d'you mean? We never have visitors. Who are these people?"

Ignoring her questions, he strode over to the window and pulled the net curtain back. Two expensive-looking cars were drawing up outside.

"Eric?" She sounded worried. "What's going on?"

He gave her a nervous glance and bit his lip as he returned to peering out of the window.

"They're here – great," he muttered to himself.

There was a loud knock and my father went to answer it. A look of relief came over his face.

"Hello, doctors. Hello, Mrs Radcliffe. Thank you for coming. This way," he said, greeting them and shaking their hands.

"Hello there, Mrs Herbert," said Dr Khan as he came in. "This is Dr Thomas, who is a psychiatrist, and this is Mrs Radcliffe from social services."

They both acknowledged Mum with a nod.

"What do you want?" asked my mother, clenching her lighter.

Dr Khan rested his leather briefcase on the arm of the sofa and started to take out some paperwork, and Mrs Radcliffe and Dr Thomas stood behind. So many adults in our tiny sitting room with nowhere to move made it cramped.

"Children, go outside for a moment while the doctors examine your mother," my father said.

We did as we were told but listened nervously through a crack in the door. I could feel my stomach tying itself in knots as we tried to understand what was going on and what it all meant.

"Mrs Herbert, do you know why I'm here today?"

"No. But obviously my husband has asked you to come for some reason."

Suddenly the door shut. Dad must have realised we were listening. From then on, all I heard was my mother's raised voice every so often. My heart raced in expectation of what might come. *They're going to take Mummy away, and this time I'll never see her again*, I thought to myself. I couldn't let it happen, not like last time, so without warning I burst into the room, my brother by my side.

"Leave my Mummy alone!" I shouted at them.

"Sally, I told you to wait outside," said Dad.

"No! I'm staying with Mummy."

My mother's hands were shaking and she was clearly frightened. I sensed she wanted to run.

"A *danger...*? What danger? What are you talking about?" she asked.

My brother and I were terrified of what might happen and stood there glued to the spot as the doctors carried on speaking to my mother.

Dr Khan, who was our GP, had always found my mum difficult to deal with and had little sympathy for her. His manner was abrupt and impatient. Dad and he were old acquaintances from their early years at the hospital, when Dr Khan was a junior doctor and Dad was a theatre technician. Dad was now a stores' manager and used to do him little favours if he was running short of medical supplies. In return, Dr Khan agreed to take us on his books at his new practice after my mum crossed her name off the last doctor's list.

"Your husband has had to report the extensive electrical damage that you've done to the council. They're worried that if it carries on you'll cause a fire."

Mum shook her head as tears streamed down. "No, no, you don't understand! You don't. Its's all lies. I haven't done anything. You have to believe me. It's my husband... he's making it all up."

"Now you know that's not true, Phyl, don't you?" interrupted Dad.

"Mrs Herbert, I'm afraid I am advising you that we're here today to section you under Section Three of the Mental Health Act. Do you understand what this means?"

Her legs gave way and she collapsed sobbing onto the sofa in a state of shock.

"You mean you want to lock me up in a mental hospital and throw away the key, don't you?"

"It's not quite like that," said Dr Thomas, stepping forward. "I understand your anxiety and no one is going to make you stay, but it would be better for everyone if you came of your own accord. It's for your own protection – just for a few days."

Mrs Radcliffe gently put her arm around Mum's shoulder and sounded compassionate.

"The rest will do you good, and the children can come and see you whenever you want. It would be better if you came now, Mrs Herbert – voluntarily."

"Voluntarily? Or what?"

"Mummy," I cried. "Mummy, don't go!"

She looked like a rabbit caught in a trap. I wrapped my arms around her neck and hung on for dear life. Will, who was six by then, looked on bemused.

"Sally, come on now, be a good girl," said my father, trying to prise my arms from Mum. "Move aside and let the doctors do their job."

He rubbed the back of his neck. "Phyl, I'm really sorry I had to do this, but we can't go on the way we are... with you like this... I'll bring the kids to see you whenever you like."

"You! You've done this deliberately just to get rid of me, haven't you? Get me out of the way – when you know I don't have a soul in the world to turn to for help. The lot of you are in it together, I know you are. I tell you, as God is my witness, what you do unto others will be done unto you!"

"Mummy – don't go with them, don't go!" I yelled.

Dr Khan and Mrs Radcliffe coaxed my mother to rise from the sofa and stood either side, leading her submissively to the door. With a look of complete despair, she turned her head to give us one last glance. Torrents of tears were pouring down her face.

"Don't you be worrying now... M...m-mammy will be back... very soon," she cried, trying to reassure us.

In protest, my brother and I rushed up to my father and banged our fists on his chest.

"Don't let them take her away, Daddy, please! You can help her, Daddy!"

"Look, I don't have a choice. It's for the best — to help her get better. Only be for a little while."

"But we'll never see her again," I cried.

"You will, Sally. Of course, you will."

"I hate you so much!" I screamed at him, as I ran to the window to watch her leave.

Dad wasn't expecting that strength of reaction and looked visibly shaken. That experience had its own effect on him, as he reminded me often for many years to come.

I ripped back the net curtain, desperate to get a last glimpse of Mum. I could smell the tobacco smoke that seemed to permeate everything. I pressed my face against the cold window pane as it steamed up from my hot breath, my saliva sticking to the glass. My heart was screaming out but no one could hear my pain as tears cascaded down my reddened face. Helplessly, I watched them escort her across the road to one of the cars. I banged on the window, longing for her to turn around and see me one last time. But she couldn't hear me, she was already in another world.

"Mummy! Come back!"

One of the doctors guided her into the back of the car, helping her duck her head so she wouldn't bang it, and Mrs Radcliffe got in beside her. I saw her rub the condensation off the window and look for us but it was too late, and within seconds they had driven her away.

Although my father explained she could only be sectioned for three days, it was several weeks before she was allowed home. He kept his promise and took us to see her. The place terrified me with its thick grey cell-like doors that were locked behind us as soon as we entered. It felt more like I imagined a prison than a hospital. It had originally been a Victorian workhouse before being an asylum and had a warm repugnant smell of its own that reminded me of sweaty leather and old people. It made me want to be sick.

I clearly remember someone in a white hospital gown run past screaming, with a fork in their hand, which was when I felt most scared. I wanted to run out of the door. *Poor Mum*, I thought, *how frightening to be in a place like this*. We sat alone on isolated chairs in the middle of a spacious room and were offered a hot Cornish pasty and a cup of tea while we waited to see her. But I was so choked with fear and emotion that eating or drinking was impossible.

When she was brought in, looking tired and forlorn, with dark circles under her eyes and her clothes swamping her fragile frame, she seemed less receptive to our hugs than she normally did and had nothing to say. Finally, she had been defeated. I felt so helpless for her but knew I could do nothing to make it better.

Then one day she was released and, somehow, we slotted back into our normal routine, whatever normal was, although she was now convinced that Dad was trying to have her put away permanently.

"He wants rid of me so he can get himself another woman," she told me confidentially. "He thinks because I've got no mother and no one to look out for me, he can do as he likes because no one will ever know."

I was waiting at the school gates, some weeks later, wondering where Mum was, when one of the mothers came over to let me know Mum was not going to be able to meet me.

"Yer mother's helping some bloke who's collapsed down near the library," she said, trying to be helpful.

I picked up my little black plastic attaché case and anxiously rushed along to find her. When I reached the library, I was surprised to find a crowd surrounding my mother as she knelt down on the paving stones and her coat was folded under the man's head. He'd had an epileptic fit and Mum was attending to him by putting her door keys in his mouth so he wouldn't swallow his tongue. Her nursing skills had never left her. After a while he recovered, got up and said he was fine. He shook my mum's hand and thanked her very warmly for her quick thinking, which, despite the fragility of her mind, had probably saved his life. After that incident, the other mothers who had been so judgemental of her before, now showed her a lot more respect. It also meant that my friendships at school started to blossom again.

There was a large green space opposite our house and, after many years of being overly protective and not letting me play on the street, Mum finally relented and let me play football outside with my brother and his friends. I relished the freedom of being able to run around, release my pent-up worries and develop new athletic skills I never dreamt I was capable of. I was 11 now and, after a summer of constant exercise, the puppy fat that had shrouded my body for so long dropped off. By the time I returned to school after our six-week summer break with a new page-boy hair style and a golden tan, the teachers barely recognised me. Despite my unstable home life, losing weight created a new unexpected confidence in me for a while, enabling me to enjoy taking part in sports day and winning a competition at the after-school club for dancing to Abba's *Waterloo*. I felt prouder than proud; but it didn't last.

Body changes and moving into puberty brought their problems. My father began to notice that I was developing and this intrigued him. Sometimes I could feel him secretly leering at me when I walked by, which made me nervous. Our house was always littered with his girlie mags and he had no qualms about it. Sex was something that should be open and talked about, he said. He hated censorship of any kind and would rant about people like Mary Whitehouse who campaigned to control expression of newly emerging liberal ideas.

More than once, if a friend stayed for a sleepover in my single bed, he'd call us very early in the morning, unexpectedly whipping back the bedclothes for no other reason than to tell us it was time to get up. If I took a bath, he had a habit of opening the door to ask me something, which I knew was an excuse to catch me unawares and glimpse my naked body. I didn't like it, so I began to lock the bathroom door so he couldn't get in. When he decided I was hiding myself from him he went ballistic and ripped the lock off the door, shouting abuse and accusing me of being a prude.

I felt afraid for my own safety with him, but what could I do? My mother's mental state was already very fragile and I didn't want to cause her any more pain, so I kept my fears to myself. I guess it must have affected me though, because I remember having a nightmare about running down the street in a terrible state of upset, with a towel barely wrapped around me, trying to hide my nakedness. I had a lot of nightmares in those days.

I couldn't hug him like I normally did, without him wanting to fondle me in a way that wasn't appropriate, trying to feel if I had any breasts.

"You're getting a big girl," he'd say. I knew he wasn't referring to my size as I had slimmed down from the dumpy child I used to be and was now slowly developing a figure.

The instant he drew close I felt sick. I couldn't even give him a kiss on the cheek without him wanting to turn it into something sexual. He'd purse his lips hard against mine and kiss me like they did in the 1930s films. Repulsed, I felt less inclined to seek affection from him, because I knew he would turn it into something else. I pulled away, but tried to do it in a way that wouldn't hurt his feelings because I knew how sensitive he was and if I upset him he wouldn't speak to me for days. All I needed from him was reassurance, especially with all the uncertainty in our life and in Mum's. We had been close, once upon a time, and I still loved him, but when he behaved that way he seemed like someone else and I couldn't cope with it. He disgusted me and the more he did it, the further it made me back off. I often cried. I'd sit on the bathroom floor with my head tucked into my knees and sob. I couldn't see a way out. I wanted him to be my dad and love me in a normal way. He was the only protection we had, and no one saw what was going on. Why couldn't he be normal like other children's fathers?

It was around this time that he developed a dependency on alcohol. In the evenings, after work, he'd just sit in front of the telly and start drinking. His home drinking had started in the mid-70s, experimenting with do-it-yourself beer kits that were all the rage, but later it progressed to strong bottled beer from the off-licence. Drinking soon became his crutch, but it made him angry and abusive. After a short while it became unbearable to be in the same room.

From then on, our family life disintegrated more and more rapidly, as we all started to live separate lives. I spent most of my teenage years at my friend Tracey's house, up the road. They were a bit rough and uncouth, but they treated me as one of their own and offered me a place to go when I needed to escape. Mrs Taddy (Tracey's mother), bore a strong resemblance to Tommy Cooper dressed in drag. Her party piece was to take out her false teeth and gurn while blowing a raspberry, while Tracey's father used to rinse his hair in the cabbage water after Sunday dinner, convinced it would make the hair sprout on his bald patch. Just being there was a real education, of which I don't think my Mum would have approved if she had known what the family were really like.

Having been well and truly indoctrinated as a child, Mum was extremely religious and slept with her Bible under her pillow every night. On Sundays, which was the worst day of the week for me because everything was shut down and so boring, she used to drag me and Will to church. I have to confess, I hated it.

The local church, St Paul's, had a new vicar. His name was the Reverend Peter Eaves and occasionally he used to appear on religious programmes on TV. Probably in his early 30s, around Mum's age, he was one of the emerging trendy types who liked to bring inspiring new ideas to the faith in the hope of increasing his congregation. One such novelty was having live music during the services, and another was to create a united feeling of love by getting everyone sitting next to each other to hold hands.

The vicar, unaware of his sultry charisma, had the looks of a Mediterranean Lothario with dark circles under his eyes, casual shoulder-length hair and olive skin. As we left the church, the knitted hat brigade was eagerly queuing up to shake hands with him and kiss him on the cheek. And Mum was no exception.

She elbowed me. "Look, look at them. They all want to meet him, so they do."

"Hmm. Yes, I can see."

She jostled her way into the queue.

"He looks like me, don't you think?"

"Mum, do you have to?"

"Ha-ha! He's good-looking don't you think, Sal?"

"Er, no."

"You don't think so, naw?"

"Mum, can we just go?"

Too late, it was her turn.

"Well, I must say, vicar, that I thoroughly enjoyed your sermon today," she said, shaking his hand and forgetting to release it.

"That's good to hear, thank you. At least I know I'm doing something right," he joked. "It's really all about bringing the community together."

"Yes, well thank you. I'm sure you'll do that alright," she said smiling. "I'll look forward to it all again next week."

Church, for quite a while, became part of our regular routine. Dad, of course, never attended because he was an atheist and thought all religions were only after your money. But Mum sat there transfixed in awe at every word the vicar said. I used to dread it when he addressed the congregation, all 15 or so of us, asking anyone to put their hands up if they knew the answer to a question. I knew Mum would want to answer, but only so he would notice her. It inevitably left me wanting to slide down the pews and out of sight. Church was a prominent feature in our lives, and whatever the event, be it Harvest Festival, church barbeque or jumble sale, we were always there. The vicarage was right next to the church and I noticed that Mum's eyes would be often drawn to this house.

Her attraction to the vicar took on a more shocking turn when life at home started to crumble further. In a cry for help, she started writing him poems and posting them through the vicarage letterbox. They were weird and made no sense, as I recall, but I doubt if she would have realised this. He lived alone, apart from his personal secretary, so I am sure it must have caused him some embarrassment.

It wasn't long then before the GP and social services were called for a second time and Mum was sent to a different psychiatric hospital for treatment. It was another austere building from the 19th century, and it gave me the creeps. Just entering the cobblestone hallway, unchanged since its days as a workhouse, I felt the ghosts watching me from its chequered past.

I was about 12 by this time and understood more than I did when I was younger, but I still couldn't comprehend why Mum kept on running herself into the ground until she suffered from chronic anaemia and nervous exhaustion time and time again. I knew my father played a big part in her unhappiness, but she had never told us about her traumatic childhood or her lack of love as an orphan. I guess she just couldn't put it into words, as it was too painful to remember.

Every time she became ill it made me more insecure, thinking that one day we would be parted forever. That feeling has stayed with me all my life.

"With your mother away, you're going to have to start doing your bit around the home," my father said. "Remember, it's only me bringing a wage into this house and I can't be expected to do everything: father, chief cook and bottlewasher. It's either that or I'll have to put you both into care."

The mere mention of the word "care" made me nauseated and jittery. Will and I had already experienced that twice and if it happened again we might never get out.

"Of course, I'll do anything, Dad," I said. "I can do the cooking and the washing and whatever else. But please, please, Dad, don't put us in another home."

And I did; although in those days we didn't have a washing machine, so I either washed by hand in the kitchen sink and drip-dried everything on the line or dragged the clothes down to the launderette in bin liners. Dad taught me to cook, and soon I was taking on the role of my mother before and after going to school.

I hated school, especially high school. I was from the baby-boom era and class sizes had vastly outgrown the original building. This meant that the teacher didn't ever know you as a person, only by sight, so you could very easily disappear into the background. Although that didn't bother me too much, I couldn't cope with the renewed taunting about my mother, followed by bullying that started when I was recognised by a neighbour's daughter. They'd pull my hair and rock my chair backwards and forwards with me in it, before the teacher came in, or call me names and push me around. Instead of sitting in the classroom during breaks, I spent my time walking around the playing field so they couldn't pick on me. I desperately wanted to run away, which inevitably I did by continually playing truant.

This caused more problems with the school board man, with him constantly on Dad's back. His relentless determination to seek me out dominated my dreams. I'd be running to get away from him, often frozen by fear so that my legs were paralysed and I couldn't move. It was my worst and most recurring nightmare. Dad would seek out my hiding places and, to my utter humiliation, take me back to school mid-morning. But even detentions didn't stop me. They simply created intrigue among my fellow classmates and I earned a sense of notoriety. It came as a surprise because I had always been 'miss goody-two-shoes' until then.

There was no counselling in those days. Teachers believed the only way to stop me bunking off school was to punish me, instead of getting to the root of the problem. I told them about the bullying and, although sympathetic to a certain extent, they weren't prepared to take it any further unless I revealed the culprits, which I was too afraid to do.

My whole life was lived in fear. During lessons, I found it difficult to concentrate and didn't seem to fit in with anyone. I felt different, and lived each day out in my own dream world. One day a teacher noticed that I wasn't paying attention in a history lesson and picked me out to answer a question. From out of nowhere, I heard my voice ask her back, "Why?" She glared at me, thunderstruck by my reply. In a split second I heard what I had said and felt my bowels churn; I had never answered a teacher back in my life. Within a panic-stricken moment I managed to turn my flippancy into another question and, thankfully, the teacher looked puzzled but relieved. The stresses of my life were obviously more prevalent in my subconscious than I knew.

And then at the age of 15 I felt so stressed that I had an out-of-body experience. I often had nightmares and would awaken to find myself falling, but this night I became aware of myself floating horizontally just a few inches below my bedroom ceiling, with my body still lying on the bed. I was absolutely terrified and anxious to be on the bed and back in my body again. I felt I had no control over myself and I thought that, maybe, I was going to die.

While dysfunctional family life was having its emotional effects on me, Mum's mental state remained unstable despite many courses of medication, which I'm not convinced she took.

Then she received the inevitable letter in the post. It was from Edna Carter, Auntie Bea's sister, in Ireland. The letter was short and to the point and advised my mother that Auntie Bea had passed away many months before. Mum was heartbroken. Although their relationship seemed to have almost fizzled out over the passage of time, Mum still looked on her with the deepest affection. Despite not having seen her for seven years, she spoke of her as a daughter would of her mother. News of her death was the final straw piled on Mum's sense of abandonment. Now, other than her children, she was alone again in the world and it wasn't long before her mental state collapsed and, predictably, she found herself in hospital, this time for a longer period of four months. I remember the date precisely, because I got the number 280 bus straight to the hospital and some kids at the back had the radio on. It was 16 August 1977, the day Elvis Presley died, and the radio stations were playing his music in memory of him.

The psychiatric hospital she was referred to this time also had medical wards on site, where she was placed for a few weeks as she was so ill that she needed a blood transfusion before being transferred to the psychiatric unit. It was the first of many transfusions over the forthcoming years, as her pattern of self-neglect never really went away. I tried to visit her as much as I could, but it was difficult alongside going to school, and looking after the family. And it was not a place I relished.

"You know I nearly died, Sal," she told me, sitting up in bed.

"Died? What do you mean Mum?"

"They said I was so anaemic that I was literally days away from death."

I shook my head in disbelief. How could she have got to this state and no one even noticed?

"No…" I didn't know what to say. "Oh Mum, Mum. How could that happen, Mum. Why?"

I wrapped my arms around her and felt a huge lump form in my throat, trembling inside at the realisation that I nearly lost her.

"I don't know, Petsey. I've got to get out of this place, but they won't let me come home yet. I've got to show them I am willing to cooperate with the treatment."

"I want you at home, Mum. But I want you to be better this time."

"And I will, Petsey, I will. I won't ever let your father ruin my life again."

And she kept her word. This must have been a turning point in her life, because it was the last time that she ever entered a mental hospital.

After a year's monitoring and agreeing to take her prescribed drugs, she somehow found the determination to survive and pulled herself back from the brink. Then, finding yet another show of strength, she returned to geriatric nursing, which she continued for eight years until my father was taken ill with cancer.

The past often haunted her though. If anyone even mentioned the word "mental" she'd suspect they were talking about her and it would send her into overdrive. Having suffered mental illness, she now felt labelled. After feeling worthless as a child and again as a wife, she felt the stigma would never go away. All she wanted was to be treated as normal. And for the most part over the next 37 years, she *was* normal. Only if she had a break in her employment, or if somebody doubted her ability, would the fragility of her mind become unsettled and old behavioural paranoid patterns start to creep back. I was the only person who recognised it, being so close to her, but I could see the key to her happiness was to constantly work and to feel needed, part of a team. Taking those essentials away from her was like pulling the rug from beneath her feet, making her feel unwanted. And then what would she have left?

If only her mother could have foreseen Phyllis's life, and the many ways she was to suffer, I wonder whether it would have influenced her decision to give her up as a baby? I guess we will never know.

PART TWO

Phyllis and Sally – Family

Chapter 10

A Trip to Ireland

September 26 2006 11:59

Dear Sally,

Further to our conversation, I am sending you information from the Bethany records.

Peggy Little (as she was known) was 20 years old when she was first admitted to the Bethany on 7 December 1936. She was in good health. She came from an address in County Wexford and her religion was given as Protestant.

Towards the end of Peggy's pregnancy, she was admitted to hospital suffering from albuminuria, (apparently a serum protein in the urine that can be a sign of kidney or heart disease). Phyllis was born three days later on 29 March 1937. Mother and baby were then readmitted to the Bethany on 7 April by which time Peggy was said to be in a weak condition.

Peggy left the Bethany on 30 June 1937 in good health, to an address in Greystones, County Wicklow.

Phyllis was baptised on 13 September, so contrary to what I said on the phone, Peggy would not have been present when Phyllis was christened.

Something I missed before, was that it appears that Phyllis left the Bethany with her mother on 4 November 1938 but returned again on 23 December that year. She finally left the Bethany to go to the North Dublin Orphanage on 16 January 1940. There is no explanation as to why her mother took her out at 18 months old but was unable to keep her for more than six weeks.

Sadly, this is the extent of the information on record, but I confirm that I will do the following:

1. Make enquiries of the orphanage records, if they allow me to act on your mother's behalf.

2. Check for a birth record for Peggy.

Yours sincerely,
Morag MacDonald

Scouring the internet for new information was like discovering a new planet. I had never been much into the web, but I was beginning to realise I could find out virtually anything I wanted by tapping a few words into Google. So, I put in the Bethany Home to see what came up. It was a place that Mum knew nothing about, only that her mother, who I discovered from Morag's letter was known as Peggy rather than Margaret as on her birth certificate, was probably sent there to conceal the illegitimate birth. To my surprise, I came across a charity that held the Protestant records for the Bethany Home for mothers and babies. They were based in Dublin and offered information about the home.

Without further hesitation I arranged a convenient time to have a telephone conversation with Morag MacDonald, a social worker, who sounded compassionate and well informed. I told her about Mum's life and how she yearned to know who her mother was. I also revealed how we suspected the secrecy might concern the woman my mother called her great aunt, or perhaps Auntie Bea's family.

"I can't promise anything," said Morag, "but I will check the records and come back to you by email if I find anything that relates to your mother."

I read and re-read the email several times, astonished and excited that after all these years, I had found out about my mother's birth. *Wow!* I thought, *there may be some hope after all. Perhaps this will lead to more clues.*

Mum was lying on the sofa in my front room, transfixed by the TV adverts, so I decided to read her my findings.

"So, Mum, what do you think of that then?"

"What do I think? Well darling, I'm amazed. I think you're brilliant to have found so much information when I never could. You're so clever, Sal."

"No, I'm not, really I'm not. I just got these people in Ireland to access your records. That's incredible, don't you think? I never thought we'd find anything."

"Yes, it is, and I'm delighted for sure! It's more than I dared hope for, although I still wonder if we'll ever reach the bottom of the truth. There's more to it than we know about – something they're not telling us. Do we even know if Peggy Little was her real name? I believe I came from money, you know."

10 October 2006 12:22

Dear Sally,

There is quite a lot to update you with, so I thought it best to send on the findings of our researcher in attachments.

As you will see, I got the researcher to search for a birth record for Margaret Little for the time period, and there are at least 16 records, but we could not find any in County Wexford, so it has not led us anywhere. However, I contacted the lady who has access to the orphanage records.

She checked all the minutes of your mother's time at the orphanage and found no reference to Miss Davidson, although it was not uncommon for people to befriend orphans. But the more important piece of information she found was the reason that your mother was there was because Peggy was living in too poor circumstances to keep her. I wonder if that ties in with why she took Phyllis out of the Bethany for six weeks in 1938, only to return her. Perhaps it didn't work out. However, it did say that when she returned her, she was now married and calling herself Mrs James Clancy.

In answer to your mother's question about how do we know that Peggy Little was her mother's real name, I have been advised that if an alias was given by a young woman booking into the Bethany, the matron would suspect that a false name had been given and write something in the ledger to that effect. But I can assure you that there was no such suspicion in Peggy's case.

I will get my researcher to look for a marriage record for Margaret Little and James Clancy.

If he finds a marriage certificate, you may need to see if your mother wants to take this any further. This piece of news may be difficult for her to receive and I hope you will find a way to share it with her. If you would like to talk about it on the telephone, just email me and we will work out a time together.

Hope to talk to you soon.
Morag

After this latest revelation about Peggy being married, I was elated beyond belief. If she had married it might mean there were other siblings around – Mum's family! Even more significantly, a marriage certificate would give us an address and other details to help trace her origins.

But it wasn't long before the euphoria left me feeling like a deflated balloon. Without a date or place of birth for Peggy, it soon became evident that it was going to be virtually impossible to pinpoint the right person. The two addresses in Wexford and Wicklow were places of residence and not birth. Not only that, but no marriage certificate could be found for Peggy and James, despite the researcher looking at a 10-year period either side of 1938, not just in Ireland but the whole of the UK. He also searched for death certificates for them both, and baptism for Peggy, but to no avail.

None of this made sense. Peggy had claimed she was married, but even after extensive searches there was no evidence. Perhaps there was a cover-up? Certainly Peggy, whoever she was, had made a good job of covering her tracks. I wanted to scream. I had come so close to finding tangible information and then, when I least expected it, found myself in a cul-de-sac. I remembered Mum's words from our car journey home that day: "Oh darling, everything was well hidden in those days. I don't know, but perhaps it was something to do with my aunt's family. They never liked me – certainly Edna never approved, and Bunty could never look me in the face."

She had always been deeply suspicious that there was a connection to Auntie Bea's family, but didn't dare ask questions out of fear and respect for their wishes.

Her guardian, 'Auntie Bea', had taken more than a passing interest in my mother though. She had gone far beyond the call of duty for an orphan. Not only had she overseen her welfare since Mum was a child, but carried on keeping a watchful eye on her into early adulthood and marriage to Dad, which led Mum to sense there was some secret family connection that couldn't be revealed because of her illegitimacy. But how could I prove a theory like that?

If my mother was right about a connection to the Davidsons, which seemed quite plausible considering her kindnesses, I knew the only way forward was to investigate Miss Davidson's family tree, looking for clues that might link her with Mum. Maybe she had a distant relation called Margaret or Peggy Little? It was going to be difficult as I knew nothing about Beatrice Davidson, not even her age. Thankfully, Mum's memory was still good and she remembered the names of Beatrice's two brothers and three sisters. She also remembered the places they had lived and knew that the family was originally English, having moved to Ireland from Lancashire. It was a start.

After months of checking census records and ordering birth, death and marriage certificates, I began to piece together Auntie Bea's family tree. But after discovering that Beatrice was born in Wales in 1901, I drew a blank. I knew the tree was incomplete as two siblings were missing, one of whom was Flory, the younger sister who Mum met in Liverpool en route to Epsom Hospital. I guessed that Wales had been their last stop before moving to Ireland.

Although in 2006, the ancestry website I used probably had the largest collection of records in the world, they did not have access to all the Irish records. Without a visit to the archives in Dublin or paying an Irish genealogist, I had little hope of going further. I found this frustrating, so I turned back to the charity and asked for their help. Their genealogist, who I was now paying privately, searched the 1911 Irish census, which revealed that Beatrice's parents had moved to Ireland after her birth, settled in the docklands area, and had two more children, just as Mum had remembered. Electoral records revealed they later moved to North Dublin and bought a large semi-detached in a fairly affluent area near Dolly Island. In 1936, there was a Little family living in that road, which raised my hopes for a while, but the genealogist discovered that to be an incorrect assumption. Finally, he suggested that we look for a will. Mum was adamant that Auntie Bea had pointedly told her, "A mother would never leave a daughter out of her will." Mum was convinced that Auntie had been referring to her. If a will could be found and Mum was mentioned in it, that could lead to proof that she was related to Beatrice.

A death certificate for Beatrice was duly found, along with a copy of her will, but it contained no clues or reference to Mum. At that point I became convinced that they could not be related. If there was a connection, it must be to another member of that family. How was I going to break this unsettling news?

"No! That can't be right. It certainly can't be," she cried, when I plucked up the courage to tell her.

I tried to comfort her but she pushed me away. "Leave me! Just leave me, Sal."

"Mum, I'm so sorry—"

How can you be sure… just how?"

"Because, Mum, she'd have been too old. In 1937, when you were born, your aunt would have been 36; she was born in 1901. The records say Peggy was 20 when she gave birth to you, which means she was born around 1917. It's too big a difference. Also, there was no mention of you in her will, which she made in 1969. She left it all to her siblings."

"But she told me specifically… she made me listen carefully… 'a mother would never leave a daughter out of…' She even made sure I knew her solicitors were in George Street. They must have made her change it after the last time I was there. I bet they did."

"Well, perhaps."

"I loved her you know… I really loved her."

"Mum, please don't cry. I'm so sorry, I really am."

"She was the only person I had, you know."

"Please Mum, don't. I know how much she meant to you'

"I used to think how we looked like each other, when she stood next to me."

"I know."

"Oh, Petsey…"

She sat there clutching at the side of the chair, head bowed and sobbing uncontrollably, the tears dripping onto her lap.

I felt devastated. I hadn't anticipated that the truth would have such an effect.

"Look," I said, "Do you want me to stop? I thought you ought to know the truth, but if it is going to upset you, then I'll stop searching. Although, having got this far, there's a real possibility I could find your mother."

She pulled herself together and a long pause hung between us. Her eyes were filled with such sadness that I thought they would rip my heart in two.

"No, you carry on," she sniffed. "It's the one thing in the world I'm really wanting to know. If it is not my aunt, then who can it be? All these years I have been praying so hard to find out the truth one day and hoping God would answer my prayers. I've suffered so much deceit in my life, being lied to, always afraid to ask those questions I need to know. You have no idea what it does to a person inside. I must know the truth about my mother. I must know who she was and why she gave me up."

23 April 2007 14:28

Dear Sally,

I'm sorry that the search for information which we embarked on together hasn't really taken us very far after all this time. I do hope ultimately that you will find some of the answers you are seeking. You have always been very reassuring with your expression of thanks and I am glad that I have been able to be of some assistance to you.

Well, I would be very pleased to meet you when you come to Ireland and may I suggest the morning of Friday, 6 July? We can firm up arrangements in due course.

Kind regards,
Morag

Having not been able to discover any more about Peggy or James, I decided to concentrate on tracing Beatrice's present-day relatives; perhaps if I contacted them, they would remember something from the past. This meant visiting them in person.

Mum remembered two addresses in North Dublin where Auntie Bea had taken her as a child. One of the houses she visited, when she was about 14, belonged to Beatrice's elder sister, Eleanor. She recalled watching Eleanor's daughter, who was seven years older, sprucing herself up to go out to a dance. Her name was Dorothy.

My brother Will, who also wanted to know about Mum's mother, had already visited Ireland and found the original house, but Dorothy had moved out 30 years before, or so he was informed by a helpful neighbour who willingly gave him the new address. When he tracked it down he was met by her husband, but disappointed to find Dorothy was out, although at least he could pass me the details.

It seemed my next plan of action had to be to visit Ireland, hopefully find Dorothy at home and ask what she could remember. And after that, to visit an address that Peggy had given while she was in the Bethany Home. It was in an area called Bush, a hamlet in Tagoat, County Wexford.

First, I wrote to Dorothy, but had no reply, so I decided to take my chances anyway and turn up on her doorstep. I also contacted a local genealogy centre in County Wexford to see if they knew this address or any Littles in the area. I thought it would be good to know roughly where the hamlet was, as it was clearly a rural location.

13 June 2007 15:23

Dear Sally,

Further to your letter of 28 May, there is an area called Bush on the road to Rosslare Strand (R740), between Ashfield Cross and the strand, and there is a gentry house in that area. Investigations so far have failed to uncover a family of Littles. The parish register for the time frame, 1912–1922 contains no reference to Margaret Little or indeed anyone of that family name. We will continue with our enquiries. You might also like to try Wexford Library or the Wexford Historical Society.

Sincerely,
Ciara

I hadn't been to Ireland since that fateful day in 1969 when Mum had left my father, so was not only curious but also apprehensive. One thing for sure, I knew I didn't want to go on my own. So, I called my good friend, Libby, whom I had been away with on two previous adventurous holidays.

"Ireland?" she said. "Well… I've never been before. But, yeah – I'm game."

"The only thing is, Libbs, I want to trace somebody my mum once knew who lives in North Dublin, and then visit an address in County Wexford. How do you feel about that? There won't be much time for sightseeing, although we'll get some in."

"Well, yeah. Sounds alright to me."

"Means hiring a car and sharing the driving…"

"Okay, as long as I don't have to do *all* the driving."

"Course not. So, we could stay a couple of nights in Dublin and then head down to Wexford."

"Sounds like a plan!"

Libby was being incredibly supportive and really quite selfless considering it was her break too; although she was happy to go along with my wishes, I felt guilty for roping her into what was essentially a road trip to uncover my mum's past. I felt even worse when our sightseeing time was eaten up by confusing road signs in Dublin city and we wasted three hours driving around in circles. We were both relieved when we finally reached our destination.

After a night at the hotel and a meal in Temple Bar we headed off, following the river north to a picturesque harbour with a scattering of shops and a pub. The house we were seeking was on top of a hill and, as we climbed higher and higher up winding roads, we took in magnificent views of the harbour below and beyond.

First stop was Dorothy's house, where we would hopefully find her in and be well received. We pulled up and parked in what looked a fairly affluent neighbourhood.

"Sal, I think this is it," said Libby, looking at the map.

She pointed to a peach-coloured bungalow with a manicured front garden and wide porch with panoramic windows.

"I feel nervous," I said. "I'm still not sure what to say. Will you come with me Libbs?"

"Of course, silly."

"What if they're hostile or turn us away?"

"They won't. Gawd, you worry too much, Sal. And if they do, then at least you've tried."

I knocked and waited.

An elderly man appeared, smiled, and was welcoming although he didn't know us. "Hello," he said.

"Er, hello there. My name is Sally… and I believe a Dorothy Reilly lives here?"

"Yes, she does, but she's out. I'm her husband, can I help you?"

My heart raced and I took a deep breath.

"Yes. I wrote to your wife earlier this year to ask if she remembered my mother and if she could tell me anything about her past. I understand Dorothy was the niece of Beatrice Davidson, who was my mother's guardian aunt. My brother also paid you a visit last year."

His face dropped and the smile turned into a frown.

"That's right," he said, remembering and looking more serious. "You'd better come in. Dorothy has gone to the dentist, but she'll only be half an hour, if you don't mind waiting. I'll put the kettle on and make us some coffee."

He led us into a long sitting room where we sat down on a comfy settee. The room was decorated on every wall with photos of their grandchildren. I introduced Libby, then started telling him about my research into his wife's family tree.

About 20 minutes later, the latch turned in the front door and a woman the same height and frame as my mother, only fuller, entered the room. Her olive skin and eyes also reminded me of Mum's. She looked surprised until her husband explained who we were.

"Well there is nothing I can tell you and I don't remember anything," she said, adamantly, before I could even ask.

I showed her my documented research of her family tree and gradually, from seeming hostile, she started to warm to me as I talked about my discoveries, which seemed to prompt some form of recollection.

"So, do you remember Beatrice then?" I enquired.

"Well yes. But my memory has faded. She died a long time ago."

"Do you have any photos of her we could see?"

"No, none."

"None?"

"None."

"Then you also remember my mother? She remembers you – getting ready for a dance and putting your hair in rollers when Aunt Bea brought her round. You'd have been about 21 at the time, Mum 14."

"No. I remember nothing. There is nothing I can tell you."

"So, you're saying you can't remember Beatrice ever mentioning an orphan or bringing her to see you?"

"No, I can't remember a thing."

"I see."

Although Dorothy had seemed quite pleasant and I was grateful that we had been invited into her home, I sensed she was putting up barriers – whether she could remember or not, she wasn't going to give anything away.

All of a sudden, her husband piped up.

"May I ask *why* you think your mother has something to do with our family?"

"You want the truth?" I asked, looking directly at them and still peeved at her reaction. "I believe that someone is related to my mother, but doesn't want us to know. That there's a cover-up of something they're trying to hide. My mother is ill; time is running out and I need to find out before it is too late."

Libby looked at me horrified.

"Sal! You can't say that! You can't go around accusing people. You don't know what went on. They've already said they can't remember anything."

There was an awkward silence.

I tried not to glare at Libby, but my feelings were brimming to the surface. I couldn't believe that she was only seeing it from their point of view. She tried to reason with me some more, but I was having none of it.

"Look! I'm just saying what I feel. I haven't come all this way for nothing. You don't know what it feels like not to know your family. Mum does and so do I. All I want is the truth."

"Well," said Dorothy, "it's not that I don't want to tell you anything. I simply can't remember. You ought to try the Carter family. Beatrice had more to do with them than us."

"Don't worry, I will," I said getting up to leave. "Listen, thanks for the coffee and your hospitality. I do appreciate it. And I promise not to bother you again."

Before I left Dorothy obliged me with a few photos and offered the use of her toilet, which I thought was kind. I felt quite bad about my outburst. I wanted to believe she was as genuine as she seemed, but the more I studied her face the more it bore a striking resemblance to my mother's.

"I'm glad you came," she said, as she saw us to the door and gave me a goodbye hug. That was the last I ever saw of her.

Next day, after a good night out in Dublin, we headed south for our hotel in County Wexford and after a jaunt around the town we found Rosslare Strand and the side road that should have led us to the house in Bush; but no matter how many times we drove up and down, we couldn't find the address I was looking for. The road was in the countryside, with some very elegant houses and well-established bungalows, but despite signs to Bush, nothing provided any clues to the address we wanted. I felt quite demoralised when we had to give up.

Before we flew home, I had arranged to meet Morag MacDonald, the social worker who had been so helpful about the Bethany Home. Libby and I took the hire car back and caught the shuttle bus to the hotel, which was close to the airport terminal. We ordered coffee and sunk down into some comfy sofas in the reception area. Morag appeared looking casually smart in trousers and a loose-fitting blouse and jacket. We shook hands and I introduced her to Libby.

"Well, thank you for coming all this way," she said. "It's nice to put a face to a case you're dealing with. I'm sorry we didn't get very far with our searches, but sadly this is often the way."

"I still believe it has something to do with her aunt's family, you know," I said. "Libby and I went to visit a niece and I can't get over how alike she and my mum are – but she wouldn't tell us anything."

"Sal," said Libby. "It's not because she wouldn't tell you anything. It's because she couldn't remember. Don't forget she was elderly."

"Elderly?" I rebuked. "She was only seven years older than Mum, and in much better nick."

"I think, Sally, that your mother probably wasn't anything to do with Miss Davidson's family," said Morag. "She was just doing her bit for the Protestant Church. Peggy's story is all too common, I'm afraid. Look, I've something to show you. I don't think you'll have seen this before, but perhaps it'll help."

She produced an A3-sized document headed FEMALE ORPHAN: a certificate transferring my mother from the Bethany Home to the orphanage. It showed Mum's name and her condition of health at the time. Below were several dates of birth, which had been queried and crossed off, but none of them was her true birthday. But I did notice the date 23 December 1937. Eureka, I thought! That was the date Mum said had been celebrated as her birthday for 16 years, until on leaving the orphanage the Reverend Parsons handed her a birth certificate with 30 March 1937 on it. Record-keeping in Ireland, decades ago, had been neither concise nor accurate. Evidently someone had misread it and assumed that 23 December was Phyllis's birthday when, in fact, it was the date Peggy had returned her to the Bethany Home after taking her out for six weeks. Perhaps it was a genuine mistake, it's hard to know, but certainly the miscommunication had created a strong feeling of distrust in Mum's mind.

An address in County Wicklow was also recorded, which was where Peggy had headed after leaving her daughter at Bethany. It read: Coolnagreine. That's an intriguing name I thought, I wonder where that will lead me next.

I arrived home feeling it had been a wasted trip. Trying to trace the family was like climbing Mount Everest. Auntie Bea's niece, Dorothy, apparently could not remember anything and I was no further along in finding any records for Margaret/Peggy Little. It felt hopeless. For a while I was on the verge of giving up completely.

But as Dorothy had suggested, I contacted another of Bea's relatives, Ronald Carter. He was her nephew and her sister Edna's son. Now retired from lecturing, he was living on the outskirts of Dublin. I wrote to him and this was his reply.

20 July, 2007

Dear Ms Herbert,

I read your letter with interest and sympathy, but unfortunately neither I, nor others of this generation, have more than a vague recollection of hearing that my aunt, "took an interest in the orphanage".

She was a very convicted Christian woman and my memory is such that I cannot believe she was your grandmother.

Perhaps you should pursue the Margaret Little line further. Age and its attendant problems mean that it is unlikely that more can be found out from this end.

Yours,
Ronald Carter

I felt my mind changing about his family's connection to my mother. Libby had tried to make me see sense when we were in Ireland, not because she was taking sides; she was looking at the situation from an objective point of view. I decided to forget about the conspiracy theories; to go back to picking through the shreds of information I had about Peggy Little and try to work from there.

Over months and then years, I carried on contacting historians and genealogists in Ireland and asking for their help. One had even worked on the television programme, *Who Do You Think You Are.* But each time they searched for birth, death, baptismal and marriage certificates, it was to no avail. It was like tramping over old ground the whole time.

By January 2009 my mother's health was in decline. She was permanently on antibiotics as she seemed to pick up one chest infection after another, and although I nagged her to stop smoking and give up work, she wouldn't listen.

"Oh, just leave me, Petsey. I'll be alright. There's plenty of life in me yet," she'd say.

Mum was the eternal optimist, but I knew she couldn't go on forever like this and there would come a point where I would run out of time to find her elusive mother and family.

Then, I remembered the name "Coolnagreine" on the document that Morag showed me at Dublin Airport. Where was this place, I wondered. I had already searched the internet and not located it. And just what significance did it have to Peggy? I emailed Wicklow County Council and they put me in touch with a helpful genealogist, who searched for the name Coolnagreine in the Greystones area of County Wicklow, but despite investigating old Ordnance Survey maps and electoral rolls, we had no luck. She thought that where it had once existed was now a housing estate, then suggested I try a local burial ground close to Greystones. I contacted the person holding their records, but no result. Even so, no matter how many dead ends I came up against, I refused to give up. Something inside just kept spurring me on.

Chapter 11

Another Brick Wall

My sixth sense never normally let me down. By the late summer of 2010 I had a nagging feeling that would often wake me in the small hours. No matter how hard she had tried to convince me that her life at work was enjoyable and gave her purpose, I could tell Mum's health was weakening and she wasn't as happy as before. There had been changes at the care home that created a more stressful atmosphere that she found hard to accept. Her way of dealing with it was to push herself harder and keep going. She forgot that at 73, and without a proper diet or enough sleep, her body couldn't take it anymore. It was a constant struggle for her to get up in the mornings and her walking was more laboured than ever. Her physical appearance also gave me cause for concern. Her skin looked grey, her hair greasy and unkempt, and her clothes drowned her slight frame. She suffered from frequent cold sores, which I knew meant she was run down. In addition to the suspicious-looking moles on her forehead, she now had a septic boil on her nose which would flare up when she was in the sun. She had stopped caring about herself. My partner Philip and I were just back from our summer holiday in Cyprus and I felt that it might be our last trip abroad for a while. Two months later, my intuition proved right.

I arrived home from work one day to a message on the answer-phone.

"Hello. This message is for Mrs Herbert's daughter. It's the doctor's surgery at Bell Hill and it's about your mother. Please ring us as soon as possible."

I played it back several times searching for clues, while my stomach tied itself in a double knot. I gathered my wits as I dialled the number.

"Pick up. Pick up!" I urged, as the phone rang and rang. Eventually I got through.

"Oh hello, Mrs Herbert," said the receptionist. "I'm afraid I need to let you know that your mother has been taken to hospital with a suspected stroke. The doctor called an ambulance when she saw him this afternoon."

The stroke, albeit a minor one, affected her down one side. By the time she realised and got herself to the doctor's surgery, she couldn't hold anything in her left hand and was dragging one leg. Thankfully, it hadn't affected her speech. I thought back to that morning after her two-day stay with me, how she had seemed uncharacteristically lethargic when I woke her up. I drove her to the station but had been impatient as I needed to get to work.

"Come on, Mother. Look at the time. I need to go now."

"Ah Sal, I'm sorry, I just can't move as quickly as I used to. I'll be there in a minute."

Why hadn't I noticed? I felt dreadful. And why hadn't she told me something was wrong? As usual she kept it all inside so I wouldn't worry, which only frustrated me when I found out. *Why does she do that?* I wondered Was it another symptom of her childhood in the orphanage, being taught not to think of herself but always put others first? That is what she drummed into us as children. Consider others first – yourself second. My father had been the complete opposite.

"Look after number one – and don't give a fuck about anyone else!" he'd say.

The hospital was in London and took four hours to reach. A team of doctors were doing their ward rounds as I walked in, and Mum was sitting up in bed awaiting their visit. It was such a relief to see that she looked fairly normal and her face hadn't drooped, but before I could greet her, the team had descended upon her and were crowding around her bed.

"So, Mrs Herbert, can you tell me how many cigarettes you smoke a day?" one of them asked.

"Oh, no more than five, I think. Yes, about five," she confirmed.

"Five!" I blurted out. "Five? More like twenty at least!"

I was aware of my blood pressure rising. In the same way that a child would try to get away with a lie, so did my mother. From being devastated that she had suffered a stroke and berating myself for not noticing, I was now furious to discover she was not being truthful with the doctors who were trying to help her.

"Naw, Sally, don't say that to the doctors. It's not true. I only smoke five cigarettes a day, you know I do."

We had an argument in front of them as they stood looking awkward and bemused. The stroke certainly hadn't affected her feistiness, that's for sure.

"Mrs Herbert, are you able to show us how you walk?" one interrupted.

"Oh yes, I can walk very well. Just look at this."

She hopped off the bed, showing off, but looked very unsteady on her feet as she ambled from side to side. Still dressed in her skimpy teenage top and black leggings, she tried to impress them with a little pixie dance.

"See," she said with an air of confidence. "I'm fine! There's really nothing wrong with me. I should be able to go home now."

A tall man, who seemed the more senior consultant, gave her a wry smile and rubbed his jaw.

"Well, I admire your determination, Mrs Herbert. Your gait looks a little unsteady, but the end of the week should be fine to go home," he said.

She came back to my house to recuperate. I took two weeks off work to look after her, while I sought help for her and let her employers know what had happened. Her local authority in South London was less than sympathetic, refusing to put any help in place until she returned home. In the end, I decided she should live with me until I could get her moved into sheltered accommodation nearby. Of course, it meant her giving up work, which she didn't want, but now she had no choice.

December 2010 had the worst snow and ice we had seen for years. It took me over five hours to get home one evening. Mum had not taken the doctors' advice to give up smoking and stood happily puffing away outside my back door, on the hour every hour, with snow drifting down onto her pink woolly hat and oblivious to the wintry weather.

"You'll catch your death of cold," I chided. But she smiled and waved at me through the kitchen window as she smoked and chomped away on popcorn at the same time.

As hard as I tried to be stern for her own good, I couldn't keep telling her off. I had to let her do her own thing. She was happy and safe with me and that was what mattered. It was no use arguing with her anyway, she always knew best.

"Look darling," she'd say. "I've nursed people in their 90s who have smoked all their lives, and it never affected them."

Although this health scare did not worry her, it made me more conscious than ever of her fragility and what might happen next. I needed to return to my search.

The name place of Coolnagreine kept drifting into my mind. Why had no one heard of it? Time to consult Google again. I played with the words and, happily, found what I had been looking for. I had misspelt the name; it was in fact "Coolnagreina".

It had originally offered safe and affordable holiday accommodation for young Protestant women who were shop workers or in domestic service. Perhaps this is why Peggy, who I believe was a domestic servant, went there after giving birth to Mum. Nobody would have known her and it may have been somewhere she could gather her thoughts together.

I decided to ring and ask if they held files on people who stayed or worked there during the 1930s. I spoke to a pleasant young man, very willing to help me but, alas, there were no records of this kind. He did, however, tell me that in order to be accepted there in the time period I was talking about she must have been a young, single, Christian woman of the Protestant faith.

Wicklow County Council had previously been helpful to me and pointed me to their Family History Centre for further help. So, I emailed them to enquire about electoral rolls for 1937–38 that might pinpoint Peggy in the Greystones area. Unfortunately, none existed.

While still persevering but getting nowhere, I had good news of a different kind. Mum's application for sheltered housing had been accepted and she was to live only a five-minute drive away. I was delighted. Although I loved Mum to bits, it made sense for her to have her own place and recoup her independence.

The accommodation was a ground floor flat with French windows looking onto a communal garden. It was so bijou that her settee had to sit across at an angle, as there wasn't room to have it flat against a wall, and her bedroom was more like a corridor; but it offered all she needed, including a lovely female warden, on site, who was very welcoming and always on hand if you had any problems. With the help of Will and his wife, who helped with the refurbishment, and after a period of adjustment, she began to love her little flat. They bought her bespoke taupe velour curtains that hung to the floor and new household items, and she moved in the spring bank holiday of 2011. I'd often pop around and we'd open the French windows and enjoy the sunshine sitting on makeshift plastic chairs, chatting away while she smoked, and surrounded by an array of terracotta pots filled with half-dead parched flowers left by the previous occupant.

Over the course of that summer, I hatched another idea to find Peggy Little's birth details to help me trace her. I had read that you could apply for information under the Freedom of Information Act. So, I telephoned the FOI department (as it was shortened to) at the Dublin hospital where Mum was born, for instructions.

Prior to this I had read online about an illegitimate woman, now in her 70s, who tried to access information about her birth mother under the FOI Act with the support of her son. The hospital had refused and the case went to court. Although a High Court judge agreed in the woman's favour for the information to be released, the hospital managed to get the decision overruled by the Supreme Court, who deemed it not in the public interest to release hospital records of this kind. The story made me feel really sad for her, but at least I realised what I was up against, and it was with caution that I spoke to the person on the other end of the line.

After explaining that I was acting on my mother's behalf as she was elderly, I asked if it was possible for her to access information about her birth. At first, the woman seemed quite helpful and told me how to apply in writing, and that she would send out a consent form for my mother to sign. But when I tentatively asked whether my mother's birth records would contain any information relating to a Margaret Little, it became like lighting blue touch paper and standing back. Her tone changed completely to one of a very officious nature.

"Any information pertaining to the birth mother was given in strictest confidence and therefore can never be disclosed," she quoted, adding, "even after the person in question has died. In fact, we have won court cases in the Supreme Court where people have challenged this."

She spoke with such pride, alongside a total lack of compassion for the enquirer, that it suggested she enjoyed being asked this question. I could see no point in pursuing anything else with her, as I would merely get the corporate line. As she spoke, I felt the muscles tighten at the back of my neck and my body tense with anger. There was an impression you could access information under the FOI Act when, in reality, if the enquiry concerned an illegitimate birth you had absolutely no chance of finding anything. In line with tradition in Ireland, the Church and the state still held all the cards and had no interest in people's suffering or individual cases. The protection of confidentiality surrounding the birth mother had to be upheld at all costs, regardless of any personal situation. To me, it felt more about a control of power than any form of legality. Discovering anything about my grandmother was going to be virtually impossible through hospital documentation. Still, I sent the form off and waited for a reply.

A letter came back, reiterating that any information relating to Margaret Little was deemed personal and would not be released. They also denied having records for a baby "Little" as some files had been lost or were missing. However, they were willing to offer the following details concerning my mother's birth record from the hospital labour ward's record book.

They confirmed that a Margaret Little had given birth to a female child, and gave its birth weight and body length, along with the date and time of birth. This was the extent of the information provided. Although I could appeal against the decision, knowing how the hospital had power to get court cases overturned I thought an appeal wouldn't lead me very far.

Even though I had expected this reply, I felt depressed and demoralised. I had hit a brick wall and there seemed nowhere else to go. How could someone give birth to a child and then disappear into thin air without a trace? It didn't make sense.

I asked Mum what she thought of my findings.

"Oh Sal, I can only think that my mother never wanted me. That's why she left me in the orphanage and made sure she'd never be found."

"But Mum, she came back for you at the Bethany Home in 1938. None of this makes sense."

"Well darling, maybe she did, but in Ireland they'd never want you to know the truth about who you are, or where you hailed from. Ah sure, they're all in it together. Having a child out of wedlock was such a sin that they'd rather take their secrets to the grave."

"Maybe that's true, Mum. But times are changing now, and people are beginning to be more open about things."

"Darling, let me tell you; there have been so many times when I felt I couldn't carry on, especially with the hell of a life I had with your father, him treating me so cruelly. Sure, I thought if my mother only knew what I was going through, she'd help me. If only I could have reached out and touched her, even met her just once, that would've made me happy... but it isn't to be.

I needed a mother so much back then. Feeling unwanted and not having anyone at all to turn to in this whole world is the most soul-destroying thing you can ever imagine. I know you're trying darling, and I love you for that. Perhaps as you're getting closer, something will turn up. My motto is – always live in hope, because without hope, what is there?"

Mum's words dismayed me and made me all the more determined not to give up. The internet was my saving grace. It allowed me to contact so many people in Ireland and ask for their assistance. I gave up on Coolnagreina, one of two addresses that the charity in Dublin had supplied, but decided to go back to investigate the hamlet of Bush in County Wexford. I reckoned that, as it was a complete address and one that had existed, it must have some significance to Peggy in 1936, even if Libby and I had been unable to locate it. My next plan was to contact Wexford Archives for advice.

The archivist had been very helpful, like so many people in Ireland, and further to my emails she sent a list of books on aristocratic houses in the area. She also mentioned a property called Bush House located on the adjoining land of Rathdowney. It was down a country lane, off the main road, and only known to the locals by that name as there were no records of it on Ordnance Survey maps. I still couldn't ascertain the house where Peggy had lived, but the archivist proffered details of a local woman, Riona, who dealt with family research.

Riona, a local genealogist, was a very kind woman indeed. She told me that she was no longer taking on genealogy projects as she was now working full time. However, she would see what she could do.

By now I was single-minded. I had searched the Wexford newspapers and discovered the obituary of a local woman who had lived in Bush all her life. Her story, which had a number of similarities with ours, mentioned the names of her family including a sister, Margaret, known as Peggy, who was born in 1917 and moved from the house in Tagoat to Dublin in 1936. Although the surname was different, O'Donnell, and they were a Catholic family, I thought I was on to something. Despite the social worker in Dublin assuring me that the matron at Bethany would know if a girl was lying about her surname, I thought it a possibility that Peggy may have done just that. I wasn't prepared to rule anything out.

Poor Riona, I thought. My email to her was two and a half pages recounting the story of Mum's illegitimate birth and my crusade to discover her birth mother. It all came pouring out of me as I had no one else to ask and every opportunity seemed like a last chance.

Riona was going to Dublin in a few days' time and would check the records office for the woman who had lived in Bush. In fact, she checked several places for linked records, both at the office and online. I noticed the time on one email: 01:20! She searched for variants of the surname "Little" in both the Republic and Northern Ireland, and typed out her findings and suggestions in a long email to me.

Her kindness and trusting nature really touched me. Although Riona put herself out for me, none of her suggestions matched the information I already had. I didn't want to burden her with my troubles any longer, so moved on to try another route.

Somewhere along the line I had read that the charity Barnardo's offered a service for children who had been brought up in industrial schools and orphanages and were trying to find their birth parents. Scanning their website, I discovered the department I wanted was called "Origins", and after explaining my story yet again they sent a consent form for Mum to sign before they could help.

While I was exploring this next lead Mum's general health had been deteriorating. Apart from continually visiting the doctor for chest infections, she was also suffering from painful joints. Walking was difficult and at my house she had to climb the stairs on all fours to use the toilet. Even stepping on and off the kerb became problematic enough to stop her popping into town by bus. She was finding any small distance increasingly difficult.

As the winter of 2011 approached, she stopped staying her regular two nights a week at my house. It took too much out of her, and alarm bells were starting to ring. Before long I discovered how tasks where she had to raise her arms, like showering, were also proving too strenuous. So, to help her remain independent, I spent every weekend doing a bit of housework for her, giving her a bath on the hoist in the communal bathroom, and taking meals over four or five times a week. Will tried to break the routine up by taking her out for weekend trips, to have her hair done, or buy lunch. But even though she enjoyed their outings they soon became more than she could cope with.

She was always appreciative of whatever I did, but my input didn't stop her growing frailer and frailer. I was deeply worried, but her X-rays and blood tests showed nothing specifically wrong and the doctors put her symptoms down to age and her smoking.

Meanwhile, Celia, the Information Counsellor at Barnardo's, listened intently as I rambled off my theory about the woman in Bush and how there might be a connection. After doing her own searches for Peggy Little, which proved futile, she suggested writing to the descendants of the woman in Bush to see if they knew anything. The process took weeks and although the family did reply, they had no recollection of an illegitimate child.

Celia also followed another lead, of a "Little" family that I had found on the genealogy website, who had a Margaret Little amongst their clan, born in 1917. Again, she wrote to the descendants but my story meant nothing to them.

She suggested a second attempt, under the FOI Act, at the hospital where Mum was born.

I explained it was probably a waste of time after the response I had previously received, but Celia thought it worth another go, and this time she would do it herself on Mum's behalf.

Communication from the hospital was very slow. Sometimes they were silent for months at a time, blaming the delay on staff shortages or such-like. To me, it seemed they were deliberately dragging their heels, but Celia was used to this procrastinating, having handled many similar cases.

Mum's health continued to go downhill, until one day when I called in after work and to my utter shock she announced that she had given up smoking. She had woken up one morning unable to breathe, which frightened her so much that after 57 years she gave up cigarettes, "just like that". It was something I thought she could never do in a million years! It also indicated to me that something more serious was going on inside her body.

Her GP showed marked concern and sent her for another X-ray. This time it showed a shadow on her lung that needed further investigation, so off she went for another CT scan. But before she could hear the results, I received a phone call from her one Saturday morning – and that was about to change all our lives.

Chapter 12

A Change for the Worse

By the time we arrived at the pub it was a quarter to 12. We finished our morning shopping and, for a change, decided to go for lunch before we drove home. Inside it seemed like a cool darkened cavern compared to the blinding sunlight outside. Philip was ordering drinks at the bar while I checked my phone.

"You have one – new – message," said the voicemail. "Beep—"

"Sal, it's Mammy here, darling. I'm in the casualty department at Downfield General Hospital. Oh, Sal, I'm in so much pain in my back, I can't tell you. I pulled the emergency cord at seven o'clock this morning, and the ambulance men came and brought me here. Ring me back when you get this message, Petsey. Beep—"

I felt a wrench in my gut. I knew something like this was about to happen. Even though she was on the strongest prescription painkillers, they had little effect these days.

Phil had returned with the drinks and couldn't help but notice my shocked expression.

"What is it?" he asked.

"It's Mum. She's been taken to hospital."

I tried to ring back but her phone was switched off. My mind darted all over the place, conjuring up the worst. Had our time run out? Was this it?

The drive to the hospital was frantic. Everything seemed to deliberately hold us up: road works, temporary traffic lights, horse boxes…

Even for a Saturday the hospital seemed busy. Having dashed through a maze of corridors we found Mum crumpled on a bed in the casualty department. She was in a frenzy, pulling out various-sized packets and boxes from a white plastic bag and creating an eruption of chaos on her bed.

"Oh, Mum!" was all I could muster.

I threw my arms around her and held her close. She felt like a tiny, clammy rag doll.

"What happened, Mum?"

"Oh Petsey, I'm so glad you're here. They keep asking me what tablets I'm on and I've told them to look in the bag the ambulance men brought from my flat. It has all my medication in it, but they won't listen to me. When I try to explain, they keep saying they're sending me home."

"Home? You're joking, aren't you?"

"No. Would you believe it naw? I've told them I'm not going anywhere until they sort out this pain in my back. D'you know, I've been here since 7:30 this morning and not even a cup of tea!"

A very young-looking nurse came over and I tried to ask about Mum's condition, but she said I needed to speak to a doctor and that once her pain relief was sorted she would be able to go. But Mum wasn't having any of it.

"Now look! I've already told you," she cried. "You need to find out what's wrong with me first and sort out this pain. I am not going anywhere and that's that. I have rights you know!"

The young nurse seemed indifferent to my mother's point of view but did agree to find the doctor.

"We're a bit short-staffed today," she said, "but I'll see if the doctor is free to talk to you for a few moments."

After two hours, a doctor appeared. He beckoned for me and Philip to talk to him outside, in private.

"My name is Gerry, Senior Houseman for Mr Patterson-Birch," he said, offering a firm handshake. "Could you tell me if there is anything wrong with your mother?"

I was puzzled. "Wrong with my mother? What do you mean? Well, she is in a lot of pain. You're the doctor. You should know."

"No, I didn't mean that. I meant... you know?"

"Know what? Are you referring to her mental state?" I gave him an incredulous look. "No. Her mental state is fine, thank you very much. She might seem a little agitated and may have had some problems in the past, but that was 40 years ago. What's that got to do with anything anyway? And what's wrong with her? I need to know."

"Ah yes," he said, putting his hands in his pocket. "The CT scan shows that your mother has two fractures to T5 and T6 of her vertebra, caused by a lower lobe mass infringing on her spinal cord. We think it is probably the result of lung cancer."

I couldn't take it in. Lung cancer... tumour... The words echoed around my head, without seeming to mean anything. I looked at him blankly. "What are you telling me?"

"The tumour, which is pushing outwards, is fracturing her spine. The consultants will be able to verify more next week," he said. "In the meantime, she can go home and we will give her something for the pain."

"You're kidding me, aren't you? You've just told me she has a tumour on her spine that is trying to break out of her back and you're saying she's fit to be released? No wonder she's in such a state."

"No, I'm not saying that. It's just that she can't stay here. We don't have enough beds and we need those we have for more urgent cases coming in."

I was stunned. "And just who is going to look after her?" I continued. "I work full time and she will need a lot of care."

"Oh, I see. Is there nobody else?"

"No. My brother's the same. We both have to work."

"Well, we will have to try and locate the social worker and see if she's free to talk to you."

He looked at his watch. "Look, I'm sorry, you'll have to excuse me. I'm afraid I have to go now."

It felt as if nobody cared. I wondered what had happened to the bedside manner that was all-important when Mum was a nurse.

My brother arrived later and by the time he left they had no option but to leave Mum in casualty until a bed could be found.

Three days later she was transferred to the Medical Investigation Unit. When I arrived, the consultants had finished their ward round and had recommended a metal-boned corset to hold her spine together. She was sitting up in bed looking like a trussed-up chicken, her white goose-pimply arms hanging over the top of an ill-fitting elasticated device that was squashing her breasts and reached up to her shoulders.

"They said I've got to wear this all the time, Sal, day and night. It's so uncomfortable and it's difficult to sleep with it on, but I don't have a choice."

I stroked her hand. "And what did the consultants say?"

"Oh, they said I need radiotherapy to shrink the tumour, but I told them I don't want any treatment."

"But why? It might help."

"Sal, these doctors think they know it all today. I'm telling you, they're not fooling around with me now. I saw enough of that as a nurse to know it's all about experimentation."

Why did she have to be so stubborn and always know best, I asked myself.

"But Mum, what's the alternative? You won't be able to walk again if you don't have the treatment."

"I'll be fine… and, sure, it won't come to that, naw."

"And what about me? Don't you care what I think? I don't want anything happening to you. What would I do?"

"Oh, now Petsey, come on. Listen, don't worry about me, naw. I'm not going to be giving up the ghost just yet. You know what they say, don't you?"

I took a gulp and put my head up but could barely look at her. "No?"

"Where there's life, there's hope."

That was her philosophy on life. Never to give up hope, no matter how bad things seemed. I wondered where that phrase had come from and why she was so tenacious. Was that because life had thrown all it could at her and she still survived?

Later that day I rang one of the consultants, who confirmed that Mum's prognosis was terminal.

"Unless your mother agrees to radiotherapy to shrink the tumour she will lose the use of her legs."

"And chemotherapy?" I asked.

"That's not really an option. She has made it quite clear that she doesn't want any form of treatment."

I felt myself shrinking into my chair as she spoke, stunned by the devastating news.

"Can I ask how long?" I ventured, feeling the phone shake in my hand.

"Difficult to say," hedged the doctor. "It depends on the type of cancer... and whether it has spread to the bones."

"How long?"

"Anything between one and five years. But we can't say for sure because your mother won't agree to more scans or tests."

I put the phone down, ran upstairs and threw myself on the bed, burying my face in a pillow. Why did life have to be so unfair? My mother had a bad start in life but never bore a grudge. And all for what? Now, after all those years of slaving, abuse and being denied love, she was faced with a painful death. The one thing, the only thing, she had wanted from life was to know who her mother was. It seemed a right that every person on the planet should be entitled to, but she would be denied it. And death now seemed closer than I could have imagined.

Having been told that her time was imminently running out, I rang Barnardo's to speak to Celia. I remember the conversation as a blur, with me blubbing down the telephone and probably not making much sense, but I suspect she was used to people getting emotional, such was the nature of her job. Although she came across as cool and collected, I know she sensed my desperation and wanted to help.

"I'm afraid I still haven't heard back about my request for information under the FOI Act," she said. "I've phoned their office and tried to speak to the person dealing with the case, but she's never there and doesn't return my messages. I'll chase them up — try emailing again — and emphasise it's urgent because of Phyllis's condition."

Mum remained in hospital for several weeks but was eventually due to be sent home with a so-called package of care. Her allocated social worker met Mum and me at the hospital.

"Hello, I'm Gemma," she addressed us both, offering a cheery smile and a warm handshake.

"A carer will come first thing in the morning, spend 40 to 45 minutes, get Phyllis up and dressed, give her breakfast and a quick wash," she said. "Then he or she will pop in at lunchtime for about 10 minutes to make her a hot drink. At tea-time, we'll give her half an hour and another drink."

"Hang on a minute," I queried. "40 minutes in the morning doesn't sound very long to do all that. Have you ever seen my mother first thing? With her arthritis it will take all that time just to get out of bed."

"I'm really sorry... Look, I do understand... but I'm afraid that's all the budget allows for. And the carers are very good. I'm sure, after a while, you'll find the time is more than adequate."

"Right. Great. And what about lunchtime? I've arranged for Meals on Wheels to bring a dinner each day, which will just need heating up in the microwave."

"Oh no! They won't be able to do that. They have to consider their travelling time so they couldn't fit it in. Their visit will be literally to pop in, check she's alright and then go."

"What – not two quick minutes? You are joking, aren't you?"

"No, that's the package, I'm afraid."

"But, it's ridiculous. I can't feed her because I work full time, and there's no one else. What is she supposed to do? Starve?"

"Well, you could prepare a sandwich the night before," she suggested, smiling and still trying to sound positive.

It was abundantly clear that the social worker's proposal wouldn't work. Mum would never cope on her own. She could barely stand up by herself, never mind anything else. How did elderly people manage on their own?

As I sat on the edge of the bed I observed scores of people in a whirlwind of activity: nurses changing a bed, a porter collecting someone for X-ray, visitors arriving and leaving. They all seemed to be in another world. It was as though we were watching from outside and they couldn't see us. Then somebody whisked in a tea trolley laden with drinks and sweets for sale.

"Get Mammy a hot cup of tea, darling, will you? I keep asking them will they bring me one, but they're always too busy. By the time they remember, it's cold."

I looked at her bedside cabinet and at two, half-drunk, now abandoned cups of tea forming a milky skin. *Would anyone notice if she didn't have a proper drink all day or night?* I asked myself.

I embraced her frail, hunched body. Her hair was limp and greasy and her cheeks sunken and grey. I asked the staff if anyone was going to give her a bath and hair wash as she had been there several weeks. But, again, I was told they didn't have time. It appeared that nobody had time for anything Mum needed. I would have to do it myself.

Her life felt hopeless. I stared at the floor, overwhelmed and choked with sadness as a mascara-stained tear stung the corner of my eye and dripped on to Mum's cold white hands. She cupped her lean fingers over mine and looked at me with a dull opaque gaze.

"Cam on naw, darling, don't cry," she said. "I'll be fine, so I will. Mammy loves you."

A few days later, after several false starts waiting for the ambulance with Mum ready to go from early morning until evening, they dropped her home around six o'clock. The hospital had lent her a nebuliser, with instructions on how to use it. It would dispense up to four hours of oxygen when she felt she couldn't breathe.

I checked up on her after work and she seemed weak but in good spirits. Then at 10:30 that night she phoned in a panic to say she couldn't breathe and couldn't remember how to use the nebuliser. An ambulance was called and they sorted her out; she did not want to return to hospital.

The warden of the sheltered housing called first thing in the morning. Mum was in a bad way and realised she had no option but to undergo treatment if she wanted to stop the pain. Less than 24 hours after coming home, she was back in hospital. It was, heartbreakingly, the last time she saw her flat.

After a course of successful radiotherapy treatment, I rang to see how she was.

"Well, Pet, I am in a lot of discomfort but at least I'll be walking again soon," she told me.

Downside General said she was still recuperating but couldn't stay there so would be moved to a small local hospital. Luckily, Henley Community Hospital, which had space for her, was only a few miles from where I lived. You couldn't imagine two more polarised places if you tried. From a large general hospital where staff shortages seriously impinged on the time and care they could afford each patient, she went to a place where each person was allocated their own "dignity nurse" to ensure that all their needs would be met.

It handled minor surgical procedures and convalescence, and had its own small X-ray department. As soon as you walked inside the door everything smelt clean and looked orderly. The nursing staff were warm and friendly, and always on hand to answer questions or be as helpful as possible. Over several months, when times were bad, they were a great comfort to me. It was a fine example of how a hospital should function.

A swab test revealed MRSA, so she had to be isolated and, for the first week, Mum was in a single room with its own en suite bathroom, lapping up all the attention she had never had before.

The change of hospital certainly did wonders for her morale; she thought it was like residing at a luxury hotel, being waited upon hand and foot. As always, she rang me from her mobile twice a day. Philip and I had just snatched a mini-break.

"Sal, it's Mammy here."

"Yes, I know."

"Sal, Sal, you'll never guess what!"

"What?"

"Mammy's got her own room! It's got its own bathroom and a television on the wall, which you don't have to pay for, unlike the other place that charged £10 a day. And the girls! Oh, Sal, they're really good to me. They bring me as many cups of tea as I want."

"Well that's really great Mum. I'm pleased for you. But you do realise that you can't stay there for long, don't you? I think it's just until the MRSA's cleared up."

"Ha-ha!" she laughed. "Ah, well naw, we'll see about that."

Oh no, I thought, *that means trouble*. By the time I arrived, as I predicted, she was causing pandemonium. The nursing staff were wheeling her bed into an adjacent room that had three other patients – and she didn't like it one little bit. She was protesting and waving her arms about.

"I have rights you know! I need a room to myself in my condition! Call themselves nurses today? They don't know the meaning of the word! I was happy there with my own little room. I don't want to be with everyone else. Tell them, Sal, tell them."

"I'm sorry about my mum," I apologised, trying to hide my embarrassment.

"It's fine, don't worry, we're used to it," said one, smiling.

"Don't apologise to them naw," snapped Mum. "What about me and my needs?"

"Mum! Please. Can't you just be nice? The nurses are only trying to help you. They're doing their best. I'm sorry, but they need the room for someone else now."

She looked at me mournfully, seeing she had been defeated.

"But I liked being on my own Sal... I did."

I stroked her brow. "I know, Mum. I know."

After a fight with the woman in the next bed over the remote control and having the television on, she finally settled down. I seriously worried how things would work out there for Mum if she carried on like this.

Never having learnt them as a child, she sorely lacked social skills in getting on with others. She would often talk over people; not listen to what they were saying but wanting them to listen to her. How could they understand that she was like this because she had missed out on the support of loving parents to show her any different? Being institutionalised, bullied and undermined had shaped her personality, making her so much more defensive and resilient about everything. It was probably one of the reasons that she didn't really have friends.

Despite a few more spats with her neighbour, and being moved to the other side of the room to keep the peace, after a while the staff began singing her praises.

"Oh, your mum's lovely," said one nurse. "She has us all in stitches with the things she comes out with."

"Really?" I said, not quite believing it.

"Well you know how much she likes ginger biscuits?"

"Yes, I should do. I'm buying her four packets a week."

"Well, she wanted to send Sister Noreen a birthday card for Tuesday and she told us to put a couple of ginger biscuits in it for her, to make her smile."

"Ha-ha," I laughed. "Well I hope it did the trick!"

But it was a local GP, Dr Jeremy Cromwell, or Jezza as he was known to the nurses, who gave the biggest boost to Mum's spirits. He worked at the hospital in between holding his own surgeries.

I had never met a doctor like him. Dispensing with all stuffiness, he was down-to-earth and approachable while always remaining professional. With a glint in his eye and a cheeky grin, he didn't just walk into a room, he sauntered in oozing charm and charisma with his stethoscope flung casually over his open-necked shirt. There was a familiarity about him that was very appealing to patients, and they took him to their hearts.

"Hiya, Phyllis. And how are you today?" he enquired, shirt sleeves rolled up and sitting alongside her on the bed.

She looked up at him and beamed a big smile when he gave her a hug.

"Ha-ha! Well I'm better now I've seen you, my handsome boy!"

He gave her a broad smile. "Sleeping alright, are we?"

"Ah, well, doctor, this corset is so uncomfortable to wear. It doesn't fit me properly and, no, I don't get a good night's sleep. It's terrible if you want to know the truth."

He scratched his head. "I can imagine," he agreed. "It's a bit of a 'one size fits all' on the NHS, although we might be able to have one specially made. But let's see if you can do without it for a while. What do you think?"

"Oooh, doctor, that would be wonderful."

"Good. Well leave it with me and I'll ask sister to have it removed."

Mum, who had been hyper all her life, was now finding it difficult to sit in bed all day. The problem of the television had not gone away: the other patients didn't want it on, but she did.

I visited one Saturday evening to find her hobbling about the ward. She couldn't stand up straight and was hunched over, but still getting around.

"Mum, what are you doing?" I asked.

"Oh Sal, I'm just going for a little walk. I can't stand to be cooped up all day."

I noticed that the television was on, but the sound was turned down.

"You don't want to watch telly then?"

"Well, it's only that Noël Cowell and the *X Factor* programme."

"You mean Simon Cowell, don't you? Noël Coward was an actor."

"Oh, whatever! That Noël Cowell doesn't know how to make music. It's a load of rubbish. Why can't they put something decent on?"

"Would you like me to change the channel over?"

"Ah no, Petsey, it's alright. The others don't want it on anyway."

"Hare, Pet!" Mum called out, catching Staff Nurse Bridie as she came in. "Can you bring me a cup of tea. I'm gasping, so I am."

"I will in a minute Phyllis. Let me finish attending to this patient first."

"But I haven't had one since this afternoon."

"I'll be with you as soon as I can, Phyllis," she said, checking the old lady's pulse.

"Mum, don't be so demanding," I chided quietly. "The nurse said she will get you one as soon as she can."

I could see she was becoming very bored being stuck in hospital, so I left the ward and spoke to the sister at the nursing station.

"How long before you think she can go home?" I enquired.

"Oh, not long. I'd think another couple of weeks. It depends what the doctor decides."

Great, I thought. *The sooner she is back home the better,* realising that I'd have to give her even more time than before she was hospitalised. *That doesn't matter*, I thought, *I'll work something out.* Little did I know what was to lie ahead.

All this time I was patiently emailing Celia at Barnardo's, but she'd still not heard back from her second attempt to access the FOI Act. Our frustration was mounting and I suspected it was a deliberate act on behalf of the Dublin hospital, who did not want to disclose any information.

One morning in early August my thoughts about Peggy Little were put on hold for a while, when I received yet another shocking phone call.

"Hello Sally, it's Staff Nurse Bridie here. I'm afraid I've some bad news for you."

I held my breath.

"Mum?"

"Yes. Phyllis had a fall last night, getting out of bed… and it appears she has broken her hip."

"How bad is it?"

"Not good, I'm afraid. Would you like to come in and see her this morning? We don't normally encourage it outside visiting hours, but under the circumstances…"

I didn't know what to say.

"Hello… hello? Are you still there?" she asked. "Are you alright, Sally?"

"A f…f-fall? How did that happen?"

"We're not exactly sure, but it seems she was getting up by herself to use the loo. We think she just slipped."

With that, instead of heading for work, I jumped in my car and tore straight to the hospital. Mum was incoherent and barely conscious.

"Mum… Mum!"

Her eyelids fluttered. "Sa-l," she mumbled, before they closed again.

"Oh dear, Mum, no…"

She drifted off into a deep sleep, leaving me sitting there distraught and wondering if hope was now dwindling away. Beside myself, my pain turned to anger and I approached the nursing station where Sister Noreen and another nurse were sitting.

I banged my hand on the counter. "Why didn't you tell me before!" I screamed at them. "Why? I could have got here earlier. Now I don't know what… I mean – how long she's…"

I burst into tears as it sunk in what a fall could mean to someone in her condition. It wasn't their fault and I did apologise afterwards, but strain and anxiety got the better of me and untethered my emotions.

Sister Noreen was taken aback by my outburst but remained unflustered.

She was kind and reassuring as I broke down in front of her, and promised they were doing everything they could and would be sending her for an X-ray to assess the damage. But whatever the result, she would have to lie on her back for at least eight weeks. There was a strong likelihood she may not walk again, if she survived. The irony hit me hard. She'd only accepted radiotherapy because she didn't want to lose her mobility, and now this had happened.

The outlook looked bleak and I started praying with a passion, as I had never prayed before. I begged God to give me more time with Mum and to help me trace her mother before it was too late. It took me back to when I was a little girl and Mum was ill. How I prayed that He would not let her die until I was a least 20 years old, which I considered to be ancient. Even when I reached 20 my prayers didn't change, although now I was asking God to keep her alive until I was 50. My world had always seemed so uncertain, but my mother's love was the one thing that saw me through. Without that love I wasn't sure if I could carry on.

Mum fought back with her usual determination, even through high doses of morphine. She completely lost interest in television, and pretty much everything else, because focusing on anything proved too difficult. She didn't even use her mobile phone to ring me as she found it too complicated through the morphine haze even to press the single key that dialled my number. Like so many other times, she found the inner strength to survive. Perhaps God heard my prayers. It took weeks before she was fully coherent and on the road to recovery, and the strong painkillers sent her into some sort of utopian world.

And then one afternoon, out of the blue, I was greeted by Mum singing at the top of her voice.

On Mother Kelly's doorstep
Down paradise row,
I'd sit along o'Nelly
She'd sit along o'Joe...

"Your mother's holding court again," quipped Sharon, smiling as she saw me entering the room.

"Mum, you sound like you're enjoying yourself. I didn't know you liked to sing?"

The patients opposite looked at her with disdain. I could see they were not amused. And Jean in the next bed, who never said anything, just sat expressionless with her mouth wide open as if in a trance.

She'd got a little hole in her...

"What me, Petsey?" Oh, yes, I love singing. I'm havin' a grand old time!"

… a hole in her shoe, a hole her sock, where her toe peeped through…

She was oblivious that she might be irritating everyone, but the nurses thought it was hilarious and goaded her on.

"I've never seen her like this," I said to Sharon, her care assistant. "I didn't even know she knew this song; it's well before her time. Do you think it's the morphine?"

"No idea," she replied, "but whatever it is, it certainly makes our day!"

A male nurse walked over and swished the curtains around Jean, wafting the smell of urine into the air. He glanced over at my mother and grinned.

"Hello, Phyllis," he said. "You sound happy today."

"Oh, I'm in fine form, Timmy. Fine form."

"She's always happy," piped up Sharon.

"Ha-ha," laughed Timmy. "Well, Phyllis I'll have whatever you're having."

I looked on, dumbfounded.

"Sing the monkey song again, Phyllis, go on," encouraged Sharon.

"Ooh, you like that one, do you?" Mum chuckled.

The women opposite rustled their newspapers in front of them in disgust.

All the monkeys in the zoo, with their bottoms turning blue…

"Again!" laughed Sharon.

So, to everyone's amazement, months after being given a maximum life expectancy of a few weeks, Mum was walking. The medical staff had worried that her cancer may have spread to the bones, in which case they may not have healed properly, but she was determined not to be beaten. She lay still for two months, as told, until she could feel movement in her hip again.

Dr Cromwell suggested that they see if she could put her weight on a Zimmer frame without toppling over. To his astonishment, and gingerly at first, she not only walked but before long was chasing him around the nursing station on her frame, albeit slowly.

"Cam here, naw. I want to speak to you, my handsome little pet," she'd say, lifting her frame carefully with each move.

"You'll have to catch me first, Phyllis," he'd tease as he played along. I looked on, speechless with delight.

But her mobility had been severely affected and she needed a wheelchair even for short distances. Her general health continued to yo-yo: one day she'd be fine, the next she'd develop a urine or chest infection which resulted in her being confused. I found it hard to deal with as we always loved chatting together, even about nothing. But when she was poorly she was like someone else who I barely recognised.

By late October the hospital was keen for Mum to go, as they felt she was now bed blocking. There had been more delays in her recovery because, over-confident as usual, she had two more minor falls that fractured her ankle and some toes.

A decision about her future became imperative and it was agreed she would give up her flat and live permanently in a nursing home. I dreaded that her mind would suffer once she lost her much-relished independence, and she might give up. But there was nothing I could do. As much as it pained my heart, her illness has gone too far.

Celia from Barnardo's emailed me. She had at last heard back from the Dublin hospital, who apologised for the delay but were now processing her application. Another month went by before they decided to uphold their original decision and tell us nothing. They reiterated the case they had won in the Supreme Court against a family who had challenged their right to information and lost. However, if we were unhappy with the decision they invited us to appeal in writing to the Information Commissioner who would make a final independent ruling. Celia and I discussed it and decided it was the only thing left I could try. What else could I do? I had exhausted every other avenue.

Before I knew it, Christmas arrived. The hospital staff were becoming more distant as they needed Mum to move on after six months. I was under pressure to find her a home but was concerned because her health was going downhill. Her face was bloated and she felt sick all the time. The staff put it down to chest infections but I instinctively knew this wasn't right. She had never suffered from nausea with previous chest infections. Who was I to say? I wasn't a medical professional. But my intuition was about to be proved right – again.

Chapter 13

No Closer

It had been snowing intermittently and, with the temperatures plummeting below freezing the roads were now slushy and slippery. I got a call at work, that Mum had been moved. The last thing I wanted was to drive in those conditions but I dearly needed to make sure she was alright, especially when she looked so frail and grey.

The nursing home had a very utilitarian façade that I hadn't noticed a few weeks earlier when I was shown around. I tapped in the security code to enter the building and signed myself into the guest book. The unmanned reception area inside was dominated by a heavy-duty turquoise carpet that swept upstairs to the main facilities. At the top I opened the landing door and my face flushed instantly with stifling heat and a lingering smell of stale cabbage. *God, it's hot in here,* I thought, as I whipped off my scarf.

I hurried down the corridor, anxiously looking for Mum's room number. My first impression was how many people they had managed to cram onto one floor; there must have been 40 rooms. Each open door drew your eyes in and down a narrow passage to a haunted face staring out at the other end. *How sad,* I thought.

Many had trays of food on their laps although the dining room and large day room were deserted. A half-hearted attempt had been made to make it look cosy with chintzy curtains and a cabinet filled with ornaments, but without people it felt lifeless. I asked one of the nurses why the residents were alone in their rooms and not in the communal areas.

"Oh, they prefer it that way, so we don't make them mix if they don't want to. We tried it a few years ago, but it didn't work," she justified.

"Really?" I quizzed, not quite believing her.

How depressing, I thought. *Do people just come here to die? Just how is Mum going to cope with this when she's so full of life?*

The nurse led me to Mum's room.

"This is tiny," I said, as I popped my head around the door. "There isn't even space for a wardrobe. Where is Mum supposed to hang her clothes?"

"Oh, I think you'll find they don't need much here. There's a chest of drawers with a television on top... and they have their own private bathroom with a toilet and washbasin."

That still didn't sell it to me.

In the middle stood the bed with Mum tucked up in it, cot sides up; it occupied most of the room. I tried to squeeze past the end to sit on a chair by the window but it was so close to the chest of drawers that the knobs dug into my thighs. *Can they really charge people a thousand pounds a week to be in a place like this?* I wondered.

"How's she doing?" I enquired.

"Oh, she sleeps a lot. Doesn't want to eat much... although we did manage to get a few spoonfuls of Rice Krispies and milk down her this morning," she replied.

Mum stirred and flickered her eyes when she heard my voice.

"Sal," she mumbled feebly. "Sal, is that you? I want the toilet; tell them I want to go to the toilet."

I gave the nurse an anxious look.

"I wouldn't worry," she assured me. "We've put a catheter in, just as a precaution. We think your mother may have a urine infection, which might explain why she's like she is."

"It's alright Mum, don't worry about that for the moment. You're going to be taken good care of here."

"Where's Will darling?" she asked.

"He'll get here as soon as he can," I said.

"Petsey, I feel so ill... so sick..." Her eyes drooped and she faded again.

I leant over the cot sides and stroked her cold, pale fingers. She was still wearing the fake emerald ring from Marks and Spencer's that I had bought her for last year's birthday. It was only cheap but that didn't matter to her. It was with an odd assortment of others, including a skull and crossbones, all on the one finger. Seeing her eclectic taste reminded me of some months before when I had to clear out her flat. One minute I'd have tears streaming down my face at the thought of her having to give it up; the next, I'd be laughing at what I was pulling out of her cupboards. A myriad of clothes was stuffed to bursting in the drawers: they were mostly black and included rubber bondage trousers, teenage hoodie tops, skimpy G-string lingerie and a pair of men's Y-fronts, all bought from second-hand shops, and none of which she would ever have worn.

Then my mind drifted to that day I gave her the ring. She had babbled with excitement when she opened the box and tried it on.

"Ha-ha, would you look at that naw? Oh, Petsey, it's lovely! You've got such good taste, so you have – and you're always so good to Mammy. What would I do without you?"

Those words hit me hard... *The truth is more like what will I do without her*, I thought.

With no improvement in Mum's condition after a fortnight, I decided I wasn't going to be fobbed off anymore, so spoke to the manager about my concerns.

"Well, if it'll put your mind at rest, I'll arrange for some blood tests," she said. "They'll give us a better indication of what's going on."

Thank God someone was listening to me at last.

When the phone rang a few days later the road outside looked hazardous and it was snowing again. Looking out from my study window, I saw people wrapped up in scarves and shawls struggling to walk through a blizzard that had come from nowhere.

"Hello, is that Phyllis Herbert's daughter? It's Dr Cromwell, here."

"Yes, it is," I confirmed. "Is something wrong?"

"Phyllis, I'm afraid..."

"What?"

"I'm sorry, but it's not good news."

"What'd you mean?"

"The blood tests came back." He took a deep breath.

"Yes... and...?"

No answer.

"Doctor...?"

"It looks as if Phyllis's kidneys are really struggling. Her renal count is down to nine – a healthy person's should be sixty."

"What are you saying? Are her organs packing up?"

"I'm so sorry. I really am."

"Is she going to die?" I dared ask." I heard myself speak the words as though another person was saying them.

"She's quite ill. Could be the tablets she's on. I'll see if lowering the dosage will make a difference."

"What do you mean about the tablets?" I asked.

"Well, this particular medication can put a lot of strain on the kidneys."

"Doctor, if she hasn't got long left, then I want to bring her home here to die. Can I do that?"

"It's not up to me I'm afraid. I'll have to get one of the care team to ring you."

"But she's my mother."

"I'm sorry, I wish I could say… but I don't have the authorisation. I'll get Judy from the care team to speak to you as soon as possible."

I put the phone down and suddenly felt the harsh thud of silence. I swallowed hard. Gazing out I watched the snow falling in a soft rumble, blanketing cars and hedges in a muted world. Nothing felt real; it was all too hard to grasp.

Mum's photo smiled down at me from the wall, reminding me of a happy day we had spent in Dorking, five years earlier. We were having a cup of tea in the market square and, as usual, she had a fag in one hand and was laughing out loud at something I'd said. I loved it when she laughed. Her unrestrained cackle was infectious, enough to lift anyone's spirits.

That had been a rare moment for us, spending leisure time together, as we were both generally working. Why hadn't we made more times like that? Why did I always think I could put it off until another day? I closed my eyes and felt my heart sink into despair.

The phone interrupted me.

"Hello, is that Sally?"

"Yes."

"It's Judy, from the care team. Dr Cromwell asked me to give you a call about your mother."

"Yes, that's right. I want to bring her home. I have just learnt that she may only have a short time to live."

"Hmm, yes, he told me. I'm so sorry to hear about Phyllis."

"Well?"

"I'm afraid it's not possible Sally."

"Why not?"

"Well… because she is being looked after in the best possible place, and she couldn't get the care she needs at home with you."

"The best possible place? More like a mausoleum, I'd say."

"I can imagine how you feel, really I can."

I tried to stay positive. "What about Continuing Care? The hospital told me that if someone is going to pass away, their care can be paid for at home or in hospital for about three weeks before they die."

"Yes, it can, but they have to be assessed first, which normally takes about two months… and your mother wouldn't get the funding."

"But why? She's dying. She hasn't got two months. When do they come out to assess? When someone becomes a corpse?"

"The thing is, you don't know that she's dying for sure."

"Dr Cromwell virtually told me she's going into renal failure. How much worse does it have to get?" I gulped and choked back my tears.

"Look, I'm really sorry. I'm sure it must be really difficult for you right now," she said. "Are you okay, Sally?" She could hear my sobs but she couldn't feel my pain.

Her words faded into the background as I was transfixed by the snow outside transforming everything into a white heaven. So peaceful.

"Sally… Sally, are you still there?"

Traffic had stopped, people had passed… the silence was blissful.

"Sally can you still hear me?

Nothingness. Tranquillity.

"I do understand, you know," mouthed Judy.

"Understand! How could you possibly understand?" My simmering fury erupted like a pent-up magma chamber, exploding for all its worth.

"Sally, I think you should calm down."

"I *need* to bring her home. Please, let me bring her home."

"I'm sorry, but it's not going to happen. There just isn't the funding."

"What if it was your mother, eh?"

"Sally, this isn't really helping."

"Go on, what if it was your mother?"

"It's not my mother though, is it? I do empathise but…"

"You'd want the same as me, wouldn't you?"

"Well, no. I'd want what was best for her. Now please try and get a grip."

"A grip? What can you know about anything? My mother is dying and you tell me to get a grip?"

"Sally, please! You must try and control yourself. Perhaps you should speak to your GP. Maybe some counselling would help you.

Without another word I slammed the phone down. I was breathless with rage, and felt my body quivering with the trauma, but I couldn't give up. I wouldn't. Mum's determined spirit had defied the odds on so many occasions, perhaps it would again this time. I hoped. I prayed. They were the only things left to cling onto.

At the end of the month I received a long-awaited email from Celia at Barnardo's.

Tuesday January 29 2013 16:27

Hi Sally,

How are you? Sorry I've not be in touch but I was off over Christmas and now only work two days a week, so it is taking longer to catch up with my backlog of cases.

I am yet to hear from the hospital about the appeal; they are frustrating me with their delays. They have advised me that my application is on a waiting list and normal processing times do not apply. I am currently in this process with another of my cases and it is the same story.

The other thing I have to tell you is that I will be leaving Barnardo's soon and you may have to continue with the appeal process yourself, but I'll leave it up to you to decide if that is what you want to do.

Talk to you soon, and give your mum my best wishes.

Celia

It was quite a blow hearing that Celia was leaving, as she had been helpful, but although it was a scary prospect I knew I couldn't give up. I would take on the appeal process and hope I would have a chance to put my mother's case before the Independent Commissioner. After all, what had I to lose?

By early February there was a slight improvement in Mum's condition, after Dr Cromwell adjusted the medication that had been affecting her kidneys. She still looked poorly but was able to chat to me again.

"Sal, ooh it's lovely to see you. Will darling is in South Africa on holiday at the moment, so I'm glad that I've got you to come and visit me so often."

"How are you, Mum?"

"Ah, Petsey, I'm feeling a bit better every day... but still not right."

"Well, I'm relieved you're still here. I thought for a while... well you know... You have to fight Mum. Understand? I don't want to lose you. You mean everything to me."

"Now don't fret, Sal. Mammy's not giving up that easily. I have been through enough in my life, and I don't give in. You always remember, darling: 'Where there's life, there's hope.'"

"I'll try. I must say though, Mum, I've never met anyone like you. I swear, you've got more lives than a cat."

"Ha-ha-ha! D'you think so, naw? How are the cats by the way? Don't you forget to give them a kiss from me."

"Oh, they're fine. Hopefully you'll see them again soon."

"Well, if they ever let me get out of this bed! They keep the cot sides up all the time and they won't let me use the toilet. It's so degrading, being put on a hoist and having to go in a plastic bag. It makes me feel like an animal."

"Don't worry, Mum, I'll have a word with the staff."

I soon discovered why they were so overprotective. The management were paranoid about health and safety and wouldn't let her walk even a few paces to the toilet by herself because they didn't know if her bones had healed from her previous falls. I could understand that, but they'd made no attempt to get her X-rayed nor see if she could be rehabilitated. What would have happened if I hadn't intervened? Nothing.

Although they kept promising to contact the doctor, after three weeks I contacted Dr Cromwell myself to arrange for her leg and foot to be X-rayed. After seeing her at his X-ray clinic the news was good: her ankle and toe fractures had healed and it was a case for physiotherapy to get her walking on her Zimmer frame, which I had to arrange.

Then the distressing calls started, with Mum crying down the phone. This wasn't like her, she never usually cried at anything.

"Sal, they still won't let me go to the toilet by myself. They keep me in this bed like a prisoner. I'm so upset, Sal! It's like I've been institutionalised all over again."

The nursing home tried to reassure me that they'd get Mum walking, but as the weeks passed and Mum's mind grew stronger, her phone calls became more and more inconsolable.

"They never come when I ring the bell. Even when I keep ringing and ringing it, they ignore me. They just leave me here to rot. It's inhuman. All I want is a cup of tea. They don't understand I'm a person and have feelings – and I'm not even old like a lot of them in here."

One evening I got an unexpected call from a very young sister-in-charge, who was finding my mother's cries for attention extremely hard to deal with.

"Is that Sally? It's Sister Dork here. I'm afraid your mother is in a very agitated state – shouting and causing a disturbance – and I don't know what to do. Can you help?"

I was surprised to get a call of that nature, but I agreed to speak to Mum to see if I could calm things down. She was sobbing heavily when I called her.

"I'm going to lose the use of my legs unless they let me walk. I'll never be able to walk again. Sal, you must tell them. Please, for Mammy now. They won't listen to me and they don't seem to care."

I made up my mind, then and there, that I was getting her out of that place. I couldn't bear to see her so desperately unhappy. But before I had the chance to look for another nursing home, she was requested to leave. She was accused of being rude to the staff and, apparently, they couldn't deal with her any longer. It was the best thing that could have happened. I soon realised that just as the care in hospitals varies, so it does in nursing homes.

Spring arrived and, with it, a final email from Celia at Barnardo's: it had been a pleasure to work on Mum's case and she was sorry that they had not been able to trace her family but, unfortunately, this often happened. She went on to say that the Commissioner's office would be in touch: it was just a matter of waiting to hear if they would grant me an appeal.

This felt like my last opportunity to find Margaret Little before the news would be too late for my mother to hear. Was I going to find another dead end? The fact that no records could be found seemed implausible. None of it made sense and time was running out for us to find the truth.

Trinity Trees, Mum's new nursing home, was a blessing. It was run as a charity by a strict order of nuns, mostly of Indian origin. Their philosophy was one of mind, body and spirit; not just about functional caring like the other place. Here was real care. They had their own convent on site, with a separate chapel for the residents, but you didn't have to be Catholic to reside there as they took all faiths. They had a hairdressing salon and an outside bowling green for the more able-bodied. Each person was treated as an individual, and everybody, from cleaners to senior nursing staff and nuns, were extraordinarily kind, friendly and filled with compassion and love.

I had viewed a few nursing homes and although some offered boutique decor with sparsely laid out furniture and village style environments, none of them seemed homely or warm. However, as soon as I walked through the doors at Trinity Trees it felt light and spacious, well decorated like a person's home, with a fire surround, comfy sofas and a television on the wall – and that was just the reception area.

The corridors were wide and the rooms spacious with plenty of place for personal belongings, and the dining room was lively with the buzz of conversation and clinking of knives and forks. The residents were even allowed wine with their meals if they liked a drink. Instantly, I knew that this was the right place for Mum.

It took a short time for her to settle in, but I saw a transformation not only in her mental and emotional state, but her physical condition too. I could not believe it. She looked better than I had seen her in years. As soon as she was assessed, the cot sides were removed from her bed and she was encouraged to hobble by herself on her Zimmer frame to the toilet in her own modern wet room. And the more independence she was allowed, the more her health improved.

"Mum, you're sitting up in the chair!" I said.

"Oh yes Petsey, I'm grand."

"You're astounding. Only a few months ago you were at death's door, but now look at you."

"Ah well, they look after me here very well, and I've got everything I need, and I'm not restricted to my room. I can walk about anywhere and do whatever I want."

How it made my heart glad, that she seemed happy at last. Although it was difficult for her to accept she would never return to living on her own, once she resigned herself, not only did she accept it but she embraced her new life at Trinity Trees.

That summer, I made up my mind that her partial recovery would allow us to maximise the time we had left together, while still making it my priority to discover her family. I fitted in as many activities as I could. We went shopping and out for tea, and even to the local zoo. We sat outside in the sunshine, me talking and her not listening properly, while she grew obsessed with trying to win on the scratch cards. My brother treated her to lunch at garden centres, and for the rest of that year and some of the next she was as fine as she could be.

In August 2013, I finally heard back from the Commissioner's Office in Ireland. They had reviewed their decision to release information under the FOI Act and gave me a date for submission. Apparently, Mum's request was the only one out of 14 to be granted an appeal. This meant an investigator would be assigned to her case, but the length of time to process it depended on the complexity involved, so it could take up to another four months.

I waited again, and by late November I had made my submission by email, explaining time was of the essence as my mother was terminally ill. At last someone agreed to speak to me on the telephone and release information. We arranged a convenient time in early December, and a pleasant woman with whom I'd corresponded earlier, rang me.

"I am sorry to say there is no new information to offer you. You have it all already," she said.

"You're joking, right?"

"No. I'm afraid nothing new has come to light. Some paediatric files from the labour ward are still missing for a few years surrounding your mother's birth. I'm very sorry, I know how much this must mean to you."

"But how do I know you're telling me the truth?"

"I can assure you I am," she said. "I'm not withholding anything but, unfortunately, I can't tell you anything that you don't already know."

It seemed like a final blow and I felt completely gutted. After so long, patiently waiting and waiting, I had reached the end of the line and found "no new information". Without further clues about Margaret Little, her date of birth or where she had come from, I had no hope of finding her. Was this the end of my search?

And worst of all, now I had to break it to Mum. I felt as if I had given her false hopes and was devastated. I decided to tell her straight away, in person, so I jumped in the car and drove down the road to the nursing home.

She was in the dining room, noisy with chatter as steaming plates of food were served to the six tables of residents. At first, I couldn't see Mum. Then I popped my head around a corner and found her on a table away from the others, gently trying to coax another resident to eat a spoonful of food. The woman she was feeding looked as if she had the mental capacity of a child, but Mum was enjoying helping her. Despite her own needs, she still wanted to care for and nurture people, who she thought were less fortunate than herself.

"Hello Petsey," she said, looking up when she noticed me.

My heart felt overwhelmed with sadness. Some of the women on the other tables heard my voice and gave me guarded looks. I could see that they had their own clique of friends and Mum would never be accepted as part of their crowd; she was different and didn't fit in. Being a good 10 years younger than most of them, she was too young to remember the war and everything associated with it, so they had nothing in common. She dressed younger than them and came across as eccentric in her behaviour, which they found off-putting. I don't think they understood 'different'.

I lowered my voice to a whisper. "Sorry, Mum, I forgot you were in the middle of lunch. I'll wait in your room, shall I?"

"Oh, that'll be grand darling. I'll be with you in a moment, when I have finished feeding Florence. Put the telly on if you like."

Paul O'Grady and his programme *For the Love of Dogs* was being repeated on ITV. I sat on the edge of the bed, with the sound turned down, distracted by woodpeckers on the giant redwood tree outside her window. They seemed so close I could almost touch them.

The door opened and Mum hobbled in on her swollen bare feet, using her walker for support.

"Turn the sound up Pet. You know I love this programme," she said. "He's a gorgeous little fellow, don't you think?"

"Who... Paul O'Grady? You know he's gay, Mum?"

"Ha-ha-ha, is he naw?" she said, laughing.

"Yes."

"Oh, but he always wears such lovely suits. I could really fancy him."

"Mother, really... behave."

"And he does such good animal programmes."

"I know, I know. But before you watch him, I've got some news to tell you."

"Would you look at that naw!"

"What?" She pointed to an obese dog. "The very size of it..."

"Mum, can you listen for a moment. I want to tell you about what the Independent Commissioner in Ireland said about information from the hospital relating to your mother."

"Oh, Pet. And what did she have to say? Have they given you some good news?"

"Sit down will you. I don't know quite how to tell you this."

She searched my face for an answer as I struggled to find the words.

"What Petsey? What?"

"Well, the woman spent an hour on the phone to me, but at the end of it she said we had all the information already, so there was nothing to add."

"Nothing to add? Oh." She thought quietly for a moment. "Oh, Sal darling, all that effort you put into it. You see, they don't want you to know anything in Ireland!"

"I don't think it's that, Mum. Record keeping was very poor years ago. I guess it is just something we have to accept."

"Accept! How can I accept it Sal? These people in high places have no clue what it feels like. They don't care. I don't believe that about the records. They must know something, they must, surely?"

"I know Mum and I do understand, really I do, but what can I say? How can I make it better? We have nothing to go on and there are no more clues."

"All I wanted was to know my mother's name. Is that too much to ask? I guess that's it now, I'll go to my grave without ever knowing who she was."

I sat beside her, took her hand in mine and looked into her face.

"Well, at the moment I really have exhausted all avenues, but I promise you – and I mean this – that as long as I live, even after you're gone, I'll keep searching for Margaret and will never give up."

She looked up at me sadly, as though she knew it was already too late.

"Well, darling, my mother may not have wanted me, but at least I have you and Will. And you both mean the world to me… so, at the end of the day… that's what matters."

With the new year Mum's health waivered again. Occasionally she felt sick and her appetite was ever declining. She stopped going to the dining room and also stopped wanting to go out for trips as it took too much energy. She was gradually withdrawing into herself. Although I remained in the doldrums about our family research, I concentrated on enjoying our time and tried to put it out of my mind.

Pessimistically, I felt Christmas 2014 might be her last. That December I bought a white Christmas tree for her room and decorated it with baubles and flashing purple fairy lights, which she just loved. I sat on her bed and we watched all her favourite children's DVDs together: *Puss in Boots*, *Fantastic Mr Fox* and *Garfield*. We talked about everything, she laughed out loud – a lot – and we enjoyed each other's company. In my heart, I pretended we could go on like this forever, but my head sensed the truth.

Chapter 14

A Last-Ditch Attempt

The white tree and purple baubles were packed away in a box marked "Mum". But she was reluctant to let the flashing fairy lights go after the euphoria of Christmas. She had loved her bedroom looking like a mini version of the Blackpool Illuminations.

"Ah Sal, can't I have them up a bit longer?" she implored.

"No, it's past the sixth so you know it's not lucky. I'll put them in my loft and they can come out next year."

My words sounded reassuring, designed to give hope, but intuitively I knew it was the last time we'd see them together.

They were little things to begin with. Sometimes, I thought it was me who had forgotten when she didn't phone, but gradually I understood that she was becoming less and less communicative.

For years, no matter where she was, she had rung me religiously every day; sometimes once, mostly twice and, more often than not, several times. We always had this close relationship. Even if we rowed we very soon put it right with half a dozen phone calls. But now our ritual of phoning each other was broken, leaving me bereft. She was changing; or something was changing.

Her concentration lapsed quite frequently, and she'd ask me to repeat something. She stared blankly at the television without paying attention. She'd tell me the clock on the wall said 2:30 when, in fact, it was a quarter to five; and she slept more and more and ate less and less. Her tired soul was wavering and, despite some residual fight to live, she was on a downward path.

I called in after work one night and noticed a pile of unused scratch cards, all lined up and sitting on her bedside locker. I felt panicked by this sight, which was so unlike her.

"Aren't you going to play anymore, Mum?" I asked.

"Oh, I don't really feel like it," she replied.

Throughout her time at Trinity Trees she'd been addicted to playing the scratch cards or the lottery, driving me and Will to distraction for her weekly fix. We bought them for her, as her meagre £30 monthly council allowance, after deducting her care fees, soon evaporated, leaving her with nothing to look forward to.

I felt aggrieved at the sheer injustice. She had been so used to spending her money freely on anything she enjoyed, and why not? Having worked like a Trojan all her life, right up until she was 73, she had well and truly contributed to paying for her future care. It wasn't as if she'd ever been materialistic. Her only joys had been second-hand shops, scrambled egg on toast in the local café and scratch cards. Her body might be that of a decaying nearly 80-year-old woman, but her mind and her spirit were much younger.

She stared into an empty space. A drip glistened on the end of her nose, hanging tantalisingly on an invisible thread.

"Here, Mum, have a tissue," I prompted, offering her the box that was lying on the bed.

"What?"

"The drip. You've got a drip on the end of your nose."

"Oh, have I? Thanks darling, I didn't realise."

"Are you alright?"

She gave me a tired smile. "Who me? Oh, I'm fine, Sal."

"Is there anything at all you want?"

"No, Petsey, there's nothing; only you. I miss you so, Sal – you'll never know how much."

Her words cut right through to my heart. I never realised. I came to see her as frequently as I could, albeit for a short time, but I suppose it just wasn't the same – nothing was. In the space of a few short years the world we had once shared of nestling up on the sofa, cosying up with the cats, watching *The Vicar of Dibley*; it had all changed. It had gone, forever.

"I thought you were happy here?"

"I am, Sal, but it's not like being at home with you."

"Oh Mum…Why didn't you stop smoking years ago?"

She shrugged and sighed. "It was normal, Petsey. Everybody did it in those days."

"We could have had more time together…"

"I know, and I wish I had, but you don't think at the time."

I observed her frail body. Her face was swollen, as were her feet, which she had to keep elevated at all times. The once emerald sparkle that had emanated from her soul was now replaced by a foggy gaze from sunken eye sockets, and a downturned smile.

"Is there nothing you'd like?"

"Like? Well there's a question. Well, you could take me away to Ireland. I'd like to go back there."

Of all the things she could have asked.

"Can't you take me there, Petsey… please?" she pleaded. "I'd really love that, you know. Just you and I together on a little holiday… and you could look after me. It'd be grand and I'd be so happy. It'd be just the two of us. You and me Sal."

Her eyes filled with hope.

"Oh dear, Mum. You know how much I'd love that; really, I would… but I'd never be able to manage you. You'd need 24-hour nursing and that costs money, which neither of us has. You know I would if I could, don't you?"

She stared back into the empty space.

"Mum? Did you hear me?"

"Yes darling… I did," she conceded with a reluctant nod.

How I ached with wretchedness. Why did I have to shatter her illusions? Couldn't I have let her dream, indulge in her fantasy? Why was I so forthright and practical and realistic? It was like refusing someone on death row their last wish. If only I'd arranged a trip when she was well, but it hadn't crossed my mind. I was just too damned selfish, wrapped up in my own problems: my work, my research, my own life.

Sister Jeanne parked her drugs trolley outside and came in briskly, breaking into my reveries.

"'allo Phyllees, darleen'. I've come to give you your medication."

Sister Jeanne was an Indian nun in her early 30s, and the sweetest person you could ever wish to meet. She nodded her head a lot when she spoke and was permanently cheerful, with a dazzling smile that lit up the room. She held out a small container of tablets to Mum and handed her a glass of pink-coloured water.

"Thank you, Pet," said Mum, as she gulped down the pills and placed her glass on the windowsill. Sister Jeanne removed the glass and swished back the curtains, letting a shaft of light flood the room with a heavenly warmth.

"Sallee, I want you to know that I love your mother," she said to me.

"Do you? Oh, that's nice," I replied, feeling awkward, not knowing how to respond.

"Yes, I do. She makes me laugh; she is always so full of fun. In fact, it's not just me; we *all* love her."

She knelt down and cupped her hands around Mum's face.

"Don't I, Phyllees? I love you darleen'."

Mum giggled and playfully brushed her off.

"Ha-ha. Ah, go on with you, naw. Where's me cup of tea, dear?"

Her loving gesture really touched me and confirmed my belief that Mum was in the best possible place. This sort of affection as a child would have changed her life.

Later that evening, I was at home watching a programme about long-lost families who were reunited. I tuned in every week and was so moved by their tragic stories that I found it impossible not to cry. During the ad breaks, an ancestry company advertised DNA kits. As a member, I'd received dozens of emails about their product but mostly ignored them because I thought they were expensive. Then something twigged.

What if I got Mum to do a DNA test? If we found she was related to someone, perhaps I could find her family. Nah, that would be a chance in a million, wouldn't it? Still, maybe it was worth one last try. What had I to lose? If I left it much longer she may not be well enough to do the test.

On my visit after work next day, I asked if she would give a sputum sample for a DNA test in the hope it would match to a distant cousin.

"Of, course, Sal, that'd be no problem at all."

"You know, Mum, you might even have brothers and sisters out there... and it might lead on to... who knows what?"

"Well, you never know," she said perking up. "I would like to do that. Really, I would."

"Then again, it might not lead anywhere. It's a chance we'll have to take."

"Darling, you can only try. We never know where life will take us or what's around the corner. Look at me! I never expected to end my days here. Finding someone would be truly wonderful, but you can only do your best. You know what they say don't you?"

"What?"

"Where there's life—"

"—there's hope. Of course, how could I forget! I think I'll remember that saying of yours, as long as I live."

A few weeks later, on an unusually hot day for mid-April, I met a couple of old friends, Nicky and Lou, for a drink in the garden of a local country pub.

"Cheers!" we all chorused as we clinked glasses and squinted in the brightness of the late afternoon sun, and pink blossom flitted down like confetti, dusting our table.

"So, how's it going with your new-found date then, Lou?"

"Oh, great thanks. I met him through a dating website. Got a couple of kids, own business and, yeah, all good so far."

"And he's good-looking and loaded," interrupted Nicky, giving me a nudge.

"Alright for some," I joked. "Let's hope it works out for you. And what about you Nicks? Are you off again soon?"

"Yep. Finished the winter season in Interlaken, and taking a coachload off to Sicily next week, followed by Guernsey in July."

"Packing it all in as usual then?"

"Of course, what else? And what about you, Sal, what's happening in your life?" asked Nicky.

"Oh, not much really. I've more or less given up hope of trying to find my grandmother and her family. Mum's really ill now, and I get stressed about it. I reckon time's almost run out. I've just about tried everything… but I'm giving it one last go with a DNA test that I got Mum to do a few weeks ago. If this doesn't work then nothing will."

"Ooh, that sounds intriguing," said Lou. "Was that expensive?"

"Let's put it this way, it wasn't cheap, although it could've been worse, but if I get a match to Mum the cost won't matter. I guess the chances are very remote. Still, you never know, you'll have to watch this space."

But then, five days later as I was about to drag myself away from browsing the internet during my lunchtime, I thought I'd have a 10-minute peek at the ancestry website. I wanted to see if Mum's DNA results had come back, although, really, I thought it would be too soon as they said processing time could be up to 10 weeks.

Ping! *You have two new messages:*

Apr 25, 2015

Hi there,

I see that we appear to be quite closely related – second cousins is the prediction. I would really like to find out how we are linked (especially as you are the closest match I've had since taking the test), and am happy to share any information. My name is Matthew and I live in Northern Ireland.

Hope to hear from you soon.
Matthew

And then:

> *Apr 26, 2015*
>
> *Sorry I've just realised that you are the tree administrator and that the person I link to through the D.NA test as a possible second cousin is someone in your tree called "P.M. (L)". I'd be grateful for any information you could share.*
>
> *Thank you, Matthew.*

I felt a strange tingle run straight down my spine and had to look again. This couldn't be true... could it? Whoa! This man called Matthew was a possible second cousin! I felt jubilant – triumphant. Wow! My thoughts went into overdrive from a place of desperation for the truth. Could this be it... the family I'd been dreaming, praying to find all these years? Had God answered my prayers?

I looked at the time. It was 13:28 and my lunch-hour had almost finished. Damn! I should get back to work, but I *needed* to reply to Matthew. What to do? I had two minutes left. My head was in a quandary. I dithered. Argh – write the email, write it quickly. No time like the present.

> *April 27, 2015*
>
> *Hi Matthew*
>
> *I'm at work right now but will email you as soon as I get home. I am so excited! P M Little is my mother!*
>
> *Regards*
>
> *Sally*

I burst through the front door, rushed for my computer and eagerly waited for it to boot up. *Come on... come on! Why are you so slow?* I was like a woman possessed. My heart was racing, anxious to get to Matthew's messages and see if he had a family tree.

I re-read his messages in case I was imagining them. Yes, he did have a public family tree on the ancestry website; one I could view. My eyes scanned for the surname. I was so excited, I almost forgot to breathe. So now, where was the name Little? At first, I couldn't see anything as my mind was darting all over the place. *Come on now, focus – concentrate!* I scolded myself.

Then I found a Mary Ann (May) Little. Well, that wasn't the Margaret or Peggy Little I was looking for, and she was married to a Joe Armstrong. *Who are they?* I wondered. *Perhaps they have children.*

They did indeed! Eight children – the eldest being a girl called Maud, born in 1913. That was Mum's middle name. That's interesting, I thought. Child number two was Jane. I moved on to number three: it was a girl, christened Margaret (also known as Peggy), who was born in 1916. Well, she was the right age but her name was Armstrong, so that couldn't be right. But I couldn't take my eyes of her and I was intrigued by her details.

Then, in the most satisfying moment of my entire search, I discovered she had married a James Clancy! Blinking heck! I pushed my chair back, refocused my eyes and checked the screen again. That was it! Margaret/Peggy Little and Margaret/Peggy Armstrong were the same person, and I had found her after all this time! She was Mum's mother and my grandmother! In that split second, I understood: she had lied about her name to conceal my mother's illegitimate birth. Instead of her married name of Clancy, or previous name, Armstrong, she had used her own mother's maiden name of Little. Mary May Little, the woman who would have been – no *was* – my mother's grandmother. No wonder I never found a trace of her; I had been looking for the wrong surname all along.

Both Mum and I always suspected that Peggy may have lied about her surname, although Morag at the charity who held the Bethany Home records claimed the matron would always have known if a girl was concealing the truth. How wrong she was.

Before I knew it I was engrossed and stumbled across an old photograph taken in the mid-1920s of the Armstrongs on a family picnic in the country. First from the left was Peggy as a young girl of about 10 years of age. She was dressed in her Sunday best – a white smock – and her hair was short, slightly wavy and fair, and she wore a very bored expression, the sort you have when you have been posing in front of a camera for ages and had enough. She was nothing at all as I'd imagined. My mother, by contrast, looked Mediterranean. Even an old boyfriend of mine, many years before, thought she could have come from southern Italy. But Peggy bore no resemblance whatsoever. This I found intriguing.

Still, I couldn't believe that for the first time in my life I was staring at my grandmother, after the endless searching, hitting brick walls and being knocked back by them. I wanted to shout from the highest building: "Hey everyone! I've found her! I've found her!"

It wasn't until I looked more closely at Peggy's details that I crashed straight back down to earth. The record told me that she had died, aged just 28 years old. Oh, no... what on earth could have happened? It dawned on me, brutally: although I could now tell Mum who her mother was, rather than it being too late because of Mum's prognosis, it was too late for any form of reconciliation as her mother had already passed away when Mum was about eight years old. I felt desolate. I was longing to phone Mum as soon as possible, but first I had to email Matthew.

Apr 27, 2015

Dear Matthew,

Thank you for your email. I have taken the liberty of looking at your family tree and am now in shock because I think I have seen my grandmother for the first time.

My mother's mother, was Margaret (Peggy) Little who said she had married a James Clancy around 1938. Neither I, nor other genealogists in Ireland, have been able to find a birth, death or marriage certificate for Peggy Little. The only thing I knew was she was 20 years old (so born around 1917) when she gave birth to my mother in 1937.

My mother's name is Phyllis Maud Little, born out of wedlock and started life in a mother and baby home (Bethany Home) and then a North Dublin orphanage until she was 16.

Is it possible to talk sometime? What relation would you be to Margaret Peggy Armstrong Clancy? Can you tell me how she died, especially so young?

My mother is still alive, although she has lung cancer and resides in a nursing home. Her life has been a sad one and I promised I would try to find out what happened to her mother before she dies. Please can you help me fill in the gaps?

Regards
Sally

After an email swapping phone numbers, the phone rang within half an hour. Matthew had a Northern Irish accent and sounded laid back and mature, probably in his early 50s, I thought.

I wanted to tell him all and everything, but I didn't know where to begin. I felt completely overwhelmed with relief and excitement. I had battled through a jungle of lost hope, dead ends and bureaucracy to finally find the rope bridge where Matthew was waiting on the other side to guide me across, and he did. He welcomed me with open arms.

"Is that Sally?" he said. "I'm your cousin, Matthew."

"Matthew! Oh... hello," I said, hesitantly.

"Are you okay, Sally?"

His accent sounded strange but familiar. It reminded me of my nan (my father's mother) who came from Londonderry.

"Oh yes, I'm fine – shaking a bit, but so thrilled at the same time. I'm trying to take it in, but I just can't believe it."

"Neither can we," he agreed.

"We?" I said.

"Yes, Mum and I were sitting here at the kitchen table when we got your email. I looked at Mum and said, 'You won't believe it, but it's happened again!'"

"Again? What do you mean?"

He spoke with an air of confidence, as though he was well informed.

"Peggy, your grandmother, had two illegitimate children. We assumed it was only one until we heard from you today. The other one was Jim, who we only found last year."

Suddenly, there seemed to be more questions than answers. My head was spinning faster than a Catherine wheel and I could feel my mouth drying up.

"You won't know, but I've been looking for 10 years without success. I've tried everything I could think of, *everything*. If it hadn't been for DNA, I'd never have found you. Can you tell me how my mother is related to you?"

"Your mother and my mother are first cousins, so I am Phyllis's first cousin once removed. My grandfather, George, was Peggy's brother."

"And what happened to Peggy?"

"You might want to sit down for this."

Sit down? I could barely keep still. I was pacing up and down like a caged animal desperately curious to investigate the world outside. As I walked past the mirror I caught a glimpse of my scarlet reflection, flushing right down to my chest.

"Are you sitting down yet?"

"Yes… yes, I am now."

"Peggy died of an illness when she was just 28 years old, two months after her last child was born."

"Her last child?" I repeated, reeling from the next revelation.

"Yes. She had four more children after your mum was born. One was a girl who died in infancy, but she had three sons who are all still alive, although one does not want to know the family."

"She has brothers?"

"Yes, Jim in Ireland, who I've already mentioned; Desmond in Canada; and another one in America."

My hand was shaking so much I nearly dropped the phone.

"Three brothers," I repeated, my mind floating off into orbit somewhere.

"Are you alright?" he checked. "I bet this has come as quite a shock."

"Three brothers! I can't wait to tell Mum. She'll be astounded."

"Like Phyllis, Jim was illegitimate and was fostered out as a baby, so none of the family knew he existed either."

"So, two babies were born out of wedlock?"

"Yes, that's right: your mum and Jim. Desmond, his sister Ethne and his other brother were born within the marriage."

"But why? Why would Peggy and James Clancy have two babies, give them away, get married and then have three more?"

"Well, that's a good question – but we have no idea. You might like to know that your mum also has an aunt, Peggy's younger sister, Eileen, who is still alive and living in Australia, aged 92. She's the only surviving sibling of the eight that lived. There was another brother called Andrew, but he died in infancy."

"What? No way!"

"And, because Peggy was one of eight children, your Mum has about 50 or 60 first cousins."

"50 or 60! But she grew up in an orphanage and thought she was utterly alone in the world. Wait until I tell her," I said, finding all this new information hard to take in.

"I'm sure Jim will be beside himself when he knows he has a sister. Can I give him your telephone number so he can call you? He's in Spain at the moment, but I know he'll be over the moon."

"And what about Desmond?"

"Desmond is globetrotting somewhere right now. I believe he's heading down to Cuba as we speak, and then will be off to Australia to meet Auntie Eileen for the first time. He only discovered Jim last year, so he hasn't met him either."

"Wow, he sounds like he gets around. Yes, of course, please do give my number to Jim, I would love to hear from him," I said.

Half an hour later the phone rang again. I hesitated.

Ring-ring – I panicked. My heart was pounding. What would I say? This must be Jim, Mum's brother, *my uncle* – after all these years. How could I tell him that Mum was… well… very, very ill?

Ring-ring – Finally, I picked up.

"Is that Sally Little?" said a soft Irish accent at the other end of the phone.

"Yes… well my name's not Little actually… but yes!" I said, feeling a bit clumsy for correcting him when I knew what he meant.

He sounded forthright and slightly impatient, "Are you my sister's daughter?"

"Yes, Phyllis, my mother, is your sister."

"I've got a sister! Oh my, I've got a sister! Can I speak to my sister, Sally?"

"I'm afraid she's not here Jim. She's in a nursing home... she's very ill."

"Oh. Well, when can I speak to her? I must speak to her. Good God! I've got a sister; I can't believe it!" he said to himself, over and over. "Well, can I be ringing her?"

"It's not that simple, I'm afraid. She doesn't always pick up the phone. It would probably be better if I was there."

"But I must talk to her. I absolutely must."

I was taken aback at his insistence, but I understood how excited he felt; first discovering a long-lost brother after all those years, and now a sister too.

"I'll arrange it as soon as I can, Jim. I promise you. Sunday afternoon is a good time, that's when I spend a few hours there with her."

After I put the phone down I was in a daze, as if it had all been a dream. I had just spoken to my mother's very own brother, someone who never knew she even existed and was now determined to get to know her as soon as possible. But how could I break it to him that she may not be around for too much longer?

My thoughts returned to Mum: *I'll ring her now*, although I knew the likelihood of her picking up the phone was remote. Once upon a time she'd been anxious for me to ring every night, now she tended to ignore the call. Simple tasks took her longer and longer as her cognitive functions slowed down considerably.

The phone rang and rang. I redialled, but still no reply. I ended up ringing the nursing home's main line and eventually Sister Jeanne answered the phone.

"Hello Sallee, you want to speak to your mother? She is sleeping I'm afraid. Would you like me to wake her?"

"No, no. Leave her. I'll speak to her when I come in tomorrow."

What a disappointment. I so wanted to share this euphoric moment with her, but she was asleep, as she seemed to be more and more these days.

The next day after work I could barely contain myself, I was so anxious to break the news.

"Mum! You'll never guess what?"

"What darling?"

"I've found your family!"

"You've what, Petsey?"

"The results for the DNA test came back. Your DNA matched with a cousin… related to your mother. The sad news is that, I'm sorry to say, your mother died, a long time ago, but you have three brothers and they're all still alive!"

"I've got three brothers," she echoed, not quite able to grasp the significance.

"Yes, three – and they're all still living! How do you feel about that Mum?"

"*Three* brothers?"

"Yes, three!"

"And my mother is dead?"

I suddenly realised that in my over enthusiasm I was breaking news about the death of her mother, whom she had always dreamed of knowing, and this must have been hard to take in.

"Yes, she is. Sadly. And she was so young too when she passed. I know that is news that you didn't want to hear, and I'm so sorry for you … but you came from a big family and you've got more first cousins than you could shake a stick at."

"Three brothers…" she kept repeating. "I've got… three… brothers."

My heart sank. She was listening and acknowledging, but it wasn't going in.

"Petsey, will you scratch my back, it's very itchy. *Three* brothers you say?"

I pulled up her top over her back to scratch where she said it felt itchy and to my horror discovered a large mound. It was in the same place where the tumour had been. I rubbed my hand over it.

"Does that hurt you at all Mum?" I asked, looking at the blood vessels stretching across the surface of the skin.

"Oh, no. Just itchy."

This was what I'd been dreading. I swallowed hard, took a deep breath and continued. "One of your brothers, who's called Jim, wants to speak to you on the telephone from Ireland. Would you like that?"

"Jim," she echoed. "Oh yes, I'd like that very much. Who's he?"

I wanted to cry. Why couldn't this have happened last year, when her brain wasn't so in the fog?

Thankfully, one Sunday afternoon when I was at the nursing home, she did get to speak to Jim. We had arranged that he would ring her phone and I would pick it up, speak to him first, and then hand it to Mum. We waited, a little fidgety for three quarters of an hour, but as he hadn't rung I nipped down the hallway to make us a cup of tea. When I returned Mum was merrily chatting away to Jim.

I could tell she was nervous because she kept using the word "right" in between laughing and winking at me. But she looked happier than I had seen her for a long time. This was obviously one of her better days. She handed the phone to me.

"Hello there, Sally. I want you to know that I think Phyllis is a lovely lady and I'm thrilled to speak to her and can't wait to meet her."

"When will you be over, Jim?"

"Well, I'm in Spain at the moment and we're not due back until the 20th of next month. Is there no way you could bring her to Ireland?"

"No Jim, she's really not well."

"But my wife, Sheila, has been a nurse. She could look after her."

"Oh Jim, she'd love to go to Ireland, believe me, but she'd never be able to cope. She's really very ill."

"I'll have to fly over then. I'll email you with the details when I get back."

After the call ended, Mum was abuzz with excitement.

"Well would you believe it naw? I have just spoken to *my brother*, Jim!"

"And how do you feel, Mum?"

"Oh, delighted I am, for sure. He's real Irish you know. I love hearing his Irish accent. When will I see him, Pet? Three brothers, I have. I can't believe it! Ha-ha-ha. Mammy's got three brothers… and after all this time."

"It won't be long now, just another few weeks," I assured her.

At last it had sunk in.

Chapter 15

The Truth Unfolds

During the following weeks emails flew backwards and forwards, thick and fast, as we started to unravel how we had found each other. Jim wrote the day after he spoke to Mum on the phone.

Hi Sally!

It was indeed unbelievable speaking to my SISTER! After all these years not knowing any of us existed. It is obvious by her giggle and sense of humour that (thankfully) the Armstrong gene is the predominant one.

He often referred to the maternal Armstrong gene being predominant and was very proud of his roots on his mother's side of the family, although his sentiment was not quite the same from his little knowledge of his father's side. But now, with a newly found sister, it was obvious that he could barely contain his happiness.

"I'm over the moon, over the moon," was his frequent refrain.

I, too, was filled with overwhelming joy. To beat all the odds and, on top of that, to discover that Mum's family were kind, warm-hearted and welcoming made me euphoric. Fulfilling her deepest wishes in Mum's last weeks was something I never believed would happen.

Yes, it seemed God had finally answered my prayers. As the reality unfolded I was staggered to work out all the coincidences and timings that had brought us together. It certainly made me wonder if it wasn't just DNA and technology that had played a part in this reunion.

In a complete contrast to his sister, Jim had lived a happy life. His foster family included siblings and had treated him well; later he married, had seven children and became a successful businessman.

Jim found out as a young boy that his foster family wasn't his biological family. For years he put it to the back of his mind, until one of his sons, Kieran, took an interest in tracing the family history, in 2013, and Jim reluctantly agreed to let him search for his birth family. He quickly found the marriage record for Jim's parents. He also found three birth certificates for Jim's siblings, although he didn't find one for my mother, or know of her existence.

Once they realised that Jim may still have two brothers out there, the hunt was on to find them. In February 2013 Kieran posted a message on an Irish web page, hopeful of attracting a response. And meanwhile, Matthew, another match to Mum's DNA, had been searching for the Clancys since 2009 and was keen to find them too. His family knew Peggy had two sons (Desmond and his older brother) but not what had happened to them. It wasn't until Matthew rooted around for more information that events began to unfold. Having already built an extensive family tree on the ancestry website, he asked his mother whom she would like him to search for next. Her resounding answer was, "Find the Clancys!"

By chance, while scouring the internet for clues, Matthew came across Kieran's message and eagerly replied. He knew nothing of Jim, so the knowledge that Peggy had birthed an illegitimate child was a shock.

Months passed and, disappointingly, Kieran didn't pick up the message. Undeterred, he tried again that November. Again, no reply. By the following March Matthew was still pondering the lack of reaction and gave it one last go. He scrutinised the email address that was originally posted, and worked out it was from a business, so sent a final message directly to the recipient instead of through the web page. His diligence paid off. This time, to his delight, he received a response from Kieran.

Result! The following July, Jim and his wife met Matthew and his mother at a hotel in Ireland. He was stunned to discover what a large family he had descended from and was at last able to learn his family history. They sat chatting and smoking outside well into the evening and from that day a close bond was formed.

He had not yet met Desmond, his brother from Canada, although he knew of his existence. Ironically, while I was searching for Mum's family in 2013, Matthew was searching for the Clancys and Kieran posted his messages online; Desmond, meanwhile, who was Irish by birth but had lived in Canada for most of his life, had been visiting Ireland!

Desmond had Clancy cousins on his father's side in the north Dublin seaside town of Skerries, and was trying to rekindle a connection after the 40 odd years since he was last there. He knew nothing of Jim or Phyllis as their births had remained a secret all this time.

While Kieran had been searching, his family had told their story to the local postman who was also interested in genealogy and eager to help.

"I know some Clancys in Skerries," he enthused. "I'll make a special trip up there and speak to the local vicar. He'll know who to contact."

The chances of him finding anyone who was even vaguely connected were pretty remote, but he insisted on trying.

So off he travelled to Skerries and spoke to the vicar, who he felt was bound to know everyone in that small community. But the vicar didn't know any Clancys, so he directed him to the butcher. The butcher said he didn't know either, but the person who regularly bought sausages might know more about it. And indeed, the person who regularly bought sausages *did* know, and so the Clancy cousins, who Desmond had visited only a few months earlier, were tracked down! The puzzle was completed when they put Jim's son in touch with Desmond. This could only happen in Ireland.

The story of how so many had been concurrently searching for each other was already mind-boggling, but more intriguing tales were to come. Now, not only did Mum have three brothers, multitudes of first, second and third cousins, in Ireland, America, Canada and spread out over the world, including eight nephews and nieces and an aunt in Australia, but I too had acquired the same relatives, none whom I knew existed. It was a case of going from the sublime to the ridiculous. From believing we had no family at all, it now seemed we had enough family to fill a small town – all thanks to DNA and a little sputum.

As these revelations unveiled themselves, Mum's health was declining rapidly. I had brought my tablet into the nursing home and Skyped her Auntie Eileen (Peggy's surviving sister) and her son in Australia, so they could see each other, as I remained anxious about time running out. Unfortunately, it didn't go as I expected. The internet reception was poor and Mum kept fading and falling asleep. She could barely sit up in her wheelchair and found it difficult to concentrate.

"Look Mum, that's your Auntie Eileen," I prompted, as she strained to see who she was looking at.

The screen seemed dark in the bright sunlight of the conservatory, the only place I could get a signal.

I tried again. "Mum, this is your mother's sister."

"Is it naw?" She looked puzzled.

"Say hello, then," I urged. "Wave."

"Hello," she said faintly, raising her hand. The screen faded into black.

"Oh damn! Try again Mum. Say, 'Hello Auntie'."

"Aww, hello Auntie?"

It was frustrating to say the least. The wi-fi was intermittent, with long silences between the screen going fuzzy and the line disconnecting. Occasionally, I could see their curious faces peering back in wonderment, but neither Mum nor Auntie really knew what to say to each other.

"Who's he?" she asked inquisitively.

"That's Auntie Eileen's son Maurice, one of your many first cousins."

She looked curiously at the screen but couldn't work it out. It was not one of her good days. Perhaps I shouldn't have forced it, but I was so keen for her to glimpse her relatives and for them to see her.

"She's got my mother's mouth," piped up Auntie Eileen.

"Hear that, Mum?" I encouraged, emphasising each word at a time. "Auntie says you've got – your – granny's – mouth."

"I've got what?"

"Her mouth."

"Who's mouth?"

"Your grandmother's!"

"Wha–t?"

She looked at me blankly as though I needed to translate.

Oh, God, this is hard work, I thought. "Mum… Auntie Eileen says you've got a mouth like your granny."

"Have I, naw? Ha-ha, very good,' she said before giving a half-hearted smile, drooping her chin and nodding off.

I apologised to Auntie Eileen and Maurice, because they were disappointed too, but there was nothing I could do. I had expected an instant rapport, like you see in the 'long-lost family' programmes. But this hadn't been stage-managed for the money shots. This was real life: two complete strangers, related but elderly, and one struggling to concentrate for more than a few minutes because she was so ill; an inadequate internet connection; both at a loss as to how to make conversation. Sad, but that's the way it was.

Auntie Eileen was an empathic person and told me how touched she was by my mother's plight. I kept in regular contact with her by email after that, and occasionally by Skype.

"Oh, Sally," she said. "When I read your email, it made me cry. It's hard to credit that my own sister could have done such a thing and kept such a well-hidden secret from the whole family. If I had known your mother was in that orphanage, I'd have come and got her out myself. I'd never have left her there to rot and be forgotten."

I asked if she could remember anything about Peggy that might suggest why she gave Phyllis up. But there was a seven-year age difference and Peggy left home in her mid-teens, while Eileen was a young child, so memories of her were vague.

"What did she look like?" I asked, intent on learning something new about her.

"I can remember she had nice legs and nice teeth," came the reply.

"Is there nothing else?" I asked, trying to imagine this person with just nice teeth and legs.

"No, Sally. Sorry, dear. I didn't really see much of her after she left." My heart sank.

As I started to analyse the birth certificates and review the information I'd already compiled about the Bethany Mother and Baby Home, I noticed that Peggy had visited to retrieve my mother on 4 November 1938 – six days before Jim was born, on 10 November.

That meant two things. One, she would have been so heavily pregnant that someone must have been helping her cope. It would have been tricky to manage the imminent arrival of her new baby and an 18-month-old toddler alone. And secondly, wherever they stayed for that short period, Mum and Jim had actually lived together under the same roof for the only time in their entire lives. By December 1938, Mum had been returned to the Bethany, and six weeks later, Jim was fostered out.

One can only imagine the agony that Peggy faced in her young life. Becoming pregnant out of wedlock would have been viewed as a cardinal sin in the context of the religious dogma that dominated everyone's lives in Ireland. In those days, Peggy, as 'a fallen woman' would have been outlawed by society and forced to hide her illegitimate pregnancy. Her situation must have been desperate to force her into refuge in the evangelical Protestant-run Bethany home. Girls like Peggy, who had fallen short of the Church's expectations because of some misdemeanour, were housed together with petty criminals, those on remand and prostitutes. It must have been a distressing environment to give birth in.

Shocking information about this place had come to light in 2010, and while searching for clues about Mum's childhood I was appalled to discover newspaper reports disclosing over 200 unmarked graves in Mount Jerome, Dublin, of children and infants who had died unnecessarily from childhood diseases, and even more shockingly, malnutrition. Mum could so easily have become one of those victims. It is a wonder she survived.

The children lived at Bethany until three to five years old, after which many were sent to poor rural families in Ireland to be used as child labour on their farms. Some, like my mother, were transferred to other institutions or were adopted by rich couples from overseas. Many reports reveal the children were physically and sexually abused.

Others, who were sick but could not be looked after by the Bethany Home, were placed in the care of people who professed to have nursed children. Tragically, many who offered help only did so for the payment, which frequently resulted in the child's neglect and subsequent death. The newspaper article also mentioned a campaigner called Derek Leinster who had set up a survivors' group and was still fighting for justice for himself and the other children who suffered in the Bethany Home. It was a poignant reminder of how the lives of children institutionalised in Ireland were affected forever, just like my own mother's, because of decisions made by Church and state.

I can only imagine, then, Peggy's anguish: longing to retrieve her daughter from this place where babies were rumoured to be left to die in their dirty nappies. That must be why she called herself Mrs James Clancy on Mum's orphan papers. She lied to try to get her out. Her marriage certificate shows the truth though: she and James Clancy did not marry until three months later, in March 1939.

What on earth happened then? Why return my mother to the Bethany Home for a second time, and relinquish her new-born son soon after?

Jim's birth certificate states that his mother's name was "Clancy formerly Armstrong", implying that Jim was born within the marriage. This being a fabrication, something doesn't quite add up; they married after his placement in foster care. Giving up her children must have been heart breaking. And why, if James Clancy was their father, did she have to anyway? Was she unduly pressurised in some way?

I resolved to ask Matthew about Peggy's upbringing, to see if that offered clues about her life and personality.

"Peggy's daddy, Joe Armstrong, was a land steward and travelled around managing large estates for landed gentry," he said.

"What, you mean the rich and famous?"

"Aye, some. You've heard of the Guinness family, haven't you?"

"Of course."

"Well, when Peggy was a wee child, like in that picnic photo, Joe Armstrong worked at Ashford Castle, which was owned by the Guinesses."

"Where's that?"

"It's in County Mayo, where the John Wayne film *The Quiet Man* was filmed."

"Really? Wow."

"There is an old story of how Joe had to gather the family up and flee, escaping by horse and cart, after a tip-off by the local priest that the IRA was coming for them. They'd already threatened to hang Joe, and pushed his wife, May, off her bicycle as she tried to cross a bridge."

"My God, that's so dramatic," I said.

"Aye, well, it was the 1920s in Ireland; a time of great troubles and turmoil, and when big houses in Ireland were being burned to the ground."

"Do you know if they ever stayed in a place called Bush, in County Wexford?" I asked. "It was one of the first places where I started looking for Peggy. She gave it as her place of residence, when she first entered the Bethany Home in 1936, although I realise it's not where she was born."

"Yes! They did," he confirmed. "In fact, I've a photo of Joe standing with a shotgun next to my granddaddy, George, Peggy's only brother. He was a boy then. He must have been working on an estate there at the time. On the back is written 'Bush, 1936'. I'll email you a copy."

My hunch was right then! Peggy had lived there, near that road we'd driven up and down. But where did she go next, I wondered? So, along with access to Matthew's family tree, I also began ordering more birth, death and marriage certificates to forage for more pointers.

Overcome with all these new discoveries about Peggy, I couldn't wait to tell Mum. I rang her.

"Your mother, Peggy, grew up in the grounds of a famous castle in Ireland, Mum. So, what do you think of that then?" I asked

"Well, would you believe it naw?" she retorted. "I knew I came from money!"

"Well, no, it wasn't quite like that, Mum. Peggy's mum and dad weren't well-off, especially with all those children. They were more like servants. Peggy's life was on the go: every few years travelling from one large estate to another, wherever her father found work... living in different houses in the Irish countryside, running barefoot in the grass and enjoying her freedom."

"Did she naw? Oh yes, I bet, she had the gypsy in her, a bit like me. Ha-ha! Did she ever go to Dublin, then?"

"Well, yes, I believe she did. Certainly, from what Auntie Eileen has told me, it's more than probable that she headed there to find domestic work, like one of her older sisters, when she left school. The bright lights of Dublin would have beckoned. I suppose that living in the country for so long would have seemed mundane."

"And what about him?"

"Him?"

"Yes, James Clancy. How did they meet?"

"Well, we don't know. No one's still alive from that generation, except Auntie Eileen, and she doesn't remember much. All I know is, their lives couldn't have been more different."

"What d'you mean Sal?"

"Well, from what I've found out, James Clancy grew up in Dublin city and was the same age as Peggy, born in 1916. He attended Trinity College, so he must have been bright. But after a while he dropped out. His wedding certificate states that when he married Peggy, in 1939, he was a clerk for the Dublin Corporation where his father worked for decades. But a few years later, in1944, he'd become a shopkeeper, making wooden toys."

"That doesn't explain how they met though and what happened after."

"I know Mum, and we'll never know for sure; we can only surmise. Perhaps they met in Dublin when Peggy was a domestic for a big family. Maybe it was her night off: the pavements damp and steaming, rain dripping down as she queued excitedly to see a film with her girlfriends, huddled under umbrellas outside the bright lights of a cinema…"

"A fil-m?"

"Yes, a film. Imagine if James Clancy is with a group of his friends, leaning back with his hands in his pockets, trying to look cool as he catches Peggy's eye…"

"Go on."

"Instantly, she's transfixed, unable to resist his charm. Peggy's an innocent young girl from the country, whereas he is tall and handsome… an air of sophistication about him with his slicked-back college-boy haircut and a dapper suit. Perhaps that's where it all began?"

"Oh yeah, I can just imagine that alright. And I'll bet he had the gift of the gab, like the lot of them. I learnt a long time ago, Pet, never trust an Irishman."

"Well we don't know what he was like really, but I have this feeling that he probably had some controlling effect on her. What do you think Mum? Mum…?"

By the time I reached the end of the sentence, she had nodded off.

Her sleeping habits and lack of appetite were becoming more and more of a worry. Every time I rang she was asleep. Concerned that perhaps the nursing home didn't know what was best for her (after all, I was her daughter), I suggested that they might be encouraging her to become nocturnal by letting her slumber until noon every day.

"Don't you realise that if you don't get her up in the morning she won't sleep at night?" I asked. "She's the sort of person that if you give her an inch she'll take a mile."

I told them how at my house I often found her still awake at 1:30 in the morning, scrabbling around in her handbag, followed by the nightmare of trying to get her up next morning before I left for work.

"But she's so tired," said an exasperated staff nurse. "We don't call her if she prefers to sleep. Perhaps you ought to speak to the manager if you're not happy."

"Don't worry I will!" I said.

So, from being the friendly daughter they enjoyed dealing with, I became the all-controlling argumentative daughter who they tried to avoid. The truth was, I was in denial. I didn't want to accept she was going to die. It pained my heart deeply that we rarely spoke on the phone now. How I missed our morning chats and hearing her cheery voice down the phone.

"Sally darling, it's Mammy here. Are you alright Petsey?"

She never even needed to ask how I was because she picked up my vibes in an instant if something was wrong.

I could offload onto her anytime, or moan about all and everything, yet she always had something positive and reassuring to say. She soothed my woes, understood me when others didn't, fussed when she sensed I was upset and put up with my rants when I was in a bad mood.

I had seen her near the brink of death quite a few times now, but she always bounced back. I told myself how that determined spirit that had driven her through thick and thin would win out, and she would survive a while longer. I adamantly refused to contemplate losing her. Now, after endless searching and at the end of her life, she could at least enjoy the triumph of finding her siblings and wider family.

Trying to understand what was happening to her, I searched an NHS website for information about cancer. Only then did it hit me: her symptoms clearly showed her to be in the final stages – stage four of the disease. Nobody had spelled this out to me, so the information came as a blow. Of course, the consultant at Downsview had said Mum's cancer was terminal, in a very brief consultation, but nothing about what to expect or how she would be. A warm handshake, a look of condolence after being told there was nothing more they could do, and we were packaged off with books to read and advice about obtaining a Blue Badge disabled sticker for the car. It was like being shunted along a conveyor belt, processed and churned out into a can at the other end. At least now though, I realised why she slept all day, had no appetite and why her cognitive functions were all over the place. Only now did I begin to appreciate what a brilliant job the nursing staff were doing in managing all her needs.

It was the usual routine for me that Sunday afternoon. I jumped in the car and drove to see her. The place was teeming with visitors and staff scurrying in and out of the rooms. A tea trolley stood abandoned in the corridor, heavily laden with cups and saucers, a plate of tempting-looking butterfly cakes and a shiny urn. The carers who had been wheeling it were distracted by an old lady in bed, cot sides up, and a very unpleasant faecal smell emanating from the room. I held my breath and hastened my pace.

Mum's door, number 52, was half open as it always was. Everything was in its normal place. The lilac chintzy curtains were drawn back revealing the giant redwood, teaming with birdlife. All the funny cat cards I had ever sent, and my brother's numerous postcards from abroad, cramped the space on her windowsill. And on her bed, proudly, sat her cuddly toys: George the monkey, who she told the staff was bisexual (much to their amusement), and Lindsay the ginger cat, wrapped in a shawl like a baby. The telly was blaring out one of her favourite DVDs, *Fantastic Mr Fox*, at full volume, while she sat contentedly watching.

"Look at that Sal – the eyes on it."

"You like this one, don't you? Was it the one Will got you for Christmas?"

"Yes darling. He knows how I love all these cartoons. Cam here and watch it with Mammy."

I laughed aloud, and marvelled at how the animated fox was brought to life by George Clooney's voice. Why, I wondered, did she have such a fascination for the television? It was as though she was regressing into a second childhood. Later I found out from Patsy, her best friend in the orphanage, that they were lucky if they got to go to the cinema once a year. She too adored children's animated films and cartoons. They missed out on a normal childhood, too busy being used as domestic labour to earn their keep, but were certainly making up for it now.

"It's very good, don't you think?" she said smiling.

"Well clever, certainly."

We were interrupted by an officious nun who strode confidently in with a cup of tea, spilling it into the saucer.

She spoke with authority. "Cup of tea, Phyllis?"

"Yes dear, just there please,"

"Cake?"

"No thank you."

"For your daughter?"

"No, I'm good thanks," I replied. I'm fussy when it comes to people making my tea.

"Shall I shut the door?"

"No, leave it dear. That's fine," said Mum.

The nun left us in peace and Mum turned to me with a smirk on her face.

"What?" I asked

"So, she's talking to me now."

"What do you mean?" I queried. I gave her an old-fashioned look. "Mo–ther? What's happened?"

"Well, I asked her if she had a boyfriend the other day… and I don't think she liked it very much."

"You did what!"

"Ha! Ha-ha!"

"What did you do that for?"

"Ah, you know I was only joking, Pet, but she took it the wrong way."

"Mu–um! That was very naughty of you."

"Ah sure, I didn't mean it. I was only having a bit of fun naw. Ha! Ha! Ha!"

She could see I wasn't amused, so changed the subject.

"Have you heard from my brother Jim?" she asked.

"Yes, I have and he is coming over on 23 June to meet you, and so is your other brother from Canada, you know… Desmond. Pleased?"

"Pleased? Oh, Petsey, I'm delighted! What a treat. I can't wait!"

"I'm piecing this jigsaw together at last… you know, how your mother came to give you up."

"Are you now?" she said, gulping her tea and still distracted by Mr Fox.

"If only we could have all met her years ago, but she died when you were just a child. So, so sad."

"What did she die of? Was it TB?" she asked.

"No, I think it says something else on the death certificate. She was only 28, you know?"

"28?" she repeated.

"Yes, you'd have been eight years old."

"So, I'd hardly have known her even then?"

"No."

She gave a deep sigh and slumped her shoulders. Sadness clouded her face, as she seemed to drift off onto another plane.

"Mum? Are you okay?"

"Yes darling, grand."

I stretched my hand over to touch her arm, but she flinched.

"Tell me what you're thinking, Mum."

"Can you be passing my mirror; it's on top of the drawers."

I rifled through the untidy mess of unwanted Telecom junk mail, tubes of cream with the lids missing, a used razor, some half-eaten sweets that had stuck to the bottom of the drawer and a tangled mess of wires from her phone chargers. I pulled out the mirror, smeared and sticky from the sweets, and handed it to her before wiping my fingers on a tissue.

"You didn't answer me. Have I upset you? Is it because you never knew your mother?"

Oblivious to my question, she held the mirror up to inspect her face, her eyes giving out a contemplative stare like a bemused child. Her mind was elsewhere.

"My mother – yes... hmmm... heh, heh, heh."

From out of nowhere, she produced a pair of tweezers and began to pluck out the few remaining hairs from her already swollen eyebrows.

"Mum! Don't! What are you doing? You know that annoys me. I've told you about it before. You'll end up with a skin infection or something."

"Ah, don't be going telling me off naw. You're always telling me off!"

"But it's for your own good. You've practically no eyebrows left as it is."

"Can't I do anything anymore?"

"Of course you can. But do you know what it looks like?"

"Alright, alright. Don't keep on at me all the time."

"Look, I only say it because I care. Now tell me what you're thinking."

"I'm not thinking anything."

"You are. You must be."

"No Petsey, I'm fine. Mammy loves you. You know that, don't you? Even when you tell me off."

"I do, and I love you too. I don't mean to tell you off or upset you. The truth is I'm frightened of losing you and I don't want you to... I really can't..."

As I said it, I felt my eyes prick with tears. I wrung my hands and bent my head in sorrow. It hadn't meant to come out like that. That was clumsy of me. Why did I say it?

"Oh darling, Mammy's not going anywhere. I'm not dead yet you know? Ha-ha. Look at Mr Foxy naw. He's cute, don't you think?" she said, trying to distract my train of thought.

I could feel my heart gripped in a state of angst by the same fear that I experienced as a child when she was torn away from me in the children's home, and later when she was sectioned and bundled into the back of the car. To be separated from your mother as a child, under such a traumatic set of circumstances, never leaves you. I knew what was coming and dreaded it with all my being. This time it would be forever. How do you face losing the one person in the world you love the most?

"Darling don't cry," she said softly. "Mammy's alright. I don't want you worrying naw. Mammy loves you, Petsey. We'll always be together."

"Together," I repeated, the words choking in my throat. "We'll always be together. I know, and I'm sorry," I said, reaching for a tissue.

"Remember, that you and Will darling mean the world to me. I am so proud to have a son and daughter like you both, and I thank you for all you've done for me."

"All I've done for *you*? You're joking, aren't you? What about all you've done for me?"

Her eyelids had started to droop and she kept blinking to try to stay awake.

"Sssh, naw, Mammy's tired now. Would you mind if I rest?"

"No, of course not. And you mean the world to me too, Mum. Always. You know that, don't you? I love you with my whole heart and whole soul."

"Yes darling, I do."

An email arrived a few days later; it was from Matthew asking if I would like to fly over to Ireland and join a big family reunion in County Meath on 26 June. He organised them once every 10 years, and it took a great deal of arranging, so it was by good fortune that it coincided with us newly discovering each other. The timing couldn't have been more perfect.

I jumped at the chance, although with tremendous sadness that Mum wouldn't be able to come, especially as she had not long ago asked me to take her to Ireland. I knew she would have dearly loved meeting all her cousins if only it had all happened a few years earlier. If only.

Desmond, who was flying from Canada to meet his brother for the first time, had decided to join Jim in visiting my mum. He had learnt about the existence of a sister while visiting Auntie Eileen in Australia, from an email sent by Matthew. Like Jim, he was blown away at the realisation that he had siblings he knew nothing about.

A plan was put in place. Desmond was to spend three weeks getting to know his brother Jim and family in his house in County

Kildare. During that time, they would take a short-haul flight to England to be reunited with Mum at the nursing home. It was to be a phenomenal moment in all our lives, maybe tinged with sadness, but one that none of us had imagined in our wildest dreams.

Chapter 16

The Meeting

Today was the day of the reunion. I woke early, feeling anxious about how everything would turn out. What would Desmond be like? What would Mum think of them? And what would they think of her, especially Jim, who had been so enthusiastic after speaking to her on the phone?

I got up to take a glimpse outside. The weather looked promising. It was the end of June. The sky was a celestial blue, only streaked by white vapour trails disappearing into the far distance. I took a deep breath. *Don't panic*, I told myself, *the day will go fine and what will be, will be.*

It was 8:30 and already I felt myself growing impatient, but there were hours to go before Jim and Desmond arrived and the time dragged. I sat on the sofa trying to watch telly, but it was impossible to concentrate. I couldn't take my eyes off the clock on the mantelpiece, watching the movement of the second hand tick around minute by minute.

I rang the nursing home to remind them that this was a very special day for Mum. I had already selected a black and beige snake-print tunic with a little metal detail around the neckline, and had hung it outside her wardrobe in preparation. I had bought it from M and S some time ago, and it was quite long so wouldn't show the obtrusive hernia that she was so embarrassed about. Like so many clothes I bought for Mum, she had never worn it, preferring to stick to her usual black V-necked jumper and leggings. However, she agreed for this occasion as it was important to look her best for her brothers.

11 o'clock came and went. Then quarter past, 20 past, and still no sign of Jim and Desmond. I was getting edgy.

Then at last, the phone rang.

"Hello…" I felt I was answering in a dream and that the person on the other end of the phone wasn't real, even though their Canadian voice sounded warm and friendly.

"Hi Sally, this is your Uncle De… here. … phone reception… not very… Can you – hear…? Sally, I'll call you back."

It rang again.

"Hey Sally it's your uncle. This is great, don't you think, us being able to talk after all these years?"

I heard an anxious voice in the background. It was Jim.

"Desmond… are you listening? Can you ask please her how we get off the M23?" he urged.

"Right, for sure. Sally, I think we're kinda lost. We left Gatwick an hour ago and followed your instructions, but I keep seeing signs for the airport again."

Oh no! They'd spent over an hour doing a complete circle. Would they make it to me on time for the restaurant booking? Eventually, they reached my town but couldn't find their way out of the high street. Desmond, who remained upbeat, called me again, so I gave him the umpteenth set of directions, hoping that this time they would find me.

"Look Des, it's easy. Just turn the car around and go back the other way. Can you see the fire station opposite?" He could. "Go past that until you see a large pub on the left-hand side, turn left, then immediate left again. Have you got that?"

"Yeah, right. Left, a pub... keep left, past the fire station... keep going left..."

He was repeating it to Jim, but not necessarily in the right order. 15 minutes later they were still lost and rang again.

"You turned the car around and went past the fire station then straight, like I said?"

"Sure did!"

"But you didn't see the pub?

"No."

"Really? There's a very large sign outside. And now you're back outside the hardware shop?"

"Yeah, kinda funny, don't you think?"

I wanted to scream, but instead I tried to keep control. I was conscious not only of the diminishing time left to meet Mum but, with her health and energy draining away every minute, this might be their only chance.

"Okay, let's try again: ... car around ... fire station... straight... drive slowly, so you see the pub..."

Next time the phone rang it was Jim. They had miraculously found my road, but driven past it. He sounded frustrated, but full of that Irish determination I recognised from Mum.

"Jim, don't move! Stay where you are and I'll come and get you!"

"You won't now."

"It's no trouble."

"No, Sally, now listen. I'll be there in a minute."

"But, Jim, I live in walking di—"

Beep-beep!

I looked out to see a little red Fiat at the top of the road and waved frantically in the hope they would see me, which, thankfully, they did.

The car crunched onto the gravel drive and one of Desmond's legs was already half out of an open door before Jim had parked. He wore a broad happy smile as he hopped out and rushed up to me for a bear hug, followed closely by Jim, who looked relieved to have reached his destination. I was filled with elation.

"You've finally made it!" Ooh, it's *so* good to meet you," I said, giving him a squeeze. "Wow! My two uncles, Mum's own brothers! I can't take it in. And I can't wait for you to meet Mum."

"And good to meet you too, Sally," said Jim, who looked as dazed as if he had stepped out onto another planet.

I had planned to invite them in for a cup of tea but there was no time now. They got straight back in and followed me the mile to Trinity Trees. I had arranged for a photographer from the local newspaper to call at three o'clock to cover the story; such a significant day should be recorded. The girl at the newspaper hadn't seemed overly enthralled and needed a bit of chasing on my part, but eventually she agreed to send a reporter along.

Sadly, my brother Will couldn't join us as he had just got back from holidaying in France and had an urgent business meeting. However, he had invited Jim and Desmond round for tea before they flew back to Ireland. Navigation skills allowing, this would work well as he only lived 10 minutes from Gatwick.

We were greeted at the main reception by Sister Michael, an elderly nun who manned the desk.

"Hello Sally," she said, with a knowing smile, as I signed in the register.

"These are Mum's brothers," I said, introducing them. "Jim and Desmond, this is Sister Michael.'

She offered them a warm handshake. "I'm very pleased to meet you both."

They struck up an instant rapport, so while they chatted I popped upstairs to fetch Mum. She was all ready: dressed and sitting in her wheelchair.

"Mum, you look lovely," I gushed.

"Ha-ha, naw. Do I, Pet?"

Sister Jeanne was standing in the doorway, beaming one of her dazzling smiles.

"Hello Sallee, we've got her all ready for you, like you wanted." I could tell by the look on her face that she was excited for us both.

"Thank you so, so much. I'm really grateful," I said.

"You're welcome my darleen'," she said.

"How are you feeling Mum?" Are you up for meeting your brothers? They're downstairs waiting for you."

"Oh yes, Petsey, of course I am," she grinned. "What are they like?"

"Oh, they're lovely, I know you're going to like them. Jim is Irish, like you, and Desmond is Canadian."

"Do they look like me?"

"I don't think so. It's hard to say... I've only just met them. You'll just have to see for yourself. Are you nervous?"

"Ah, Petsey, what have I got to be nervous about naw?"

"Right, let's go then."

I took a deep breath, wheeled her to the lift and we descended to the ground floor.

Jim and Desmond were waiting patiently by the reception and still chatting to Sister Michael. They spotted Mum and walked slowly towards us. There was apprehension in the air and I had a feeling of fear in my gut, even though I had imagined this moment for so long.

"Mum, I want you to meet your two brothers," I said, my voice trembling, as I wheeled her up to meet them.

They both looked overwhelmed. I don't think either of them was expecting to see her looking so pale and fragile, her haunted face staring back meekly. They must have realised in an instant, on this special day of being reunited, that their time together as a family would be short. There was a tense moment of silence as Mum gazed at them in wonderment and then looked up at me.

"My brothers?"

"Yes, Mum. Your very own brothers."

I wiped away a tear that was trying to fight its way out.

"Hello, I'm very pleased to meet you," she said, offering a limp hand and a warm smile.

"Mum, this is Desmond, from Canada, and this is Jim, from Ireland."

"Phyllis!" cried Jim. "It's a pleasure, so it is. I am so thrilled to meet my sister at long last!" He cupped Mum's hand in his, shook it vigorously and pecked her on the cheek.

"Ooh, I love your accent," she said, giving him an impish grin. "Yer sound real Irish, yer know. Whereabouts are you from?"

"Dublin, originally, although I live in County Kildare now."

"I'm from Dublin too. I was born there."

"I know," said Jim. "Our mother had us both there."

"Sure, did she naw?"

I realised then how much she had missed hearing the Irish brogue and all the colloquialisms that were familiar to her. It was pure joy to see her so happy.

Desmond too shook her hand, then gave her a gentle hug. "I just can't believe that we're only just meeting after all these years. This is quite an amazing experience, I have to say."

"No, I couldn't imagine it either," she said. "I never thought that my mother might have had more children after she gave me up. I thought I was the only one in the world. This is quite fantastic to find out I have brothers."

"Yeah, right. I kinda know what you mean, because I only found Jim last year myself," said Desmond.

"You sound foreign. What accent is that?"

"He's Canadian, Mum," I butted in.

"Oh, is he naw. Ha-ha-ha!"

I checked my watch; the sooner we were seated in the restaurant, where we all could relax, the better.

"Will I be getting a cup of tea soon?" she asked.

"Of course, you will," I said. "Come on, we'd better go before they stop serving. We're already late."

"Here, let me do that," said Desmond, taking command of Mum's wheelchair.

He pushed it with an ease that indicated he knew exactly what he was doing. He wheeled it out of the nursing home and up a slope to the adjacent building, which was the original Victorian convent before a new one was built. It seemed strange watching him interact with her, as if he'd known her all his life – and yet it was only 10 minutes after they had first met.

Jim and I traipsed slowly behind, while he smoked a cigarette. It was a time for contemplation, rehearsing what might have been. Over all those years never knowing they were related. A lifetime they might have shared, yet they now found themselves thrown together by fate in a very short window of remaining time. It was sobering, but did nothing to answer the questions why. Why did they never know about each other? Why did Peggy and James want to keep secrets that had impacted forever on their children's lives?

We entered the grand dining hall and were seated near a gothic window overlooking the landscaped gardens. It was like sitting in a stately home, with its huge ornate ceiling, wood panelled walls and oil paintings hanging on them.

Seeing Jim, Desmond and Mum together for the first time in their lives was an emotional experience. They were each so individual in appearance and personality that it was difficult to imagine they shared the same DNA and had the same parents.

The brothers were a similar height, around five foot eight. Desmond, who was wearing a blue-checked short-sleeved shirt, was the more filled-out of the two, with a good head of coarse grey hair and a short beard, slightly tinged with white. He was 70 years old, though I would have easily passed him off as 59. I could tell from his looks that he must have been a handsome chap in his prime. Now widowed for nearly 10 years, after nursing his late wife through multiple sclerosis, he had a casual charm, which I later discovered hid painful memories.

Jim, too, had the kind easy-goingness of the Irish, although he seemed more organised than Des. Leaner than his brother, he wore glasses and wore a shirt and navy V-neck jumper with the Guinness logo on it. He had a good head of hair too, although it was almost white, showing off his recent Spanish holiday tan. But, despite his colouring from the sun, Jim appeared rather frail. He walked at a laboured pace, stopping every so often to catch his breath. The journey here, coupled with not being able to find his bearings, had been challenging. Aged 76, and still absorbing the shock of discovering two siblings, he looked fragile.

I took a few photos of the three siblings together before we all sat down.

"Mum, tell your brothers what it was like in the orphanage," I urged.

"The what? Oh, that place… don't remind me. It was a terrible life and I'll never forget it."

"Describe it to them, Mum,"

Jim and Desmond listened intently.

"Like a prison it was – a prison! We were always hungry and we felt as though no one cared. They'd hit you for the tiniest little thing and made you feel useless and worth nothing in life. Many's the time, I asked myself *what am I doing here*?"

Jim was taken aback. "Oh Phyllis," he said tutting and shaking his head. He touched her arm. "I'm so, so sorry. I had such a different upbringing. I was just lucky."

"What was your childhood like then, Jim?" she asked.

"My life? Well, I was fostered out at six weeks old. They didn't have proper adoption laws until about 1952 in Ireland. But I went to a lovely family. I had siblings and I grew up happy. I thought they were my real family."

"So, when did you find out you were a Clancy and not related to them?" I prompted.

"I only found out when my sister took me to school with my birth certificate… when I was 12. It was the first time I'd seen it, and the mother and father's names on there weren't my foster parents at all, but 'Margaret Armstrong' and 'James Clancy'."

"That must have come as a bit of a shock," said Mum.

"Sure, it did. I also had to change my surname to Clancy from the one I'd grown up with all those years."

"How did that make you feel?" I asked.

"I went mad when I found out," he said. "I thought: if they didn't want to know me then, well, I'm not bothered about finding them now!"

"Jim, d'you realise this is probably the second time you and Mum have met?" I prompted.

Jim looked puzzled.

"In the records of the mother and baby home, Peggy, your mother, came back for Mum 18 months after leaving her there. The date she collected her was the fourth of November 1938 and you were born six days later. Mum was only sent back just before Christmas the same year, which means you would have been together, with your parents, for about six weeks."

"Well, would you believe it naw!" piped up Mum.

"Jasus!" exclaimed Jim. "You're not kidding? So, we were together as babies for a short while?"

"That's right, although why she gave you both up remains a mystery, because she married James Clancy three months later."

"That sure is weird," intercepted Desmond.

"Definitely," I agreed. "Peggy had Mum and Jim, gave them up within a few weeks of each other (Mum for a second time), then she got married to your dad and went on to have three more children. It seems so cruel. Why would she do that?"

"Well, I've always thought my mother never wanted me," said Mum.

Jim took her hand. "I'm sure our mother did want you, Phyllis; it's just that times were different... and we don't know what happened."

"Yes, you're right, times were different. I hoped I'd meet her one day... but Sally has done well to find you. It's like I'm dreaming. And I am thrilled to bits that you've both come all this way to meet me."

"Oh, it's our pleasure Phyllis," said Desmond. "I only found out about you last month, while I was in Australia visiting our Aunt Eileen, Peggy's younger sister. I never knew about her either."

"Didn't your father tell you anything of your family, Des?" I asked.

"No. I didn't even know I had grandparents. He told us nothing when he emigrated to Canada... that was in 1956. I thought the only family I had was my brother and some cousins on my father's side from Skerries, off the north Dublin coast."

"So, you had no notion about meself and Jim?" Mum asked.

"No, none. Knowing I had siblings has come as a real shock."

"So, you're the youngest, isn't that right?" I asked.

"Yes, I was born in 1945. Peggy died two months after giving birth to me, so I never knew her."

"That was hard on your father. D'you know what she died of?" asked Mum.

"No, I don't. Sally might."

"It said 'aplastic anaemia' on her death certificate," I offered. "It can be brought on by pregnancy sometimes, but having five children in eight years must have taken its toll on her body."

"I'm sure it did," said Jim.

"Did your father get remarried?" asked Mum.

"Yes, he married Barbara, my stepmother, in 1947. She brought us up until my father wanted to move to Canada when I was 11. She was the only mother I ever knew."

"But she didn't go with you?" asked Jim.

"No, we were packed off on a boat, by ourselves. Our father had gone ahead 14 months beforehand; he found work in Quebec and sent tickets for all of us to follow, but Barbara refused to come."

"But why? Why wouldn't she go?" I quizzed. So many unanswered questions were tangled in my brain. So much to know... and yet none of us had answers.

Our musings were interrupted by the waitress serving our meals, leaving those questions hanging in the air.

Mum, although very happy and enjoying the craic, was looking tired. She started to cough and I wondered how much longer she could carry on talking before she needed to lie down.

Jim noticed my concern. "Phyllis, are you alright?"

"Oh, don't you worry about me Jim. I'm fine naw."

Mum ate her scrambled eggs tentatively and wiped her mouth with a tissue.

"Sal darling, when am I going to get my tea? I'm dying for a cup of tea, you know."

She enjoyed her tea more than her food, in which she had little interest these days.

"I'll call over to the waitress and—"

Jim interrupted. "Sally, when she comes, tell her I don't want a main course, just the starter. I'm going out for a quick cigarette," he said as he waved the packet.

"Okay Jim, will do."

Not only had Mum lost her appetite, but Jim too. I watched her pushing her food around and my heart sank. I knew it was the cancer, making her nauseous all the time, but she would never tell me.

"Would you like me to cut your food up for you?" I asked.

"No, darling, I'll be alright... I'm grand," she said.

"Hey, this is real good," said Desmond, who was heartily tucking into his pasta. "Great place too. Just a shame I can't connect with the wi-fi."

Desmond, who was an artist, was keen to show us his drawings and photos on the iPad, but the area was surrounded by trees so the signal was abysmal.

"Glad you like it." I said. "I believe it was one of the places where Churchill conducted covert meetings with his cabinet in the war years, before it became a convent."

Jim decided to abandon his broccoli soup in favour of popping out several more times for a cigarette.

"Are you alright, Jim?" I asked.

"Oh, fine I am. I just don't seem to have much of an appetite lately."

As the afternoon progressed and three o'clock drew near, I suggested we return to the nursing home for afternoon tea and cake, and to meet the photographer. He never turned up, which niggled me but wasn't a huge surprise considering the lack of enthusiasm the girl had shown on the phone.

We sat in the conservatory and, this time, Desmond took the photos while Mum chatted merrily away to Jim about his wife and his family. It was a delight to see how well they got on, given the circumstances. Then we took them to see Mum's room. I stood in the doorway observing them interact. They had all lived such different lives and had experienced many different things. Mum had grown up in an orphanage, became a nurse, married, had children, but suffered ill health from her childhood and unhappy marriage, yet she had a positivity that saw her through many a turmoil. Jim, a confident and proud man, who had been happily fostered, went on to have his own successful business in Ireland, a large sprawling family, including 10 grandchildren, and had enjoyed life to the full. And Desmond, who I would describe as a laid-back thinker, started his childhood with no stabilising influences in Canada, studied at art college, became an accomplished artist and married the love of his life, Elaine. Their life changed when she developed a life-limiting illness after seven years of marriage, but they remained happily married until her death 37 years later. How wonderful it would have been if Mum, Jim and Desmond could have shared their lives, their families, their highs and lows and been a comfort to each other throughout those years.

As I stood pondering these thoughts in the doorway, I tried to hear what they were saying, but it was impossible against the clatter of cups from a tea trolley outside. Mum remained animated, despite her tiredness, and was laughing away. She had found the family she longed for but time was not on her side. A creeping sorrow diminished my joy. Sadly, they said their goodbyes and hugged. The day had flown by.

"I can't tell you how great it's been to meet you Phyllis," said Jim. "I'll bring Sheila with me in the new year, you'll love her. Don't you worry – you'll see me again. I'll make sure of that."

"Oh, I'd love that, truly I would," she said, giving him a cheeky grin. And I knew that she meant it.

Chapter 17

A Hope for the Future

The journey to my brother's house was about an hour's drive. The plan was that Desmond and Jim would follow me, as I didn't want them to still be circling the M23 when their flight was leaving, and besides I could see Jim was getting tired. Desmond, however, decided to come in my car, to get to know me better. I was apprehensive about Jim driving alone, but Desmond was quite insistent, so I drove at a slow pace so Jim could keep up.

Although unplanned, it was a good opportunity to chat to Des about his past and his family life, of which I knew very little. We seemed to both find it easy to have an open conversation, about his life and Mum's, and experiences growing up that had affected them both.

Like me, Desmond had many questions about why the three siblings had been separated all their lives, but with the knowledge I had gained from Matthew, the story began to unfold.

After Peggy's unexpected death, Desmond's father, James Clancy, was faced with bringing up his two sons by himself. Being Catholic he turned to the Church for support with childcare and they dutifully obliged, but only for a limited period as they expected him to find a new mother for his children.

Two years after Peggy's death, in 1945, he visited his in-laws, Joe and May Armstrong, who were now living and working on a gentry estate outside Dundalk, County Louth. He explained this was the last time they would see their grandchildren as he would be making a new life and emigrating to Australia. Whether it was his original intention, or whether he wanted to cut ties with his late wife's family, no one knows. However, he did not go to Australia but, instead, he remained in Dublin for a further nine years, developing his carpentry skills by making and selling toys in a shop. He met his second wife, Barbara, who he married in 1948, in a big Catholic ceremony in County Tipperary. I asked Desmond what she was like.

"Oh, she was several years younger than him and came from Clonmel. I think she was a shop assistant when he met her. She was easy-going and carefree... she loved to sing around the house. My brother and I were always taking the mickey out of her singing."

Desmond recalled how it was good in the early days, when his father and stepmother seemed genuinely affectionate towards each other, but over time his father's true colours started to show through.

"Get off my clean floor," he remembered her yelling at James, as he would deliberately walk across it in thickly muddied boots, with a clear disdain for her hard work.

He continued, "People's feelings didn't matter to him; basically, my father didn't give a shit."

"Why was that then?" I asked.

"He just didn't give a damn about anyone unless they were useful to him. He liked money in his pocket but never paid the bills... people were constantly chasing him for owing rent or the likes. He was always smartly dressed... he had a mop of brown slicked-back hair... very self-assured. He was extremely clever – quick witted – and knew how to manipulate people within a few seconds of meeting them."

"Did he have any friends then?"

"Oh yes, he had friends, but only ones who he considered his intellectual equals. One of his friends was the mayor's son, but there were others too, who were happy to do him favours. If it wasn't for his solicitor friend, Tim, helping me when he went off to Canada, I'd be illiterate. Tim took an interest in me and taught me how to read and write; he was really kind. I was 11, and still didn't know my alphabet, but with his help I made progress. I owe him a lot."

"Canada... tell me about Canada," I asked, "and how you ended up the other side of the world."

"One day, my father came home and announced that we were all off to Canada. He'd have to travel first and find work, but once established he'd send tickets for us to follow."

"How did you feel about that?"

"How did we feel? Oh, my brother and I were giddy at the prospect. I remember a popular song by Mario Lanza which went something like, *Oh, oh, I wanna go to Africa, Africa, Africa...* but we inserted Canada to the same beat!"

"And what about Barbara?"

"Barbara had no say in the matter. She was just left to look after us while he sailed off to Quebec for 14 months."

"But how did she cope? Did she work?"

"No, in those days women generally didn't work; their husbands supported them."

"So, what did you live on?"

"We struggled to survive. Lived on hand-outs from Dad's friends, who called round every so often with a few shillings or a food parcel. We'd eat well for a while after they had gone, but then things got rocky again. We were reduced to growing onions and potatoes in our small backyard just to survive."

"Oh God, that must have been hard. Didn't he send anything in the post to help out?"

"Strange as it sounds, I didn't realise the situation was that bad. I was only a kid and thought it was normal. He sent some money once, but generally it was comics, or small items Barbara could sell on the black market. Customs often caught those deliveries."

"Tell me what happened when the tickets finally arrived? Didn't Barbara want to go with you?"

"No. I reckon she'd had enough by then. And she'd been having an overnight visitor to the house. He was a Sean McMurphy, and he drove the number 17 bus that terminated at Capps Road. I rode it a number of times and vaguely remember the thrill of the free bus ride, as I do his stacks of coins all lined up on the kitchen table when I came down for school in the morning."

"Did you ask her about him?"

"No, I didn't think anything of it – I was only young. It wasn't until later, in Canada, that I realised the significance, when I had to go before the courts and give evidence in my father's divorce, that she was an adulteress."

"So, what next?"

"The tickets came in the post and Barbara tried to cash hers in, but a wife could only do that with her husband's signature. The shipping company sent a telegram to my father, so he knew before we left that Barbara wasn't coming. The next thing I remember was a woman called Mrs Powers (another of my father's friends) coming to collect us. I think she was well-off and financed our trip."

"And where did you go?"

"Mrs Powers took us to a Dublin train station, from where we had to change three times to reach Cobh, in County Cork, where the SS *Saxonia* was harboured. On the way there, she insisted we stop at a church, but my older brother was having none of it. She soon realised that was a mistake – trying to push him against his will – and she backed off. A smaller boat took us from Cobh Port to board the main ship, so Mrs Powers said goodbye there. We sailed for eight or nine days, by ourselves, and weren't bothered by anyone. In fact, people were really kind. We were on this big adventure and had a great time. The dining room was a sight to behold. We'd never seen so much food – spent half our lives starving – so we gorged ourselves on the buffet! So much that I remember a sway under my feet and I immediately knew I was going to vomit... and vomit I did, like I've never vomited before or since."

"Weren't you scared? You were just a little boy. Didn't you miss Barbara?"

"Ah sure, yeah, I was just a kid, but there were plenty of distractions. The ship had its own cinema and we watched *Seven Brides for Seven Brothers* and a sci-fi film called *Them*, about ants. It was only later I missed Barbara, when we sailed up the St Lawrence River, stopping at the base of the citadel in Quebec City. I could see the Château Frontenac, really impressive from the deck. I felt really sad and uncertain just then... an uncomfortable feeling in my stomach that become pretty familiar in years to come."

He explained how his life was never stable again once they were reunited with his dad. He and his brother were left to fend for themselves, often without any food, and they were forced to steal from local supermarkets to survive while his father was out dancing and seducing women. They moved from house to house, as well as changing schools numerous times, so his studies suffered. He told me he felt retarded when he was a young teenager, far behind everyone else, and that the shame and stigma lasted for years. Sometimes they were abandoned for weeks. Without parental love or guidance Desmond grew rebellious and ended up in the care system after smashing a window and stealing a bicycle. But rather than it doing him more harm, he began to flourish. He put on weight, got good grades at school and was happy for the first time.

"My foster folks looked after me real good. It was the first time I ever got to see a doctor," he said.

He stayed in Canada for the rest of his life, but often wondered about his past; a past his father would never talk about.

By the time we arrived at Will's house, Des and I were both reeling from the unfolding stories. So many secrets; lies that were kept well-hidden until now. Peggy and James must have thought that no one would ever find out about the misadventures in their lives, but little did they know what the future would hold. If it hadn't been for modern-day technology and the discovery of DNA, I would never have pieced this jigsaw together.

"Well then – I'll see you Friday!" I called excitedly from the car window as I waved goodbye. "If you're absolutely sure?" This wasn't to be goodbye after all – it was only the beginning.

Within days, I was walking out of Dublin Airport's Terminal One, to be warmly greeted by Desmond and Jim's wife, Sheila, who I hadn't met. Jim drove us to his home, where we all sat round the kitchen table eating Sheila's Irish stew. It was so wonderful to be chatting and getting to know my amazing Irish family who I never imagined existed. I was introduced to Jim's sons, my first cousins, who welcomed me with big hugs and a friendliness I could have only dreamed of.

Next morning, Jim drove us to a hotel in Slane, County Meath. The area had a historical significance to us as generations of the Armstrong family had lived nearby. It was also a good halfway point for the numerous cousins who lived both north and south of the Irish border. The evening was fabulous with everyone spilling out into the gardens and seated under canopies on what turned out to be a sultry night. Matthew, his mother Anna, Sheila and I sat literally rocking our seats with laughter over a shared joke, while Jim and Desmond stood at the top on the steps looking down on us fondly. I was staggered to meet such an array of Mum's first cousins and I posed for photographs with them, in place of her.

She would have been in her element a few years earlier, revelling in the attention and joining in the craic with her unmistakeably Irish sense of humour. My happiness was tainted with a sadness too, that she had missed these life-affirming moments.

I rushed to the nursing home to tell Mum about the wonderful visit I'd experienced and hear her feedback about her newly found brothers.

"My brothers? ...Yes, of course it was wonderful. I'm sorry I didn't have more time with them. But, darling, what I'm most pleased about is that you'll still have them even when I'm gone, Pet."

The words stabbed at my chest. That was so typical of her. Always thinking of my feelings and putting others before herself. The irony of it nearly broke my heart. I had tried so long to find her family and now I had, she wouldn't be there to appreciate them with me. How tragic and bittersweet it now all seemed.

Before I knew it, the end of August had arrived and it was nearing my holiday time. I took Mum to the local hairdressers, which she relished for all the unfamiliar attention and fussing they bestowed upon her. Despite being barely able to walk, she wanted her hair to look nice. Afterwards we went back to my house for a cup of tea.

"The room seems small," she said. She looked around as if it was an alien place she hardly recognised.

"We're going away next week – to Majorca," I told her.

"Oh, Petsey, d'you have to?"

I felt torn in two. Neither Phil or I earned very much and we had saved frantically all year to go on holiday. When we booked we had never envisaged Mum would become so ill. The previous year she had been on such an even keel that I assumed she could go on forever.

"It's only a week, Mum. I'll be home before you know it,' I tried to reassure her.

That wasn't strictly true; it was actually 10 days, but I was guilt ridden and keen to make it sound shorter. Even as I spoke, I was telling myself that she would not die, at least not yet.

"Oh, darling, please don't go," she pleaded.

"Mum, I have to. I'm really sorry and you know I'd rather stay, but I have Phil to consider too… and if we don't go, we'll lose all the money."

"But you don't have to, Sal. Stay with Mammy, please stay."

Why didn't I listen to her? Why did I let my head rule my heart instead of the other way around? She was the most unselfish person I have known and never asked anything of me, ever, except for this one time. I still berate myself when I think about it.

The week before we left, she was more and more confined to bed. She even stopped wanting her beloved television on. It was as though she just sought peace and tranquillity as she grew weaker and weaker by the day. I was so concerned that I asked a doctor to come and examine her.

The lady doctor acknowledged that Mum was probably going downhill, so I asked her if she thought I should cancel my holiday. She said that, in her opinion, Mum could go on for several more weeks, which I queried in my head considering she was scarcely consuming food or fluids, but I trusted the doctor and wanted to believe what she was telling me. It was still a tough decision, because I knew that Philip, my partner, would not have been happy to forfeit his holiday, and his voice was constantly in my head.

"Your mother's tough as old boots, she's not going to die. She could go on forever."

By now, Mum was looking emaciated. Her aversion to food and drink was the worst it had been. I popped in to see her on my way home. Her small square of a sandwich and tiny portion of jelly and cream sat untouched on its tray.

"Tell them to take it away, Sally. I don't want it."

I gazed at the bird-like portions in horror.

"Is that all you're eating now?" I enquired.

"Oh, Petsey, I have plenty you know, but I just don't feel like it."

"Mum, you need food to give you strength. If you don't eat, you'll starve."

"Just let me drink my tea, that's all I want."

I felt the side of the mug. "It's cold. Would you like me to make you a hot one?"

"No darling, I prefer it cold. That's how I like it."

"Mum? You've never liked cold tea. You'd only ever have it if it was piping hot."

This behaviour, saying and doing quite the opposite of her regular habits, was happening more frequently. On one visit she told me I could go the moment I arrived! None of this was her normal personality; the cancer was progressing and causing the wires in her brain to malfunction.

Just over a week later, and with a reluctant heart and a guilty conscience tearing away at me, we took off for Majorca. I had persuaded Phil that if anything should happen to Mum we would be on the next plane home. Still, even with him agreeing to this, I was riddled with anxiety about leaving her.

"Sallee, you go," said Sister Jeanne. "We have your mobile number and the telephone number of the hotel. Don't worry. Phyllees will be fine. You have a lovely time."

Having a good time was the last thing on my mind when I discovered my brother was going away at the same time. Unbeknownst to me, he and his wife had booked a driving holiday to Germany that overlapped with our dates abroad. This was really bad timing but we weren't great at communicating and I only discovered it at the last minute.

Majorca was pleasantly warm and, with no oppressive heat, we sat idling around the pool most days. There was even an occasional cooling breeze, when Phil would take himself off for solitary walks and I would read a book. In the mornings, around 11 o'clock, I called the home to speak to Mum. The staff had to bring the phone to her, but at least I heard her voice. But by day three of our holiday, she was either sleeping when I called or her voice was so weak that I could hardly hear her. I thought if she could just hear my voice it might keep her going until I got back.

"Mum, I know you can hear me, so just know that I love you very much and I will soon be home." It was all I could think of to say.

With nagging doubts tormenting me, I regretted coming abroad and longed to return to her. A foreboding hung over me, along with an ache inside that came and went, always returning in quiet moments. The days started to drag. We had settled into a routine of not doing very much and trying to relax, but my mood wasn't lifted by the built-up location around us and being some distance from the beach. The evening entertainment was mostly bingo calling, followed by a late-night show, by which time we were ready for bed. And there was a distinct lack of people our own age. We weren't young by any means, but the number of people on walking frames made me wonder if we had come to the right place and continually prompted me to think of Mum. She dominated my thoughts morning, noon and night, making it difficult to read a book or do anything without constantly worrying about how she was.

On day seven, I received an unexpected text message from Will. He had never been one for mobile phones or texting, so I opened it with apprehension.

"Sal, I'm broken down in Germany. Just received phone call from nursing home to say Mum taken a turn for the worse – going in and out of consciousness. Problem is can't get back for several days – will take that long for engineer to repair car."

The news swept through me like a hurricane and my mind raged in a state of blind panic.

No!!! I screamed inside. *This can't be happening.* Quickly, I texted my brother.

"Don't worry Will," I replied. "On next plane home. Will reach nursing home today, whatever it takes."

Immediately I rang the home.

"Yes, Sallee, you need to come as soon as you can," urged Sister Jeanne.

I felt overwhelmed. Philip had just returned from his walk and was unaware of the state I was in until I looked up.

"What's the matter?" he asked, as he pulled his T-shirt off over his head and wiped his face which was drenched in perspiration.

"Mum! It's Mum... We have to go... and now!"

"What d'you mean?"

Agitatedly, I collected my belongings into a bag, dropping things in haste, knocking over my soft drink onto the concrete tiles and banging my head on the umbrella.

"She's going in and out of consciousness. Will texted me and I rang Sister Jeanne. We have to get home, right now!"

Philip looked taken aback by my reaction. "Sal... How do you know that this isn't another false alarm? She's been like this before, remember?"

"No, she hasn't! Not like this, Philip. She's dying for God's sake. And we need to get home now. Lend me the money for the air fare. I haven't got my credit card with me."

"What about your brother? Can't he get back?"

"No, his MG has broken down again and he's stuck in Germany and he can't get it repaired for several days. Anyway, you agreed that if anything happened we'd return straight away, didn't you?"

"Yes, I did. Okay, I'll lend you the money and we'll go and pack."

After a tearful meeting in the travel rep's office, he quickly arranged our flights home and for a taxi to take us to the airport. By four o'clock, we had left the hotel in a mad dash and were heading for a plane due to fly that evening. We arrived at the nursing home at quarter to 11, a miraculously fast trip. Philip accompanied me up to Mum's room and as I hurried along the corridor, my heart still racing, we were met by Sister Jeanne carrying a little plate of food wrapped in clingfilm.

"Hello Sallee, my darleen'. I thought you might be hungry after your long trip home, so I've had some sandwiches made for you, and we've prepared the room next to Phyllis's if you want to stay the night."

I felt choked. "Thank you, thank you... you're so kind. Yes, I'll stay."

As I pushed open the door, with Philip behind me, my eyes fell straight on her skeletal body. My stomach tightened as I recoiled in horror. Her eyes were rolling backwards in her head. She looked like a silhouette of her former self; like some poor ravaged victim from a concentration camp, her features wore a deathly pallor and her face was sucked in by a desperation to live. I felt the wind howl in my soul.

I kissed her head and stroked her brow. She felt cold. I wanted to talk and keep her close, like it used to be.

"Mum, oh Mum..."

Phil touched my arm. He too was visibly disturbed by the vision of my mother that was laid in front of us. He hadn't imagined she would ever look like this, but then neither had I.

"Shall I pick you up in the morning, or would you like me to stay?" he asked.

"No, you go, I'll be fine. I'll ring if I need you."

That night I sat with her and held her hand, and prayed to God that she wouldn't die just yet. I didn't want to let her go. My heart was soaked in grief. After a while I went next door, lay on top of the single bed and eventually dropped off into a sleep of sorts. In the morning she was the same, but she had survived the night.

Phil took me home for a while and to my utter astonishment when I returned later that morning, Mum was sitting up in bed and being fed breakfast. Neither the staff nor I could believe it!

"Mum – darling!"

"Oh, hello Petsey," she said, "I'm so pleased you're home."

"Mum, do you know how ill you were last night?"

"No. Was I?"

"I stayed with you. I didn't think you were going to wake up... I thought you were... The staff let me sleep in the room next to you."

"Did they, naw? Well, would you believe it. Heh-heh-heh! Oh, they're very good to me here."

She looked bemused, totally unaware of what was going on. *I've got her back*, I thought. *She'll go on for some time yet.* It gave me a glimmer of hope. She continued to rally for a few days, still not eating and only drinking occasionally, but by the next week she was unable even to take fluids. The carers dabbed a lemon swab around in her mouth to keep it moist. It was heart-breaking watching her still fighting to survive. By the Wednesday, I called in about six o'clock, and saw a clear deterioration. She was stretching her arms out, wanting people to get closer so they could hear what she was saying because her voice was barely a faint whisper. Carly, a carer she was fond of, came in to check on her.

"I love you. I love you,' she told Carly, her voice hardly audible.

It seemed she was so full of love for everyone, but for a moment I felt a pang of jealousy inside. Mum didn't love her. She was just saying that. She was my mother and I was the one she loved.

Then she stretched out her arms and looked longingly for me, drawing me close. Her strength was weakening and everything was a strenuous effort. I wondered how well she could see me because her eyes were clouded and grey.

"Sally..." She struggled to get the words out. "Sally... I – want – you – to – know... I love you so much. I – LOVE –YOU – SO..."

"Sssh... stop, Mum, stop," I interrupted, as I held her close. "Save your breath. I know you love me, and I love you too with all my heart. Remember, we will always be together. Understand? Together."

She closed her eyes, and her face shone with contentment as she relaxed back into my arms. She mouthed the word, "together' and smiled. I shook my head in denial, I didn't want to let her go. Tears trickled steadily down from the enormity of what I was witnessing and I was falling apart. This was it. After all these years, she was finally leaving me. The grief was a boulder in my throat, choking me, pushing my pent-up pain back deep down inside. I too struggled to express the words I longed to say, but eventually I won.

"Mum, I will never forget you for as long as I live. You have been the best mother I could have ever wished for and you will always be with me in my heart and soul. One day, Mum, I'm going to tell people about your life, the life you had but didn't deserve, and write a book, and make you famous. Would you like that?"

She could no longer speak and her eyes remained closed, but she gripped my hand with all the strength she had left in her, and the corners of her mouth creased upwards. And then I knew, I just knew, I had to tell her story.

That was the last time we spoke. Next day she slipped into a coma and died peacefully on the Friday evening with my brother Will, his wife, and Philip and me by her side. Seven nuns who had nursed her wheeled in a table and lit candles before saying prayers and singing for her in melodious harmony. One knelt beside her bed and said the Lord's Prayer. The other six lined up with me against the bedroom wall, like a row of blackbirds on a washing line. I stood transfixed, numbed by pain, as they took over for us. Silent tears were dripping one by one in huge globules. They said she died a beautiful death, if there is such a thing. Well maybe that was a fitting tribute, because no matter what had happened to her in life, she had always remained a beautiful person. She had been the kindest, most forgiving and compassionate soul that I have met on this earth. She taught me many things, but the one overriding thing that she wanted me to remember was that no matter what happens, never give up: because where there's life, there's hope.

Epilogue

Jim was the first person I telephoned as soon as I arrived home that evening, to tell him of Mum's passing. His voice quivered. It must have come as a shock; he had been hoping to see his sister again one day.

I liked Jim. Although I hadn't known him long, he came across as an extremely generous person, with a deep compassion in his heart for people less fortunate than himself. He was also astute and had easily tuned into Mum's personality. A few days later he sent me this email.

Dear Sally,

I have been thinking about how lucky I was to meet Phyllis earlier this year and, although she was poorly at the time, I could plainly see the twinkle of devilment in her eyes, in spite of the extremely difficult times she suffered in her life. It is hard to realise the cruelty she had to put up with, but the Armstrong gene was predominant, and she was some fighter.

Thankfully she had a unique daughter, who loved her with all her heart and more. She was blessed to have a daughter like you.

Death is no stranger to us and the feeling of loss never goes away, but life goes on and we must face the future bravely. Phyllis is at peace now and thankfully did not suffer.

Have no doubt that we are all here to help in any way we can, always. So just pick up the phone anytime day or night.

Your uncle, Jim

Sadly, Jim himself was very ill when he wrote this. A week after he met with his sister in England, he was diagnosed with the same condition and was now undergoing a gruelling course of chemotherapy to fight off the disease. Because of this he was unable to attend Mum's funeral, but his wife Sheila came instead, and one of their sons who, despite never knowing his Auntie Phyllis, stood next to me in the church and shared our grief.

Jim did not survive the cancer. Eight months later, almost to the week that the siblings had met for the first and last time, he passed away.

It was cruel losing Mum and then Jim so soon after, and it made me wonder what it had all been for. All that searching, all that energy expended on finding everyone, and then time runs out: no way to enjoy each other's company. But Jim was right. The loss may not go away, but life goes on.

The event that I had feared most had come and gone, and although I never thought I could live without my mother, I did. I survived. The grieving was at its worst while she was still alive, but now she had gone I needed to carry on. Life is precious and, as common wisdom tells us, we need to make the most of it while we're here.

I challenged myself to fly to Australia. I had never flown that far by myself and was frightened at the idea, but I wanted to meet Auntie Eileen, my grandmother's only living sibling, who was nearly 93. I spent a week at her bungalow in a small suburb north-west of Melbourne with her and her son Maurice, one of my mum's many first cousins. It was a unique time and one I will never forget. Auntie Eileen and I continued to correspond for a number of years. She was always thrilled to hear my 'newsy emails' as she would call them, and see any photos of the family get togethers that we had. Sadly, she never quite made it to her 96th birthday, as she passed away in November 2019. However, although she has gone, I am still in contact with Maurice her son and a whole host of family members all over the world.

Discovering this family has been a completely joyous experience and has opened up a new world for me. We have already had mini family reunions over the last few years, with more planned for the future. Having no extended family when I was growing up, it really is my dream come true. I too felt devoid of relations, yet here I am with my enormous family spread out all over the world. Although Mum is no longer able to join in, I am able to talk to them about her, so she is never forgotten.

Matthew, the cousin whose DNA matched Mum's, is the main reason that the family are so closely linked. He is in contact with me every few weeks and has been over to stay, as I have with his family. It feels so natural, as if we have always known each other. Not only is he my second cousin, but also a very dear friend, for which I feel extremely blessed.

Thanks to his genealogy skills, he set up a Facebook page with another cousin, and many new members of the clan have joined in after taking a DNA test. And thanks to the wonders of technology we communicate with our family in other countries, particularly in America, all of whom have individual stories to tell.

Desmond has remained in contact ever since we first met and has ventured back to England as well as paying many visits to his birthplace, Ireland. We have gradually begun to know one another well, and are catching up on the years we missed. He is a very dear uncle. Whenever I am in Ireland, I try to visit Jim's family, who are my first cousins too.

If only Mum had been able to do all that, not just with her lost family, but also her friend Patsy who grew up with her in the orphanage.

While burrowing for yet more information, I tracked down Patsy, who is now aged 82. She filled me in on those years that I knew little about, when Mum left Ireland to fulfil her dream of being a nurse in England. Apparently, they worked alongside each other in several jobs. Wherever Mum found work, Patsy followed, and they shared laughs along the way. Although they lost contact, as Patsy moved to many locations over the years, she had never forgotten her old friend.

In 2012, when Mum was hospitalised with lung cancer, Patsy was living in the same town south of London that Mum had left only the year before. She lived with her husband in sheltered accommodation, and had sent him to search the record offices to see if he could track my mother down. 12 months earlier they might easily have bumped into each other in the high street, since they lived less than a mile apart.

How ironic, that if fate hadn't intervened, they might have enjoyed each other's friendship again after nearly 40 years. But life, as they say, never goes according to how you plan it. I thought that when I found Mum's family I had come to the end of this story... little did I know there are always more revelations to come.

As I have grown to know my grandmother's side of the family, I also became friendly with cousins on my grandfather's side, the Clancys. A second or third cousin, not a Clancy by name but related on the maternal side, kindly took a DNA test at my request in September 2017. It had always bugged me why there was no father's name on Mum's birth certificate and yet there was on Jim's. Both babies were given up by Peggy, but why did only Jim have the father's name?

I was shocked to find that James Clancy, who married Peggy soon after she gave up her two children, was not related to me or Mum. The Clancy cousin only matched to Desmond's DNA. This could only mean that Peggy had a relationship with someone else before James Clancy. It also meant that my late mother and I might still have family out there from her father's side. But who was he and where to look?

I was intrigued but thought the chances of new evidence were pretty remote. Then, out of the blue, on Christmas Eve, I was viewing our DNA matches and worked out by a process of elimination that Mum matched to a first cousin once removed, or second cousin, on her father's side.

I contacted this person straight away, asking how he thought we were connected. After a little prompting by a second email, he explained that it was through his mother's side; they originated from a tiny fishing village called Loughshinny on the north Dublin coast, which lies next to Skerries.

The coincidences were too great. This was the place where James Clancy's parents had retired to. Why had Peggy been in that area? And did James Clancy know the man who got her pregnant? If so, was she manipulated by James Clancy into giving up her two first-borns? He certainly seemed to have had a hold over people; so, did he know something about them? Or was it a love triangle, and naivety on Peggy's part that forced her to hide the facts? There are so many unanswered questions that I may never find out. But, as long as I live, I am going to keep searching for the whole truth, because I know in my heart it's what my mother would have wanted.

A sketch of Mum by her brother, Desmond

Acknowledgements

They say that lightning never strikes twice, but for me, finding my long-lost family and then someone accepting my book for publication, has illuminated my world. It has literally been a dream come true, which would not have been possible without the belief, help and support of the following people, who encouraged me from the beginning and helped make this dream become a reality.

First of all, I would like to thank the fantastic team at Mardle Books, Jo, Mel and Kaz. Also, Jon Rippon of Adlib Publishers. What an amazing bunch of people you are, who have worked tirelessly to bring this book to the market and show it in the best possible light. Jo, I would like to thank you especially, for appreciating this heart-rending story and realising its potential to inspire others, who may have had similar lives themselves.

Helen Stockton, after four years from this book's inception and several drafts later, even though you must have felt like having to keep your eyelids open with matchsticks at times, you're still here. I thank you so much for all your encouragement and support over the years. You know that I couldn't have done it without you. Dawn Austin-Locke, your suggestions and advice have been invaluable, I am so glad to have found you.

Matthew, my cousin, who made finding my mother's long-lost family only possible because of his DNA: I will be eternally grateful not only for that, but also for welcoming me into the Armstrong and Little folds and making me feel part of the family that I always wanted. That means so much. I only wish Mum could have shared that, too.

Des, I'm very proud to have you as an uncle and I thank you for your contribution to this book. Not only for the stunning sketch of Mum, but also for your memories of your father and childhood, some of which I know were difficult to share. Kieran, thank you too, for your accounts of how you found Des and the family, and always offering your kind support.

Libby, you are a true friend to have been so selfless on our Irish road trip. I will never forget that. Rita Edwards, if ever there was a good Samaritan it was you for showing such kindness. And the same with Brian Garland. So glad that we became friends, Brian. I will always remember what you did for me. And finally, my dearest friend Sawmill Steph. I love you Steph for showing such an interest in this book throughout the years and believing in what I was doing.

Thanks also for the many people who contributed information about my Mum's early years, but who do not wish to be named. Your recollections really helped enlighten me on what life was like for Mum in the orphanage and after she left there.

Oh, and there is one person I forgot. John. You said a few decades ago that I should write a book. So, guess what? I did.

Mum with her brothers Jim (left) and Desmond

About the author

Sally Herbert was born in 1962 and grew up in Surrey, before moving to Sussex in her late thirties. She lives with her partner Phil, and elderly cat, The Big Boy, and works for an animal charity.

After nearly a decade of searching for her long-lost family, she likes nothing better than to make trips to Ireland for reunions and get-togethers. When she is not doing that, she enjoys going for walks on The South Downs and researching her ever-expanding family tree.

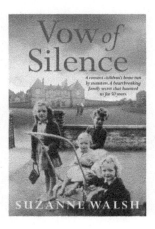